ESSENTIAL LOCAL GOVERNMENT 2000

RON FENNEY

The recommended textbook for the examinations of the National Council for the Training of Journalists

First published 1983 as Local Government for Journalists
Seventh Edition 1996
Eighth Edition 1998
Ninth Edition 2000

Price £14.95
ISBN 0 904677 91 5

Published by
LGC Information
Greater London House
Hampstead Road
London
NW1 7EJ
Telephone: 020 7347 1828
Fax: 020 7347 1815
email: samina.ghadiali@lgc.emap.com
Web site: www.lgcnet.com

LGC Information

emap PUBLIC SECTOR MANAGEMENT

Printed by Black Bear Press Ltd

ESSENTIAL
LOCAL
GOVERNMENT
2000

RON FENNEY

Contents

Preface

The National Council for the Training of Journalists Public Affairs Board devises the Council's syllabus and sets its exams. Part of the assistance which the NCTJ gives to students is to arrange for the publication of this book and its companion, *Essential Central Government*. I was asked by LGC Communications to rewrite this book, having written two of the earlier editions of it in 1996 and 1998 – and its companion, *Essential Central Government*.

This book does not attempt to give a complete account of what local government does, but, instead, concentrates upon the requirements of Part I of the NCTJ syllabus and outlines the background to those aspects which can give rise to stories. In places, I have ventured beyond facts, to express a few personal opinions – again, those opinions are entirely mine, based on 30 years' experience of local government and they are included to raise questions for discussion.

In the preface to the previous edition in 1998, I referred to the arrival of the New Labour Government and the prospect of considerable change in relations between central and local government. Those looking for change have not been disappointed. At the time of writing this book, various pieces of legislation are still going through Parliament, not least the Local Government Bill which will have a revolutionary effect on the internal workings of local authorities over the next few years. Much the same can be said of the Care Standards Bill in relation to personal social services and, to a lesser extent, education. Although it is possible for those Bills to undergo significant changes on their way to the Statute Book, it is unlikely that there will be a fundamental departure from the outline of them in this book. However, when they become the Local Government Act 2000 and the Care Standards Act 2000, it will be necessary to ensure that any fundamental changes are tracked.

Ron Fenney
March 2000, Leicester

1 Structure and Functions

The development of the local government structure through successive reorganisations — the allocation of functions to the various types of local authority

How it all began — Town and Country

Up to the end of the 19th century, local government was a pretty hit-and-miss affair and probably would not be recognisable as such in our terms. Such bodies that did exist were unelected and fairly patchy in their geographical coverage and performance — representing the people and the delivery of services to the public was not their prime concern.

Local government structure has a longer history in the towns than in the country areas. Many of the towns or boroughs had been granted their own charter by the Sovereign — some for hundreds of years before the 19th century. The charter granted rights and privileges and a certain degree of freedom from Crown control, often in return for a fairly significant payment into the Royal coffers.

By the 18th century there were over 300 such boroughs, usually governed by a mayor and council. When a vacancy arose on the council it was filled either by the councillors appointing one of their friends or by election from a very limited group of wealthy ratepayers. Any public service, such as repairing roads and bridges, was undertaken by the council for the main purpose of supporting local trade, rather than for any altruistic public motive.

The larger towns sometimes established Improvement Commissioners, to lay drains and improve the paving and lighting of streets, paid for by levying rates on householders, but these 'improvements' seldom extended beyond the town centre.

In the 18th century, no new charters were granted, so towns expanding rapidly as a consequence of the Industrial Revolution, such as Manchester or Birmingham, were not self-governing, although they could set up their own Improvement Commissioners if Parliament agreed.

In the rural areas outside the towns, such local government as there was rested in the hands of the local Justices of the Peace owning land worth more than £100 per year. The JPs met four times a year in Quarter Sessions and licensed public houses, appointed and supervised the parish constables, the surveyors of the highways and the overseers of the poor — and collected the rates from the local householders to pay for it all. In the event, most of the JPs appeared to be more interested in punishing poachers than repairing roads.

This, then, was the background against which the reform and development of local government started — the first phase of which was to take from 1835 to 1894 to complete.

Municipal Corporations

The first step in the reform process was the Municipal Corporations Act 1835 which abolished the self-serving and ineffective town governments. The Great Reform Bill of 1832 had extended the Parliamentary franchise to 'ten pound householders', but the 1835 Act went further by extending the Municipal franchise to all local ratepayers, regardless of the value of their property. For the first time, towns were governed by an elected council consisting not only of the wealthy local landowners but also of middle-class shopkeepers and, even, Dissenters. This change in the structure of local government in the towns was not matched by a similar reform in the rural areas, which continued, for a time, to be governed as before.

The promotion of public health

The cholera epidemics of the 1840s promoted interest in public health and this started the steady increase in functions given to local government. Borough councils which started life in 1835 largely for policing, lighting and paving of streets and making local bylaws, saw their responsibilities steadily increase to cover: control of the building of houses; the sanitation and health of the borough; transport to enable workers to travel to and from work; public libraries; a range of municipal utilities such as gas and water supply; and education.

Public health provided the impetus for further growth in local government structure. The Public Health Acts 1872 and 1875 established urban sanitary and rural sanitary districts covering the whole country. The urban sanitary districts included the boroughs, improvement commissioners and local boards. The rural sanitary districts included the areas of the poor law unions outside the urban sanitary districts.

County and District Councils

The Local Government Act 1888 created administrative county councils covering the whole of England and Wales, effectively taking over the functions previously carried out by the JPs in Quarter Sessions. However, at the same time, those boroughs with a population of 50,000 or more were given 'county borough' status — independence from the county council — that is, they were given the powers of the new county councils, in addition to those which they already enjoyed as municipal boroughs. In modern terms, they were the new unitary authorities of the 19th century.

Boroughs with less than 50,000 population remained as 'non-county' or municipal boroughs, with the county council providing a number of services (such as police, education and fire-fighting), while the non-county borough councils provided public cleansing and lighting.

The Local Government Act 1894 effectively completed the process by renaming the urban and rural sanitary districts as the new urban and rural district councils.

So, by 1894, the country outside London had a structure of local government (county councils, county borough councils, non-county or municipal borough councils, urban district councils and rural district councils) which was now elected by the ratepayers and accountable through the ballot box for what they did. In some ways, it is remarkable that this structure, put in place before the invention of the motor car, survived largely unchanged until 1972.

Cities

Many people think that a City is synonymous with a large local authority. In fact, city status has nothing to do with the type of local authority involved — it is to do with privilege.

A city was originally a borough which had (or at some time in the past had had) a diocesan bishop — but not always. Other areas could also acquire city status by Royal Letters Patent, or through their Royal Charter or even by custom and practice (that is, they have been cities for so long that nobody can remember why!). As the urban population increased during the 19th century, the Church of England had to increase the number of its dioceses — with an increase in the number of towns which gained city status. However, the mere possession of a cathedral did not mean that a town would automatically be a city, nor did a new city necessarily need to have a cathedral before it could come into existence. For example, when Birmingham was granted the status of a city in 1889 it had yet to acquire a cathedral, because it had grown so quickly as a consequence of the Industrial Revolution. It was even possible for there to be a city which was not a borough — an example of this was the City of Ely, which was then an urban district. In more modern times, it is the Home Secretary who advises the Sovereign on which towns should be granted city status, usually (but not always) to commemorate particular events: Lancaster was made a city in 1936 on the coronation of George VI and Derby gained city status in 1977 to celebrate the Queen's Silver Jubilee.

The present total of 58 cities is to be increased. A 'Millennium City' will be created, although at the time of writing this book the result of the competition, in which 39 towns took part, has still to be announced. There is, it seems, to be another competition for city status in 2002, to commemorate the Queen's Golden Jubilee.

London County Council

London has always been different from the rest of the country. The City of London (the 'Square Mile') has had its own Corporation for hundreds of years, since mediaeval times — and retains it to this day, unaffected by the various reforms of local government which have taken place around it.

The area of London outside the City had a structure of local government which developed in a way which was different from the rest of the country and at different times.

The Metropolitan Board of Works, the forerunner to the London County Council, was created in 1855. Indirectly elected by the vestries and district boards, it covered most of built-up London — as it was in those days. Its functions included sewerage, drainage, paving, cleansing and lighting, with the later addition of the Metropolitan Fire Brigade. The Metropolitan Police Force was established in 1829 but has never been subject to local control.

In the year following the creation of county councils in 1888, the London County Council was created, to succeed the Metropolitan Board of Works. The London County Council had more powers than the other county councils (it had a housing function unlike the rest of the counties). But it proved too powerful for central government and, at the turn of the century, some of its powers were transferred to the newly-established metropolitan borough councils.

Various changes in the London County Council's functions followed. In 1929, it became London's social welfare authority in place of the local boards of guardians which had been established in 1834. This involved the management of some 70 hospitals, which the council reorganised and modernised to form the largest unified hospital service in the world. These powers, in turn, were removed, as they were from the rest of local government, when public hospitals became the responsibility of the National Health Service in 1948.

London reorganisation

The move to reorganise local government in London began in 1957 with the establishment of the Royal Commission on Local Government in Greater London under Sir Edwin Herbert. The use of the word 'Greater' reflected the vast expansion of the built-up area since London County Council was established, and recognised that no logical distinction could be drawn between 'inner' and 'outer' London.

The Herbert Commission's report led to the London Government Act 1963, which extended the administrative area, taking in parts of Essex, Surrey, Kent and the whole of Middlesex.

The 1963 Act established, on 1 April 1965, the Greater London Council (GLC) and 32 London borough councils. The Act confirmed the position of the City of London Corporation, the only local authority without a democratic basis.

The GLC was predominantly a strategic authority. But, even so, the distribution of functions between the GLC and the London borough councils was ill-defined and frequently disputed, particularly in respect of housing and planning. These disputes came to an end with the abolition of the GLC in March 1986 (see *The 1986 reorganisation*, below).

The 1973 reorganisation of Northern Ireland

Prior to 1973, the local government structure in Northern Ireland was broadly similar to that in England and Wales — county, county borough, non-county borough, urban district and rural district councils. There were, however, special arrangements in two areas: Fermanagh and Londonderry.

The 1973 reorganisation produced 26 district councils, but more significantly, the transfer of functions from local government to central government. The 26 district councils are listed in Appendix A; the position on functions is explained in Appendix B.

The 1974 reorganisation

In 1966, Richard Crossman as Minister of Housing and Local Government in a Labour Government, set up a Royal Commission under the chairmanship of Sir John Maud (later Lord Redcliffe-Maud) to review functions and areas in England and Wales (excluding London). It was, however, not expected to consider local government finance (possibly involving the introduction of a new local income tax as an alternative to the rates); this was regarded by many people, albeit some years later, as a missed opportunity.

The Redcliffe-Maud Commission reported in 1969, proposing that more than 1,000 existing local authorities should be replaced by 61 new local authority areas. Of these areas, 58 were to be 'all-purpose authorities', based on enlarged county boroughs and given the name 'unitary'. In the other three areas — centred on the Birmingham, Liverpool and Manchester conurbations — Redcliffe-Maud suggested a two-tier form of metropolitan-style government, similar to that in London.

The Labour government accepted the Report, but with modifications. For their part, the Conservatives disliked the Report, probably because of their long-standing affinity with two-tier shire county government. They committed themselves to maintaining the existing two-tier system. When the Conservatives won the 1970 general election, Peter Walker became Minister of Housing and Local Government (the post was soon upgraded to Secretary of State for the Environment) and he made it clear that the unitary structure proposed by Redcliffe-Maud was too revolutionary. Instead, the reorganisation of local government under the Conservatives was to be evolutionary.

This evolutionary approach found expression in the Local Government Act 1972. The 1972 Act recognised the special needs of the major centres of population by introducing two-tier metropolitan-style government in six areas. These were the three areas proposed by the Redcliffe-Maud Commission (West Midlands, Merseyside and Greater Manchester) together with West Yorkshire, South Yorkshire and Tyne and Wear. In the event, the six metropolitan county councils only survived until 31 March 1986.

For the rest of the country, a two-tier structure of county council and district councils was introduced. Many of the new districts successfully applied for Royal charters to be called boroughs. The aim was to reduce the number of local authorities and the consequent amalgamations at county and district level brought a drastic reduction in the number of authorities — 39 counties and 296 districts in England, eight counties and 37 districts in Wales.

The two-tier structure may well have been regarded as traditional, but many people were upset because old counties, like Cumberland, Westmorland and the three 'parts' of Lincolnshire, disappeared. New counties like Avon, Cleveland, Cumbria and Humberside in England and Clwyd, Dyfed and Gwent in Wales, were created. Many of these new counties were regarded as artificial and were deeply unpopular — and the most unpopular have now ceased to exist, as a consequence of the rolling programme of reorganisation post-1992.

The two-tier system meant that county boroughs, the all-purpose authorities regarded by many as the most efficient form of local government ever devised, were swept away. They found themselves having to transfer some of their more important functions, such as education and social services, to the county council. Outside the metropolitan county areas, the big cities like Nottingham, Bristol, Leicester, Derby and Norwich were relegated to district council status — the same status as other districts only a fraction of their size. The only consolation, if it was such, was that they could keep the title 'city'. Again, the larger county boroughs have since regained their all-purpose status by becoming unitary authorities in the post-1992 rolling programme of reorganisation.

The 1986 reorganisation

The Conservative Party included in its 1983 general election manifesto a promise to abolish the Greater London Council (GLC) and the six metropolitan county councils (MCCs).

The manifesto suggested that these authorities were a "wasteful and unnecessary tier of government". In reality, the Labour-controlled GLC (based on the opposite side of the Thames at County Hall), under the leadership of Ken Livingstone, had become a thorn in the side of the Conservative Government — which explains Tony Blair's fear that Ken Livingstone might repeat that role if he was the first elected Mayor for London in 2000. The manifesto promised to abolish these seven authorities and return most of their functions to the boroughs and districts within them, with those services which needed to be administered over a wider area, such as police and fire, being run by newly-established joint boards.

Although its passage through Parliament was at times difficult, the Local Government Act 1985 received Royal Assent in July 1985, with the seven authorities ceasing to exist after 31 March 1986. The absence of a strategic local authority for London remained an issue for debate for the succeeding decade and was addressed in the proposals for a Greater London Assembly mentioned in a later section — *London 2000*.

The Inner London Education Authority (ILEA) was retained as a directly-elected authority, responsible for education in inner London but it did not last long in its new form, being abolished by the Education Reform Act 1988 on 1 April 1990. Each inner London borough council then became responsible for education in its area.

The work in winding up the affairs of the GLC and the MCCs was handled by a series of 'residuary bodies'. Set up in London and the metropolitan counties in September 1985, they assumed responsibility for dealing with the assets and liabilities of the former authorities and were themselves wound up when they had completed their work.

New police authorities were set up for the metropolitan county areas of Greater Manchester, Merseyside, South Yorkshire, West Midlands and West Yorkshire. In addition, the Northumbria Police Authority was extended to take in Tyne and Wear. Action in relation to the police in London was unnecessary because the Home Secretary was already the Metropolitan Police Authority for that area. All of the metropolitan district councils nominated councillors to serve on the new police authorities but, as in county police authorities, one third of the membership of each police authority had to be non-elected magistrates appointed by joint magistrates committees. These magistrates did not have to live in the county area. The constitution of these county police authorities was changed on 1 April 1995.

Seven new fire and civil defence authorities were set up in the areas administered by the abolished authorities. In London, each of the 32 London boroughs, plus the City of London, nominated one councillor to serve on the London Fire and Civil Defence Authority. In the six metropolitan county areas the number of nominations of each district depended on its size.

Six new passenger transport authorities were set up in the metropolitan county areas. Their membership was based on the same criteria as the fire and civil defence authorities. London local government has not had any involvement in passenger transport since London Regional Transport, a government appointed body, was set up in 1984 to take over GLC underground and bus powers. The position is now somewhat changed, as described in the *London 2000* section later.

On waste disposal, the position was varied. In London, one borough — Bexley — was allowed to go it alone; for the remaining London boroughs, three non-statutory and four statutory bodies were set up. In the metropolitan county areas the position varied, with Greater Manchester (except Wigan) and Merseyside having joint boards, while in the other areas, such as the West Midlands, there were voluntary joint arrangements.

Mechanisms for review prior to 1992

Since the end of the Second World War, there was a series of boundary and other commissions charged with examining boundaries or structure, or both. Most seem to have had little success. The Local Government Act 1972 set up Boundary Commissions for England and Wales, with powers to recommend the abolition of a local government area, the amalgamation of authorities, the abolition of any 'principal' area of local government, or the constitution of parishes.

The English Boundary Commission was charged with reviewing all counties, metropolitan districts and London boroughs between 1984 and 1989. Some county boundaries were changed in 1985 and there were recommendations for places like Humberside, but the Boundary Commission itself did not have a major effect on the structure of local government.

Local authorities were able to make proposals for changes to their own boundaries and these had to be passed on by the Commission, with their comments, to the Secretary of State for the Environment.

District councils had a duty to keep parish boundaries under review. They could propose changes to the Boundary Commission. They had to act on a request for a review from a parish council, or from at least 30 parish electors.

The 1992 reorganisation in Scotland

Prior to 1992, local government structure in Scotland consisted of regional councils with district councils within them, although three councils covering the islands (Orkney, Shetland and Western Isles) were unitary councils. In some parts of Scotland, the regional councils, in population terms, were significantly larger than the English county councils.

In 1992, the regional/district structure was replaced by a further 29 new unitary councils, bringing the total to 32. Unlike England, the process of change was a 'big bang' approach. The Scottish unitary councils are listed in Appendix A.

The 1992 process of phased change

One aim of the 1974 reorganisation was to make local government simpler for the general public to understand. It seems to have failed in that respect, and the later reorganisation in London and the metropolitan county areas did nothing to improve matters. The new authorities created by amalgamation in 1974 and the division of functions between the different levels meant that people were unsure about which authority was responsible for providing which service to them. Confusion could also be caused by the titles of authorities: county councils were clearly identifiable, but shire district and metropolitan district councils could variously be known as district council, borough council or city council, with no indication of their precise place in the local government framework.

In late 1991, the government announced its intention to undertake a major reform of the structure of local government by the creation, where practicable, of 'unitary authorities' responsible for most local authority functions, either directly or through joint arrangements with other authorities. These new unitary authorities would be similar to the Maud Commission all-purpose authorities, the old county boroughs and the present metropolitan boroughs. Cynics thought that the announcement might have been made to distract attention from the Government's U-turn on the Poll Tax, announced at the same time!

The first step in this reform process was the Local Government Act 1992, which replaced the English Boundary Commission with a new Local Government Commission for England, under the chairmanship of Sir John Banham.

No similar Commission was established for Wales, the process there being directly handled by the Secretary of State for Wales, without the benefit of advice and recommendations from a Commission. This difference from the process adopted in England was the subject of much criticism in Wales. The existing eight county councils and 37 district councils in Wales were replaced (on 1 April 1996) by 22 unitary authorities (see Appendix A).

The Local Government Commission was given the task of undertaking consultations, considering the structure of English local government, area by area, and making recommendations to the Secretary of State. The Secretary of State could decide whether or not to accept the recommendations of the Commission and he could refer its proposals back to the Commission for further examination, if he was dissatisfied. Although the final decision rested with the Secretary of State, it was felt that the Secretary of State did not have the right to impose a solution of his own which had not been previously considered or recommended by the Commission as part of its consultation process. It is important to understand that the Commission was independent of the Secretary of State — an independence which was emphasised from time to time.

1992 review in tranches

The 'big bang' approach of the 1974 reorganisation, when all authorities changed on the same date, was discarded for England. Instead, the process involved the Commission's work being undertaken area by area, in tranches, with implementation dates being phased over a number of years. The original time-scale envisaged completing all reviews by 1997; the Secretary of State then decided to accelerate the process and called for the review process to be completed by December 1994.

Each review was expected to be completed within eight to 16 months, depending on the complexity of the area. The time actually taken depended on how long it took for the Commission's part of the process to be completed; for the Secretary of State to reach a final decision on the Commission's recommendations; and for the Secretary of State to secure the approval of Parliament to the proposed changes for that area.

The original time-scale slipped in some areas, because of the Commission expanding its consultation process; or legal challenges to the process itself or the Commission's recommendations; or the Secretary of State not being satisfied with the Commission's first recommendations; or combinations of these factors.

The task of the Commission was not an easy one. The Secretary of State laid down detailed guidelines to the Commission which required the Commission to reflect the identity and views of local communities, as well as the need for effective and convenient local government. The Commission also had to take account of: people's preferences; work, shopping and leisure patterns; and the topography, geography and the history of the area. Any change had to be worthwhile and cost effective.

One surprising guideline was that there was to be no fixed minimum or maximum size for the new authorities, a departure from previous reviews, although there are none under around 100,000 population — with one exception. The Secretary of State, after some hesitation, approved a unitary authority for Rutland, with a population of 33,700, even though this solution was regarded as having implications for the people of Rutland in terms of costs and service delivery.

Unitary authorities everywhere?

Although a uniform solution throughout the country was not necessarily envisaged, there was nonetheless, at least initially, a clearly expressed preference by the government for a unitary-type system with one principal layer of local government in any area, but with the parishes continuing as before. The original guidelines to the Commission required it to look for structures consisting of unitary authorities, unless there were clear reasons for different arrangements.

This was interpreted by many districts as meaning the demise of the county councils and their own elevation to unitary status. This led to a campaign at national level, at times difficult, between the two local authority associations representing the two types of local authority involved — the Association of District Councils (ADC) and the Association of County Councils (ACC).

At local level, as the Commission's process got underway, similar campaigns were mounted by local authorities seeking greater status and by local authorities fighting for their continued existence — quite often involving commissioning their own formal public consultation exercises, alongside those undertaken by the Commission, in order to establish the strength of the evidence for supporting one option rather than another.

The actual results which emerged from the Commission and/or the Secretary of State were markedly different from the initial impression that there would be unitary authorities covering most of the country outside London and the metropolitan county areas (see Appendix A).

The results of the 1992 reviews

The first areas emerging from the review process involved the creation of new unitary authorities: a single unitary authority for the Isle of Wight (the obvious solution favoured by most of the people on the island) and four unitary authorities in each of Avon, Cleveland and Humberside (often described as the 'unpopular' and 'artificial' counties created by the 1974 reorganisation).

However, in some 10 counties the Commission recommended no change at all — the *status quo* (Cornwall, Cumbria, Hertfordshire, Lincolnshire, Northumberland, Oxfordshire, Suffolk, Surrey, Warwickshire and West Sussex). Elsewhere, a hybrid solution was adopted, involving a combination of one or more new unitary authorities and the status quo in the rest of the county (for example Leicester City and Rutland County unitary authorities, with the status quo in the rest of Leicestershire). Many of the new unitary authorities were former county boroughs which lost that status in 1974.

Following the resignation of Sir John Banham as chairman of the Commission, the Secretary of State announced that he was setting up a newly-constituted Commission under the chairmanship of Sir David Cooksey to re-review some areas, starting in July 1995. A total of 21 districts were the subject of further review to establish whether they should achieve their wish to be unitary authorities, having been disappointed with their failure to do so in the earlier review.

The Commission adopted a somewhat different approach for this review, involving considerations of the "stability, viability and identity" of any new unitary authority and the rest of the county without that unitary authority — with some emphasis on economic development and regeneration.

The Commission produced its draft recommendations in September 1995, suggesting the creation of 10 new unitary authorities — eight being existing districts and two, in the 'Thames Gateway', created from the merger of two existing districts each. The draft recommendations were the subject of consultation before final recommendations were made to the Secretary of State. The results of that last stage in the process appear in Appendix A.

If the aim of the 1992 process was to introduce a more simplified and coherent structure to local government, then a glance at Appendix A will demonstrate that it has failed — indeed, it has made matters even more confused.

London 2000

As already mentioned, following the 1986 reorganisation abolishing the GLC, London lacked a strategic local authority. In New Labour's manifesto for the 1997 General Election it was said: *"London is the only western capital without an elected city government. Following a referendum to confirm popular demand, there will be a new deal for London, with a strategic authority and a Mayor, each directly elected".*

The referendum on the creation of a Greater London Authority (GLA), on 7 May 1998, attracted a 34% turnout, of whom 72% were in favour of the proposal. The GLA which has emerged is fundamentally different in concept from the original GLC and, at the time of its creation, from any other local authority. In addition, the elected Mayor of London should not be confused with the Lord Mayor of London who is appointed by the Corporation of the City of London.

Following the referendum, the government steered the Greater London Authority Act 1999 through Parliament. In combination, the elected Mayor and the 25 member Assembly constitute the GLA. The first, separate, elections for the Mayor and the members of the Assembly took place on 4 May 2000 under different forms of Proportional Representation (PR). The Mayor was elected under the Single Transferable Vote (STV) system. The Assembly elections were carried out under the Additional Member (AMS) system, similar to that used for the Scottish Parliament and Welsh Assembly. Each elector had two votes: the first vote was for one of 14 *Area Members* elected for new constituencies, consisting of one or two London Borough areas. The second vote was used to elect the remaining 11 *London-wide Members* from lists of party representatives and independents, elected to achieve an overall share of the seats, proportional to each party's share of the overall vote. A description of the different forms of PR appears in *Essential Central Government.*

The Corporation of the City of London and the 32 London Boroughs retain their respective responsibilities for the local services within their areas and the Mayor is expected to work with them in exercising his or her London-wide executive responsibilities. The Assembly has no executive powers but acts as a check on the Mayor, scrutinising his or her executive decisions and agreeing the budget. It is important to bear in mind the distinction between the collective title Greater London Authority (GLA) and its two components, especially the Assembly.

The GLA is responsible for four bodies:

- *Transport for London* (Underground, buses, taxis, most main roads, and Docklands Light Railway);
- the *London Development Agency* (economic development);
- the *Metropolitan Police Authority* (a new police authority in place of the Home Secretary); and

- the *London Fire and Emergency Planning Authority* (replacing the existing London Fire and Civil Defence Authority).

The Mayor appoints a proportion of the members of each of these bodies and thus enjoys a degree of personal patronage unknown elsewhere in local government. The Mayor also has responsibilities (but in collaboration with other bodies) in relation to the Environment (air quality, waste and noise), land use planning (the overall planning framework for London but not individual planning decisions), culture (tourism, arts, and sport) and health (health improvement, but not running the health services).

The English Regions

As a consequence of devolution in Scotland, Wales and Northern Ireland, there will be increasing pressure for some sort of devolution in England, although whether the New Labour Government responds positively is another matter. This is discussed in *Essential Central Government*. If some sort of regional devolution takes place it is likely to be based upon the Regional Development Agencies but will almost certainly not result in an increase in the powers of existing local authorities. In fact, some commentators believe that if this development comes about, it may be at the expense of the English shire county councils which could disappear altogether — but that remains to be seen.

Local Government Bill

The *Local Government Bill* (LGB 2000) affects all local authorities other than the Greater London Authority and the Corporation of the City of London. The LGB 2000 is very significant for local authorities but it is not about areas or structure (and therefore is only mentioned here as a pointer), but about internal organisation, ethics and a 'power of general competence'. The various parts of the LGB 2000 are described in the relevant places in the following Chapters.

English parishes

All parishes and parish councils survived under the Local Government Act 1972, but without the added powers which were proposed for them by the Redcliffe-Maud Commission, whose recommendations envisaged their being the only tier of local government under the large, all-powerful unitary authorities. The 1972 Act required all parishes with more than 150 people to have a council.

Parishes are very much the grassroots of local government and as such can be important pressure groups. Their articulation of the local viewpoint can be 'inconvenient' for the 'principal' local authorities, but it is quite common for parish councillors to serve as district and/or county councillors, which means they have an additional platform for advancing the cause of their parishes.

Parish councils (often retaining traditional titles of town or, very occasionally, city council) vary enormously — from the 150 minimum population to more than 30,000. There are nearly 200 in metropolitan county areas. After the 1974 reorganisation, a number of 'disappearing' authorities, mostly with a population under 20,000, gained special dispensation to continue in parish form (known as Town Councils).

Parish councils have to hold an annual meeting and at least three other meetings a year. The chairman of the council may call an extraordinary meeting at any time. In addition, there must be a parish meeting, open to all electors, every year between March and June. The parish meeting may discuss any matter of interest to the parish. A vote can be taken, with all electors present entitled to take part, but in most cases the vote is not binding on the parish council. Further parish meetings may be called by the chairman, two parish councillors or six local government electors for the parish.

Welsh community councils

These are the Welsh parish councils. They automatically took over where there was a parish council before the 1972 Act. All former Welsh boroughs (except Cardiff, Merthyr Tydfil, Newport, Port Talbot, Rhondda and Swansea) and all urban districts became communities on 1 April 1974 and had to have a community council if the former authority demanded one or the Secretary of State for Wales insisted.

It is easier to get rid of (and recreate) a Welsh community council than an English parish. After five years, a meeting of electors can abolish a community council; on the other hand, after two years an electors' meeting can bring a council into existence.

Functions of 'Principal' local authorities

'Principal' local authorities are: unitary authorities, London borough councils, metropolitan borough councils, county councils, shire district councils — and, of course, the Corporation of London. Parish/community councils are not 'principal' local authorities.

Local authorities exist to provide services to the public, apart from their role in the political and democratic processes at local level. The responsibilities of a particular local authority will depend upon what functions have been assigned to it by the relevant legislation — what those functions are will depend upon which type the authority is and whether there are any agency or joint arrangements which have been adopted locally to improve service delivery or share resources.

Agency agreements are frequently set up between counties and shire districts within a two-tier area, whereby the district carries out work within its area as agent for the county council. The agreements vary from area to area — they are most common in road maintenance. Agency agreements are not allowed for education, social services, police and fire.

London borough councils and the metropolitan borough councils in the former metropolitan county areas have existed for many years now and their functions and any inter-authority working arrangements are well-established. One of the criticisms of the 1992 reorganisation process was that the far more important issue of the distribution of functions to, and between, local authorities was not included in the review. Some eminent commentators believed that this was a lost opportunity by the Government.

Unitary authorities are broadly similar to London borough councils and metropolitan borough councils in terms of their functions. As already said, the 1992 review concentrated on structure rather than detailed arrangements for the allocation of functions. Little guidance was forthcoming from the government about how it saw services being delivered in the future by the unitary authorities which it established. In essence, the issues were left to the unitary authorities to sort out between themselves and with any residual county council within whose overall area they existed.

Joint arrangements for some county-wide services, particularly the small specialist services, needed to be made if those services were to survive — possibly by one authority agreeing to act as 'lead authority'. But this solution depended upon all of the authorities involved reaching agreement at a time when they were preoccupied with ensuring that basic services continued to be delivered within the financial framework decreed by the Government (see the Chapter on *Finance*).

The two exceptions to what is said in the previous paragraph are the police and fire services. New police authorities were established on 1 April 1995, making them much more independent of local government. Where one or more new unitary authorities were created within the area of an existing shire county council, a new statutory combined Fire Authority was established to ensure a continued county-wide fire service managed by a single authority. Although these arrangements secured the continued effective delivery of the police and fire service, their very existence called into question the rationale of the rest of the reorganisation process and their creation was viewed by many as yet another extension of the quangocracy.

Functions of parish councils

Parish councils exist, for the large part, in rural areas. Parish councils can exist in urban areas, but are much less common there. Most services provided by parish councils are concurrent with the district council in whose area they exist. Transport services may be undertaken with the permission of the county council. In addition, the district council, if requested, must notify the parish council of all planning applications concerning the parish council. The parish council may then comment on these applications.

Functions of all local authorities

The basic distribution of functions to particular types of authority is described in Appendix B.

2 Councillors and Officers

The role of the councillor — types of officer — the councillor/officer interface — officers giving advice — political assistants

Councillors — what are they for?

As explained in Chapter 1, local authority councillors have existed in some urban parts of the country since the Municipal Corporations Act 1835 and county councils have existed since 1888. For most of the time since then, the majority of people, if asked to define the role of councillors, would only have a vague idea of what they did — probably not able to go much further than a characterisation of someone performing unpaid public service. The next few sections of this Chapter attempt to shed some light on why people become councillors and what role they perform.

The modern lack of knowledge/interest in the role of the councillor was neatly summed up in a piece in the *Guardian* newspaper in mid March 1998, by Kay Holman, Director of Public Access Partnership, under the heading *Hit Squad Time:*

> *"Talk to friends and neighbours and most will have only a hazy idea of what the council is, the difference between councillors and officers, what they do, and why any of it matters. When there is some point of contact, it's often a source of irritation, incomprehension or frustration.*
>
> *A survey in Newham, east London, asked young people what they thought of councillors. They needed further explanation, before deciding that it sounded like they might be a good idea — presumably under the impression that the concept was being market-tested. ...*
>
> *We have seen education hit squads and social services hit squads. Might we soon see democratic renewal hit squads?"*

In referring to 'democratic renewal hit squads', Kay Holman was echoing the kinds of initiatives trailed by the New Labour Government in its first 1998 Modernising Local Government Green Paper — Local Democracy and Community Leadership, as the means of improving communication between local authorities and their electors/consumers — focus groups, citizens' juries and opinion polls. The proposals in this and the other Green Papers connected with modernising local government issued that year were picked up in later legislation, especially by the Local Government Bill (LGB 2000), which is considered later.

Councillor — who wants to be one?

What kind of people decide to become a councillor? Robert Gifford, then the Leader of Milton Keynes District Council, in an article in the *Municipal Journal* in late June 1994 about the training needs of members, had these thoughts to offer:

- *"Elected councillors come in a number of shapes and sizes. Some are strategists, seeking to put in place a particular policy covering the locality (as in, say, economic development or health).*
- *A second group are the community activists. These seek to remedy a particular local problem — a hole in the road, for example — and realise that the only way to achieve that is by being elected on to the council to do something about it.*
- *The third group comprises those who are the last in the room when nominations are handed out. ...*
- *The fourth and final group is those who wish to repay something to their local community. At other times, this group might be active in the National Trust or the World Wildlife Fund. Above all, they want to undertake some kind of voluntary service, supporting the town in which they live.*

No councillor fits into just one of these categories".

More recently, in March 1998, the Local Government Management Board (LGMB) published the results of the 1997 first national 'census' survey of councillors in England and Wales. The response rate achieved by the LGMB (98% of local authorities and 67% of councillors) was impressive for this kind of voluntary survey. The published results give an insight into the profile of the councillor 'population' and may dispel (or confirm!) some myths about the kind of person most likely to be a councillor:

- **Gender, ethnicity and disability**

male	73%
female	27%
white	97%
ethic minority	3%
disabled	11%

- **Age**

The average age was 55.6 years, with most councillors in age groups over 45 years.

- **Employment status**

full-time employed	30%
part-time employed	8%
self-employed	15%
unemployed	3%
retired	35%
other not working	8%

Of these people, 25% regarded themselves as being 'full-time' councillors, that is, spending at least 30 hours per week on council work of any kind, with or without other jobs.

• Current occupation	
managerial/executive	33%
professional/technical	28%
lecturer/teacher/researcher	12%
admin/clerical/secretarial/sales	13%
manual/craft	14%
• Sector of employment	
private sector	60%
local government	11%
central government	4%
NHS	5%
other public sector	14%
voluntary sector	6%
• Education and qualifications	
degree/higher degree/NVQ4/5	32%
professional qualification	21%
HNC/A level/ONC/Diploma/NVQ3	12%
GCSE/CSE/NVQ1/2/other	18%
none	17%

Councillors — what do they do?

In 1972 the *Bains Report* on the, then, new (created by the 1972 reorganisation) local authorities' management and structure also examined issues of effective management, including the role of the councillor, and confirmed that the ultimate direction and control of the affairs of the authority should lie with the councillors; that the councillors should take the key decisions on the objectives of the authority and on the plans to attain them; and the councillors should keep under review the progress and performance of the services.

The *Widdicombe Report*, on the conduct of local authority business, published in 1986, included:

> *"Local government has derived strength over the years from a complementary relationship between part-time councillors drawn from and representative of the general public, and full-time officers with professional expertise. We accept that this cannot be a rigid or static model. Some councillors will need to devote considerable time to council business, and there has sometimes been too great a stress on officer professionalism. Councillors moreover have the right to ensure that their*

decisions, for which they are statutorily responsible and accountable, are implemented by officers. Nevertheless a merging of rôles is not desirable. Councillors should leave the day to day implementation of council policies, including staff management, as far as possible to officers, and officers should demonstrate that they are sensitive to the political aspirations underlying those policies".

In 1990 the Audit Commission joined the discussion in its paper *We Can't Go On Meeting Like This*. Although the main thrust of that paper was about more effectively defined internal working arrangements and reducing the number of committee meetings, it had, nevertheless, some interesting things to say about the modern role of councillors.

The Audit Commission argued that councillors had three key rôles: as *politician; representative;* and *board member*. As *politician*, they were concerned not only with public service but also with social change. As *representative* of the electorate, they acted to ensure that the local authority was held to account for service priorities, allocation of resources and ultimate performance. As *board member*, they had a constitutional duty to share collective responsibility for the local authority organisation and its activities, in a way similar to non-executive company directors — but with an important additional dimension. That dimension lay in the additional pressure of accountability through the ballot box every four years and the Draconian statutory sanction of surcharge if they made a serious mistake in the decisions they were expected to take. As a consequence of the Local Government Bill 2000 (LGB 2000), surcharge will no longer exist.

The post-2000 role of the 'modernised' councillor, as envisaged by New Labour in the LGB 2000, is discussed later.

Councillors — how much time do they spend on their work?

The 1986 *Widdicombe Report* referred to much earlier research, carried out in 1964, which had shown that in 1964 the average number of hours spent by a councillor on council duties was 52 per month. Research undertaken in 1985 for the Widdicombe Report itself showed that by that year, that figure had risen to 74 hours per month.

In the context of supporting its assertion that too much councillor time was spent in meetings, the 1998 *Modernising Local Government* Green Paper — *Local Democracy and Community Leadership* referred to a survey carried out in 1992 for the Joseph Rowntree Foundation by Nirmala Rao, published as *Managing change: Councillors and the New Local Government.* That survey was much smaller than the previous surveys and its conclusions therefore need to be treated with some caution, but the Green Paper used it to support its proposition that by 1992, the average time commitment had increased further to 97 hours per month.

However, some further research, involving a more reliable sample of 1,682 councillors in 53 local authorities, had been undertaken by Ken Young and Nirmala Rao to supplement the 1992 report. The conclusions of that further research had been published in April 1994, in *Local and Central Government Relations Research Paper 27*, again under the auspices of the Joseph Rowntree Foundation, as *The role of local government councillors in 1993*. That report made some interesting observations which are worth repeating here:

- *Councillors spend on average 74 hours a month on council business, exactly the same as indicated by the Widdicombe survey of 1985.*
- *Nearly 70% of councillors feel the overall time they spend on council business is 'about right'.*
- *The majority of councillors give first or second preference to their representational work. Only a small minority give first preference to participating in policy-making or the overall running of the council. Carrying out the party programme is the main concern of very few councillors.*
- *Despite this preference for representational work, councillors spend a majority of their time (56%) on council, committee and party meetings, preparing for them, and meeting officers.*
- *Strikingly, this broad allocation of time does not vary much between councillors with very different responsibilities, and has remained remarkably stable through four national surveys conducted over a period of 30 years. Councillors in general do not experience their committee and sub-committee work as burdensome.*
- *The present system of decision-making commands the overwhelming support of councillors, with only a small minority in favour of a more streamlined system. Satisfaction is less among newer and younger councillors and those from minority parties.*
- *Proposed changes in decision-making structures are seen as concentrating responsibility in the hands of too few councillors, thus removing ordinary councillors' incentive to serve on councils.*
- *However, proposals for Westminster-style scrutiny select committees and for decentralisation to local areas with greater member involvement evoke widespread interest.*

Over the last decade, there has been an increasing tendency for the most senior councillor in the larger authorities (usually the Leader of the majority party and, therefore, of the Council) to become, to all intents and purposes, a full-time councillor, with a consequent increase in his or her personal allowance to reflect the additional work. This tendency was recognised by the proposals in the LGB 2000 discussed later.

Modernising Local Government — the Local Government Bill (LGB 2000)

Some of the comments reported in the previous paragraph need to be remembered when looking at the proposals included in the LGB 2000. The LGB 2000 had its origins in the New Labour *Modernising Local Government* Green Paper — *Local Democracy and Community Leadership.* The proposals in that Green Paper, and the one which followed it, *Improving Services through Best Value,* are mentioned in the next Chapter.

In this context, it is useful to consider the implications of the LGB 2000 for the role of the individual councillor. One might speculate on the real attraction to a prospective councillor in having to choose between an executive role or a representational role when taking on the role of councillor, as suggested in *Local Democracy and Community Leadership.* That presupposes, of course, that the choice is actually offered to the new councillor by the political hierarchy already in place. Under the pre-existing system, backbench councillors were already often uneasy and even suspicious about the power wielded by the more senior councillors, even from their own political party; the LGB 2000 has now increased the likelihood of this polarisation.

The polarisation between frontbench and backbench councillors is institutionalised by the LGB 2000 proposals for elected Mayors and Cabinets, replacing the existing committee system as a means of taking executive decisions. If the object of the exercise is to make the local government councillor appear to be a more attractive occupation and thus attract candidates of higher calibre, then it is difficult to see how the LGB 2000 can achieve this. LGB 2000 limits the size of the Cabinet and it is to be expected that the existing senior councillors will want to be members of it — it is unlikely that a newly-elected councillor would be 'parachuted' into the Cabinet, without having served an apprenticeship first. There lies the problem, because the only place where that apprenticeship can be served is, under LGB 2000, in the non-executive or scrutiny arms of the authority. Councillors who are not members of the Cabinet will have to be content with looking after the interests of their constituents, dealing with non-executive functions and scrutinising the activities of the Cabinet.

However they are dressed up, non-executive and scrutiny activity will almost certainly be viewed as a second-rate role — the real action (in terms of taking executive decisions which make a difference) will be in the Cabinet which, under LGB 2000, will be able to (and, therefore, probably will) meet behind closed doors. It will be difficult for the Cabinet to keep the other councillors, let alone the public, informed of what it is doing. The position is even more difficult where only one person, the elected Mayor, is exercising executive responsibilities. The LGB 2000 also has implications for the officers — these are discussed later.

Departments

Any local authority obviously needs to employ staff to implement the policies determined by the councillors. Each local authority can determine what staffing levels it needs or can afford, but it is obliged by law to appoint certain officers.

The staff are employed within the local authority in one of a number of departments, usually headed by a professionally qualified officer or an experienced manager. Each department usually reports to one or more committees. Over the last decade, the number of departments within each local authority has tended to reduce as a consequence of rationalisations to achieve 'efficiency' savings. Under LGB 2000, for executive activity in discharging the local authority's functions, departments will now report to the Cabinet or the elected Mayor (as the case may be). Departments will still relate to those committees which will continue to exist — connected with the other, non-executive, activities of the authority and with the internal scrutiny of the executive.

There are two types of department: *service* department and *central* department.

Service departments are responsible for the delivery of the authority's services to the public — for example: education, social services, housing, technical services and leisure services. This service delivery can be achieved in one of three ways: firstly, directly from within the service department itself; or secondly, through a direct labour organisation (DLO) or direct service organisation (DSO) attached to the department, where compulsory competitive tendering (CCT) has resulted in this semi-independent form of organisation; or thirdly, by using external suppliers as agents under contract. The use of external suppliers can arise in a number of ways. Often, the use of an external supplier offers the best and most cost-effective means of service delivery and, in this case, the local authority has decided to become an *enabling authority*, rather than a direct service provider. Sometimes, the local authority had no choice but to use an external supplier, because it lost the right to provide the service itself through a DLO/DSO, when it failed to succeed in a CCT process for that service. The issues around CCT and DLO/DSOs are dealt with in more detail in the next Chapter.

Central departments provide the corporate core of the local authority and also provide support to the service departments — for example: chief executive, finance, law and administration, and personnel. Again, if a process of CCT has been applied to these support services, they may be provided through a DSO or an external supplier.

The names of these departments can vary greatly from authority to authority, as can the title of the officer at the head of them.

Chief Executive — Head of the Paid Service

The senior officer in most local authorities is usually called the *chief executive* but may sometimes be called clerk, principal officer or general manager. The role is to act as the principal policy adviser, manager and co-ordinator for the authority.

There is no recognised professional qualification for the appointment but the majority are still lawyers or accountants with an increasing number of other disciplines.

The number of women chief executives is still relatively small, but it is steadily increasing. When a local authority is appointing a chief executive it is looking for somebody with the experience and maturity to be the principal adviser, who will be responsible for seeing that its wishes, if lawful and practical, are put into effect.

The local authority will need a first class manager who can motivate all staff to produce results and who is politically sensitive and neutral, but not politically committed. The idea of a chief executive was widely introduced at the time of the 1974 reorganisation, largely as a result of the 1972 *Bains Report* mentioned earlier. Bains espoused the concept of *corporate management* — that is, moving away from the former department-led approach in managing the authority towards an approach which transcended departmental boundaries and considered, instead, the management of the authority as a corporate whole. The chief executive then envisaged by Bains was a stand-alone officer, free from departmental responsibilities so as to have time to oversee the development of the corporate management of the authority.

Since their introduction, for a variety of reasons often connected with the relationship with the political leadership, a few authorities have critically examined the continued relevance of their chief executive. In the early 1980s, some councils used the excuse of financial cutbacks to question the post and sought to replace it with a triumvirate of chief officers or some other management structure not involving a chief executive post; however, this trend did not catch on generally. In many authorities, for reasons of cost-effective management (or chief executive self-preservation!), the post of chief executive reacquired some departmental responsibilities of a central or corporate nature.

Authorities were required by the Local Government and Housing Act 1989 to nominate one officer as *Head of the Paid Service*. This post was usually held by the chief executive, clerk or principal officer. The Head of the Paid Service has a statutory duty to report to the authority on the co-ordination of functions; numbers and grades of staff; and the organisation, appointment and management of staff. The authority must consider this report within three months but does not have to agree to its proposals. In practice, individual Heads of Paid Service choose to comply with this duty in different ways — not always by producing a specific 'Head of the Paid Service' report but raising any less fundamental issues through more informal links with the political leadership of the authority.

These new responsibilities of the Head of the Paid Service have the potential for difficulties with the council. Because of this, the Government introduced a requirement for authorities to make provision in their Standing Orders for the process to be followed in dismissing or disciplining the Head of the Paid Service. The process must include a 'designated independent person' to ensure fair treatment. In reality, the post of chief executive is so close to the political processes of the local authority that if there is a breakdown in mutual confidence between the chief executive and the council leadership, the matter usually resolves itself into negotiating severance terms, rather than fighting the disciplinary action itself.

This close connection of the chief executive with the political process is likely to be increased by the LGB 2000. Whichever model the authority adopts — elected Mayor or Cabinet — the chief executive will find it increasingly difficult to avoid becoming even more closely associated with the executive arm of the authority. This may result in two developments. Firstly, some existing chief executives may decide to leave for greener pastures, if they are uncomfortable with the concept of having to depart from the existing tenet that all officers (including the chief executive) are there to work with the authority as a whole. Secondly, there may be an increase in the number of fixed-term contracts for chief executives, linked to the authority's electoral cycle and the probable life of a political administration, because many of the councillors engaged in Scrutiny (certainly the opposition parties and possibly even the backbenchers of the administration) may come to regard the chief executive as the 'Cabinet's person', if nothing worse. The position becomes even more pointed in an authority which adopts the elected Mayor and Council Manager model of modernisation.

Other Statutory Officers

Local authorities must also appoint an officer, the *Chief Financial Officer,* to be responsible for making proper arrangements for the administration of their finances. The officer must be a member of an approved accountancy body. Like the Chief Executive/Head of the Paid Service, the Chief Financial Officer may be given a different title (for example, County Treasurer, Director of Finance) and the individual may also have responsibility for other central support services (for example, Director of Finance and Administration). The position can become rather confusing if the post is responsible for a range of central support services and the chief officer post is known as, for example, Director of Central Services. The key to where the statutory responsibility actually lies is to establish who is the *Section 151 Officer*, which refers to the statutory provision under which the appointment is required. There may be times when, because of his or her statutory responsibilities, the Chief Financial Officer has to give advice which is not very popular with the political leadership of the authority. This can put the Chief Financial Officer in a potentially difficult position and the LGB 2000 recognised this by extending to Chief Financial Officers the special procedures in relation to discipline and dismissal previously applicable only to the Head of the Paid Service.

Local authorities must also nominate an officer as *Monitoring Officer.* The monitoring officer must report to the authority, in consultation with the Head of the Paid Service, Chief Financial Officer and Chairman of the council on any contravention of law or a code of conduct or an act of maladministration (what amounts to maladministration is discussed in the Chapter on *Propriety and Ethics*). The authority must consider the report within 21 days and must not give effect to any proposals which are the subject of the report before it has done so. Formal reports of Monitoring Officers are not that frequent and are usually regarded as the last resort either where informal action has failed to resolve the problem or where there has been patent maladministration or activity which was potentially unlawful.

Originally, the authority had some discretion as to who it could appoint as Monitoring Officer, including the Head of the Paid Service, but *not* the Chief Financial Officer, who had to be a different officer from the Monitoring Officer. In practice, in most authorities the Monitoring Officer is the chief legal officer, because of his or her professional training and ethics. However, in some authorities (the smallest ones where a lawyer might not be employed at all) the Head of the Paid Service was also sometimes the Monitoring Officer.

Opinions differed about this duality of role in the same person. Some chief executives claimed that they had always carried out this role, but had done so with the sensitivity that was necessary to achieve results, rather than by threatening their local authority with a statutory report. Others took the view that the chief executive was necessarily too close to the political processes of the local authority and the role of Monitoring Officer was better carried out by someone less closely connected with them and able to apply objective judgement to the issues involved. On balance, most people concluded that propriety was better served if the chief executive was not, also, the Monitoring Officer. The LGB 2000 put the issue beyond argument when it introduced a prohibition on the Head of the Paid Service also being appointed as Monitoring Officer. Because of the fact that individual Monitoring Officers could also find themselves in difficulties similar to those of the Chief Financial Officer, the LGB 2000 also extended the special disciplinary and dismissal procedures to Monitoring Officers as well.

The Councillor/Officer Interface

The vast majority of the paid employees of a local authority will seldom, if ever, come into direct contact with councillors of that authority. Contact between councillors and officers tends to occur at the more senior levels of the officer structure — either in the formal/informal decision-making processes of the council or in dealing with constituents' complaints when those councillors are fulfilling their representational role.

It is at this level that attention has been given to the relations between councillors and officers — most notably in the *National Code of Local Government Conduct*, the *Widdicombe Report* and the *Nolan Report*. One feature remains constant in this continuing debate — that there are no easy answers.

How the councillor/officer interface is managed in practice will vary from one local authority to another and it is unlikely that any two authorities will deal with it in the same way. Much will depend upon the political balance of the council, the conventions and practices which have evolved over time and the personalities of the people, both councillor and officer, involved. At times, tensions will inevitably exist in the relationship, which have to be worked through in the interests of the effective running of the local authority's affairs.

The *National Code of Local Government Conduct* issued in 1990, replaced the original version previously issued in 1975. This statutory Code covered councillors only. On the subject of relations between councillors and officers, the Code stated:

> *"Both councillors and officers are servants of the public, and they are indispensable to one another. But their responsibilities are distinct. Councillors are responsible to the electorate and serve only so long as their term of office lasts. Officers are responsible to the council. Their job is to give advice to councillors and the council, and to carry out the council's work under the direction and control of the council, their committees and sub-committees.*
>
> *Mutual respect between councillors and officers is essential to good local government. Close personal familiarity between individual councillors and officers can damage this relationship and prove embarrassing to other councillors and officers".*

The LGMB later produced a parallel voluntary, non-statutory, Code for local government employees which, on the subject of relationships, effectively repeated the terms of the two paragraphs quoted above.

The Third Report of the Committee on Standards in Public Life under the chairmanship of Lord Nolan, *Standards of Conduct in Local Government* (the *Nolan Report*) published in July 1997, considered, amongst other things, defining the working relationship:

> *"There have been a number of attempts to define the proper working relationship between officers and members. The present national code states [quotes the two paragraphs above]... This passage illustrates the limitations of the present national code. In practice, the simple split of policy (councillors) and implementation (officers) is neither always accurate nor illuminating. It is clear that there exist enormous variations in local government in the way the relationship works, both broadly and in detail, and that these relationships cannot be summarised in a code designed to apply nation-wide. In our draft principles we have therefore included a simple statement of the need for councillors to respect the position of officers and treat them with courtesy: it goes without saying that the same is true for officers and their attitude to councillors".*

These various Codes and the Nolan Report provided the basis for the proposals in LGB 2000 which are considered in more detail in the later Chapter on *Propriety and Ethics*. The LGB 2000 provides for the Secretary of State to obtain Parliamentary approval of General Principles of Conduct for Local Councillors in England. In the context of the councillor/officer interface, the consultative draft of those General Principles (which would be included in a new National Code) suggested:

> *"You should respect the role of the council's officers and employees and treat them in a way that engenders mutual respect at all times".*

Officers — political neutrality and sensitivity

It is of paramount importance that both councillors and officers understand the duties upon the officers to provide honest and accurate advice to the council *as a whole* — but advice which is nonetheless politically sensitive. As a matter of principle, most would argue that this should still be the case in an authority which has adopted one of the executive models under *LGB 2000*. That advice may not always entirely suit some councillors' political objectives, but the councillors would be vulnerable without it. The strength of local government depends upon the officers being able to offer impartial advice to the councillors, while at the same time understanding that the councillors are also able to reach their own decisions in the light of that advice. This requires a degree of mutual understanding and a willingness to discuss and resolve any misunderstandings as they arise.

The area of policy advice is obviously a sensitive area, where precise definition of what is appropriate is often difficult. The context is best set by considering what the Widdicombe Report had to say on the subject. On the evidence given to the Widdicombe committee on the subject of officer neutrality:

> *"The overwhelming view in the evidence we have received has been that officers (subject to very limited and closely defined exceptions) should continue to serve the council as a whole. This has not been a source of difference between officers and members, between majorities and minorities, or between right and left. There has equally been wide agreement that the public service tradition of a permanent corps of politically impartial officers should be retained. That is to say that the majority party should not use their voting strength to appoint officers on the basis of political sympathy with their position".*

Widdicombe also offered the following comments on the officer as adviser:

> *"We do not believe from the evidence we have received from them that councillors are looking for advice which* ***reflects*** *their political point of view, but rather advice which is factual and honest and which* ***shows an understanding*** *of their political aspirations and constraints. There is no*

reason in principle why an officer should not be able to give advice of such a kind to all political parties represented on the council. Nor, to the extent that officers might in practice give advice on a fuller and more regular basis to the majority party, is there any reason why they should not continue to do so just as effectively when there is a change of political control".

The LGB 2000 introduced a new factor in this discussion — officer support for the executive, non-executive and scrutiny arms of the authority. The DETR Guidance on new council Constitutions under LGB 2000 (see the next chapter for more information on Constitutions) built on the foundations laid by the Code, Widdicombe and Nolan when it commented (on officer support for the executive arm):

"Officers will continue to work for the authority as a whole. Nevertheless, as the majority of functions will be executive functions, it is likely that in practice many officers will be working to the executive for most of their time. The executive will have to respect the political neutrality of the officers".

On the avoidance of misunderstandings between officers and members under the LGB 2000 models, the DETR Guidance suggested:

"Councils are encouraged to consider developing appropriate conventions setting out the roles, responsibilities and rights of officers and members and establishing the key principles governing officer/member relationships".

On the subject of officer support for Scrutiny, the DETR Guidance had this to say:

"Overview and scrutiny committees will need properly resourced and effective support. Where the same officers are supporting both the executive and overview and scrutiny committees there is also the potential for conflict. Overview and scrutiny committees will be questioning the executive's decisions which will usually be based on officer advice. This might discourage officers from leading an overview and scrutiny committee down a fruitful line of enquiry.

The Government does not believe that a formal separation of officer support between the executive and overview and scrutiny is necessary. Indeed the Government recognises that, particularly in smaller authorities, it will not be possible to separate support in this way. However, some authorities may, depending on local circumstances, decide that some separation of officer support between these roles is necessary. The legislation does not prevent or require this and it will be a matter for local choice. Where a council does decide to separate officer support it will be essential to ensure that there is appropriate exchange of staff to and from the two 'sides' of the officer corps and that all staff have rewarding career development opportunities and are treated fairly at all times.

Similar conflict may occur for officers supporting both the full council and the executive, particularly in the budget and policy setting process. Again it will be a matter for local choice how councils choose to organise support for the full council in its roles and, in some cases, it might be appropriate for there to be dedicated support for the council and committees which discharge non-executive functions".

So, no easy answers here. Local authorities will have to find their own local solutions to the problem of officer/member relationships arising out of the LGB 2000 modernisation.

Officers — politically restricted posts

Arising from Widdicombe, the Local Government and Housing Act 1989 disqualified a paid officer of one local authority from being a councillor of another local authority (except parish and community councils), if that officer was in a *politically restricted post*. This was intended to put an end to 'twin tracking', under which some councillors were allowed large periods of time off by their employing authority to enable them effectively to become full-time councillors of another neighbouring local authority with a similar political complexion.

In addition to this, an officer in a politically restricted post cannot hold posts in political parties, act as agent, canvass, or speak publicly on political issues. The prohibition also extends to being, or for standing for election as, an MP or MEP. When these provisions were first introduced, some officers objected to them on the grounds that they interfered with their ability to take part in political activities as individuals. NALGO (as it then was) took the issue to court, challenging the legality of these provisions, but failed to impress the court with its argument.

The post is to be listed as *politically restricted* if:

- *the gross annual salary exceeds a specified level (in excess of £19,500), equivalent to spinal column point (scp) 44 of the local government national pay scales (£28,839 in April 2000); or*
- *the officer is the Head of the Paid Service, the Monitoring Officer, a chief officer or deputy chief officer or is otherwise involved in giving advice to councillors on a regular basis; or*
- *the officer is responsible for regular contact with the media on behalf of the council, such as press officers.*

The list is maintained by the local authority. The second and third criteria can be a matter of opinion and a person who is aggrieved at his or her post being listed as politically restricted may refer the case to an Adjudicator appointed by the Secretary of State.

Political assistants

However, it must be remembered that local authorities are political bodies and councillors are, first and foremost, politicians. Widdicombe recognised that there would be times when the political groups required advice of a political nature which it would not be right for the paid officers to be asked to provide. Most political groups rely upon their local party organisation to supply that political advice, but Widdicombe put forward the idea of *political assistants* — officers specifically employed for the sole purpose of giving political advice to a political group, rather than professional advice to the whole council.

On the issue of *political advice*, Widdicombe said:

> *"In some authorities it might be considered that the political groups' need for advice cannot be fully met by the chief executive and by those staff reporting to him or her through the normal officer hierarchy. This might occur where the chief executive is by natural disposition more a manager and less a political operator. It might occur where a council is hung with three parties all holding the balance of power, or it might happen simply because the political temperature is that much higher.*
>
> *In the evidence, a sharp distinction has been made between overt arrangements of this kind and covert arrangements whereby officers beneath chief officer level in the main officer hierarchy have become singled out by the political parties as being sympathetic sources of advice. This latter practice is highly damaging to chief officers' management authority and blurs rôles insidiously. We believe it is quite wrong and should be stopped, and this view is widely reflected in the evidence. On the other hand, there has been widespread acceptance in the evidence of limited overt appointments. They are regarded as providing some flexibility within the system and thereby taking some political pressure off the main officer hierarchy without challenging their authority".*

The Local Government and Housing Act 1989 made it lawful for a local authority to employ political assistants — but not many have chosen to do so. Obvious difficulties can arise between the political assistants and the chief officers whose role is to advise the local authority as a whole. It was because of those difficulties that strict limitations were imposed on the appointment of political assistants:

- the council must have made Standing Orders relating to the appointments before any appointments can be made;
- the council cannot have more than three such posts;
- each political group can only have one post allocated to it;
- the appointment is made on merit and in accordance with the wishes of the political group concerned;

- the gross annual salary for each post cannot exceed a specified limit, which is adjusted by the Secretary of State from time to time — from October 1995 (last time reviewed): £25,044 p.a.;
- the posts are regarded as being 'politically restricted' for the purposes of the 1989 Act;
- contracts are fixed-term and have to terminate no later than 12 months after the next council election;
- political assistants can only carry out work for members of political groups in their capacity as councillors, not for other political purposes; and
- the council cannot delegate any of its functions to political assistants.

The LGB 2000 provides that, where there is a directly elected Mayor, a fourth assistant can be appointed by the Mayor in order to advise him or her. Political assistants do not have a right to attend executive meetings but may do so if invited.

3 Decision-making, Information and Quality

Chief officer management — delegation — the formal committee system — informal systems — politics — how meetings work — access to information and meetings — Cabinets, Leaders and Elected Mayors — general information — CCT — Best Value Citizen's charters

The previous Chapter considered the role of the councillor, the statutory chief officers and the interface between councillor and officer. It is against that background that this Chapter now looks at how decisions are reached in practice and how the local authority is managed internally. The first part of this Chapter deals with the position prior to the Local Government Bill (LGB 2000). As the provisions in LGB 2000 (described later) are implemented in individual authorities — some may take until 2002 to adopt the LGB 2000 models — the process for taking executive decisions will change quite dramatically. Until that time, the following sections of this Chapter will still be relevant and most will continue to be relevant thereafter for the non-executive and scrutiny arms of the modernised authority.

It is best to look at the officer management processes first, since they underpin the more fundamental councillor-based mechanisms. Just as councillor- based mechanisms will vary from one local authority to another, the same is true of the systems devised by the officers (with the approval of their council) to undertake their part in the running of the local authority.

Chief Officers Management Team

In the previous Chapter, mention has already been made of the Bains Report and the introduction of corporate management and standalone chief executives. The main feature of corporate management put forward by Bains was the Chief Officer Management Team (COMT). Although most chief executives now have some kind of departmental responsibilities, the COMT (or something broadly similar) still exists in most principal local authorities.

The COMT will probably meet periodically — sometimes once a week or fortnight — to discuss corporate policy initiatives which might be put forward for councillor consideration or issues originating in one department which might affect the other departments. In effect, the COMT provides one of the mechanisms by which the Chief Executive/Head of the Paid Service exercises the co-ordination role.

Not all chief officers may be members of the COMT. Where the number of departments is large, only those chief officers managing the central departments and the larger service departments will be members of the COMT. This makes for a more compact and focused COMT. The chief officers of the smaller service departments are not excluded, however, since they will still meet with the COMT members periodically, but less frequently, in a broader-based officer meeting.

Separating service planning from service delivery at officer level

Some of the larger authorities have developed their officer management structures so as to separate service planning from day-to-day responsibility for service delivery. In this model, the Chief Executive/Head of the Paid Service will be joined by a small number of 'strategic directors' in a much smaller corporate management group, which may or may not have functions similar to a 'normal' COMT. These 'strategic directors' will not have management responsibility for service delivery but will concentrate, instead, on reviewing and producing a broad strategy for the future delivery of all council services, which can then be debated by the council. Responsibility for existing service delivery is placed with a much larger number of 'heads of service', responsible for individual services.

Delegation

Local authorities are *creatures of statute*, that is, they owe their existence, their powers and their duties entirely to Acts of Parliament. The implications of this are explored in more detail in the Chapter on *External Controls*.

In theory, all decisions needed to apply those powers and discharge those duties can be taken by the council itself. In practice, that is not possible for a local authority of any size; so, some of the powers and duties can be (and are) delegated to officers and to subsets of councillors (committees and subcommittees). The only powers and duties which a local authority cannot lawfully delegate to an officer or a committee or subcommittee are fixing the amount of the Council Tax/precept and the consideration of a report from the Monitoring Officer.

Although powers and duties can be delegated to a single officer, prior to the LGB 2000 it was not lawful to delegate powers and duties to a single councillor, such as the chairman of a committee (a committee must consist of more than one person) — which meant that primary legislation was required to implement the executive mayor proposals of New Labour, which now appear in LGB 2000.

Where powers and duties are delegated to **officers**, this will be by means of a decision of the council, or of a committee/subcommittee which itself has been given delegated power by the council — giving either **general** authority to take decisions in a particular area of activity or **specific** authority in a particular case. The delegation can be withdrawn at any time and the officer to whom the powers have been delegated may be expected to report periodically to councillors on how that delegation has been used in practice. Whatever the nature of the delegation, general or specific, it will be recorded in the minutes and details of it will need to be included in a specific register of such decisions, which is open to public inspection.

Terms of reference of committees

Where powers and duties in a particular area of activity are delegated to a **committee** or **subcommittee**, this will usually be reflected in one of the main constitutional documents of the local authority — usually called the *Scheme of Delegation* or *Terms of Reference of Committees and Subcommittees,* under which the committees and subcommittees are established and their remit defined by the council. The remit will usually distinguish between those areas of activity where power to take action has been fully delegated and those areas where the council has reserved the final decision to itself after receiving the comments of the committee/subcommittee. In addition, this general scheme of delegation can be supplemented by *ad hoc* delegations to a committee or subcommittee in respect of a particular issue.

Standing Orders

The other important constitutional document of the local authority is its *Standing Orders*. The Standing Orders may be boring to read, but they are relatively important since they regulate and control how business is to be transacted at the meetings of the council — how questions and petitions can be submitted, and how any debate is to be conducted. A councillor would normally take the trouble to become familiar with the Standing Orders, to avoid being wrong-footed at a council meeting. Standing Orders of each council are worth studying so that procedures and manoeuvres are understood.

During a debate, councillors can raise *points of order*, usually to claim that something which has been said or done during the meeting is contrary to Standing Orders.

Standing Orders now have to contain some basic provisions prescribed by the Secretary of State — including the appointment of chief officers and disciplining the Head of Paid Service, Chief Financial Officer and Monitoring Officer.

The council meeting

Local authorities usually operate through a system of full council meetings held either monthly, bimonthly or quarterly, supplemented by committee and subcommittee meetings. There will usually be a special meeting of the council each year to decide on the revenue budget.

The full meeting of the council usually receives a report from each committee on details of action taken under delegated powers, and what recommendations the committee wishes the council to endorse. The range of items included in a committee report will vary enormously from one kind of authority to another. For example, the larger the local authority, the greater the degree of delegation (to officers and committees) and this means that only those items which require a decision of council will reach the full council, so as to keep the business (and the meeting) to manageable proportions. On the other hand, some smaller local authorities will insist on the full council receiving the minutes of all the committees and subcommittees, effectively giving the councillors a further opportunity to go over ground already covered by their colleagues. Apart from lengthening the meeting, this practice can have the disadvantage that the councillors receive (and have to read) detailed documents which most of them do not really need.

The Mayor or Chairman's role is to manage meetings of the full council and see fair play during debate and the due expedition of business. The role is largely ceremonial, but it must be remembered that the Mayor or Chairman is still a councillor and probably a member of a political group. This means that if the political balance on the council is critical, the Mayor or Chairman will be expected to vote on any important issue, according to group wishes. In this context 'Mayor' is fundamentally different from the directly elected Mayor under LGB 2000.

Where a single political party has an overall majority, the real power is vested in the councillor who leads that party — usually called the *Leader of the Council.* The position is not so clear where the authority is 'hung' or politically balanced; each political group will appoint its own *Group Leader* to deal with negotiations and discussions with the group leaders of the other political parties.

The agenda for the meeting will have been prepared by the appropriate chief officer (usually the Chief Executive or the Secretary or the Director of Administration) and will list the items of business to be transacted and the order in which they will be taken. Although the order of business can be changed, it is unlawful for an item to be considered at a meeting of the full council which is not on the agenda — gone are the days of 'any other business'.

All meetings begin by seeking approval of the minutes, the record of what took place at the last meeting. Minutes are written by the officers in a form which is intended to make them accurate and comprehensible. The officers must sometimes use legalistic terms to ensure that a minute cannot be challenged in a court of law or by an ombudsman or at audit. All decisions of the meeting will be recorded in the minutes, starting with the rubric: "RESOLVED that..." .

Questions usually occur at the start of the meeting of the full council. Councillors give prior written notice of questions they wish to put to committee chairmen about any matter within the competence of their committee. Questions from members of the majority party are often framed so that the chairman can paint a glowing picture about some enterprise which the majority party wants to publicise. Questions from opposition members are usually tabled in a bid to show that the majority party is not doing what it should, or is doing it too slowly or badly.

There may also be a procedure for members of the public to have a limited opportunity to ask questions of committee chairmen. If there is such a procedure, the council's Standing Orders will explain how it is to be used and any limits on its use.

The next item of business is usually *petitions* from electors, which are formally presented by the relevant local councillor, but are then usually referred to the appropriate committee for examination. If there is a debate on the issue, it takes place at the later committee meeting and, if necessary, at a future meeting of the full council. Petitions usually highlight some newsworthy, local issue.

At some stage in the meeting, the committee reports will come up for consideration and debate — a debate will particularly arise where issues of political controversy are involved. Often the positions of the respective political groups on the issue will have been decided at group meetings a few days prior to the council meeting and may be known before the item is reached in the debate.

Not all decisions of committees will be available for debate again at the full council — many, fairly routine, decisions will have been made by a committee acting under its delegated powers — sometimes referred to as *resolved items*. However, there may be an internal procedure under which a minimum number of councillors can object (within a specified period) to a decision made by a committee under delegated powers and this decision then has to be debated again at the council meeting — the issue is usually political and the objecting councillors presumably hope that the second bite at the cherry will produce a better result from their standpoint.

If an individual councillor opposes a committee recommendation, there is a number of courses of action available to that councillor — although he or she may find themselves obliged to follow any political group instructions. The councillor may propose that the matter should go back to the committee for further consideration — usually called the *reference back*. Alternatively, the councillor may seek to *amend* a committee proposal or move its *rejection*. Any of these actions can open a debate. Any formal proposal requires a seconder before it can be debated — very occasionally the proposer of a motion fails to attract a seconder and, at that point, the motion falls without debate. It is useful to keep track, during a debate on an item, of whether the debate is about the original proposal/motion; or a proposal to amend the original motion; or the revised motion arising from a successful amendment to the original motion.

The agenda may contain *notices of motion* given in advance in accordance with Standing Orders, either by individual councillors or political groups, to raise an item for debate which is not covered by the committee reports. The council may decide that the issue covered in the notice of motion be referred to a committee for examination; or be approved or rejected; or be amended in some way. Where a notice of motion involves significant additional expenditure, the Standing Orders may require that the issue be referred to a committee, anyway, before it can be debated at the council — to avoid any surprise increases in the overall budget.

Committees and subcommittees

As already explained, committees and subcommittees are subsets of the full council, established to look after an area of activity in more detail than is possible in a full council meeting. All committees and subcommittees are supported by professional officers.

The committees/subcommittees can be permanent, or *standing*, and councils may be required by law to appoint a standing committee for a specific function — a so-called *statutory committee*. Local authorities which have social services functions must appoint a social services committee, although this requirement no longer applies for an authority which has adopted one of the LGB 2000 models. The previous requirement on local education authorities to appoint an education committee was repealed some years ago.

Occasionally, the standing committees/subcommittees are supplemented by a temporary, or *ad hoc*, one to deal with a specific issue in even greater detail, without clogging up the normal business of a standing committee. Once the issue has been fully explored, the *ad hoc* committee will report its conclusions to its parent body and will then disband.

There is an increasing trend to establish *area-based committees*, often with some measure of influence or control over a delegated budget. These area committees usually include representatives of the local community, so as to broaden public participation in the running of the local authority. These area committees can also be expected and encouraged to raise policy issues for examination within the main committee system.

Although some parts of the council's Standing Orders will also apply to committees, committee meetings will usually be less formal than meetings of the full council, with, for example, no limit on the length of speeches or the number of times an individual councillor may join in the debate. Nevertheless, there will still be an agenda and there may be provision for questions from councillors and members of the public and for the presentation of petitions. Unlike the full council, it is possible to discuss items which are not listed on the agenda — but the ability to do so is limited, by law, to those items which the chairman of the meeting (in his or her absolute discretion) has decided to require to be discussed at that meeting on grounds of their being too 'urgent' to wait for the next meeting. As a matter of good practice, the chairman would usually be expected to give reasons for his or her decision.

The Policy and Resources Committee

The committee system will usually consist of committees and subcommittees covering either the central or corporate activities of the local authority, or the delivery of services to the public. This central/service split is similar to the same kind of split usually found in the officer management structure.

When the Bains Report advocated the introduction of corporate management, the chief executive and chief officer management teams, it also made recommendations about committee structures. Those recommendations included the establishment of a *Policy Committee*, or where it was also responsible for resource (finance, human and land) co-ordination, a *Policy and Resources Committee.*

The Policy and Resources Committee usually manages, in overall terms, the use of the local authority's resources. This overall management function gives it a pivotal role in determining how the local authority operates.

However, even more influence comes from its role as policy co-ordinator. In theory, whenever a service committee wishes to propose a major service development for full council approval, the Policy and Resources Committee will be given the opportunity to add its own comments to the service committee's report to the council.

When the full council meets to consider the revenue budget for next year, although each service committee will have looked at its own share of the budget, it will be the Policy and Resources Committee which reports and makes recommendations to the full council on the overall amount of the budget, on how it is to be shared between committees and on any proposals for increases or reductions in service needed to balance the budget.

For all of these reasons, the Policy and Resources Committee is usually characterised in the media as 'powerful' and/or 'influential'! The adoption of one of the executive models in LGB 2000 is likely to bring with it the demise of the Policy and Resources Committee.

Appointing committees

Where no single party has overall control, there will be a lot of political wrangling over committee composition and chairmanships, though they must now, by law, reflect the political complexion of the council as a whole, under what are usually known as the *proportionality rules*. These rules are mentioned later.

In some authorities (where the political balance is well and truly hung) there may even be no standing committee chairmen — a councillor is elected at the start of each committee meeting to act as its chairman for that meeting.

Committees may decide to co-opt people who are not members of the council. Where the committee has **delegated** powers, the co-opted members may speak and give advice and otherwise contribute to the work of the committee, but they **cannot vote** — the one exception to this being church representatives on any committee exercising education functions. Where the committee is purely **advisory** and has no delegated powers, co-opted members can speak **and vote**. By contrast, the co-opted members on the new police authorities have voting rights.

The voting rights of 'ex officio' members have also been removed. There had been a fairly widespread practice of mayors and council chairmen, and leaders of controlling groups, being regarded as 'ex officio' members of all committees with power to vote at meetings. They can still attend and contribute to the debate but have no voting rights unless they are also full members of the committee or subcommittee, counting as such under the proportionality rules.

Working parties

It is becoming increasingly common for working parties of members and officers to be appointed to examine a subject or proposal and to report back to a committee. Proceedings at working parties will probably not be covered by Standing Orders and, therefore, are often much more informal than committee meetings. While the use of working parties has much to commend it, in terms of members having a greater input into proposals coming before committee and a greater understanding of what they are actually deciding, a degree of caution is necessary.

- Working parties can allow for a much fuller and frank discussion of the topic than will ever take place with the media and the public present, because there will be no temptation during the meeting to play to the gallery or pressure to follow, slavishly, a party line. However, working parties can be used as a cloak for secrecy. The law is clear. Working parties are legal and need not be open to the public and the media provided their functions are purely deliberative and advisory and not decision-making. They cannot be subcommittees in disguise.

The concept of working parties is often taken one step further, by setting up advisory bodies almost wholly composed of non-councillors, to look at specific areas of service provision. Such bodies are usually referred to as 'forums' and are often used to elicit the views of service clients not normally represented amongst the councillors — for example, services for young people.

Political balance on committees and subcommittees

The composition of committees and subcommittees must reflect proportionately the political balance of the whole council. On education committees, the existence of church representatives (who can vote) is taken into account in determining how many seats constitute a working majority. In reviewing political representation on committees, local authorities have to have regard to the following principles:

- not all seats to be allocated to the same political party;
- the majority of seats to be allocated to the majority party;
- the number of seats a political party has on committees etc. to be the same proportion as it holds of the total seats on the council.

If it so decides, with no councillor dissenting, the council can decide to disapply the proportionality rules in favour of some local *ad hoc* arrangement which suits the council better. This approach was used by those authorities who wanted to set up a 'non-proportional' Cabinet and Leader model in advance of the LGB 2000.

The allocation of seats is left to the political party, which may appoint, and terminate the appointments of, their members.

This task can be made more difficult by the need to ensure that the same members do not sit on both the client committee awarding contracts and on the committee controlling a DLO/DSO which may be tendering for work under Compulsory Competitive Tendering (CCT). With the extension of the scope of CCT there was a view that, in some small authorities, it might become impossible to achieve this separation and also comply with the requirement to achieve political balance. The replacement of CCT with *Best Value* substantially reduced this problem.

These proportionality rules do not apply to working parties.

Party politics

The previous few sections of this Chapter point to the increasing politicisation of local government. This politicisation has been overtly recognised by the introduction of political assistants under the Local Government and Housing Act 1989 — as described in the previous Chapter.

Most local authorities are now run on party lines with group meetings. Although some people may regard this as being at odds with 'public service', party politics in local government is now a fact of life. It must be remembered that it has not been imposed by law — it has evolved spontaneously to become part of the established order of things.

Party politics in local government does, of course, have considerable merits. Voters have a far better knowledge of what candidates stand for, since most parties — and even bodies like residents' associations — publish election manifestos setting out their general policy.

The emergence of the Liberal Democrats as a significant party in local government has reduced opportunities for one party decision-making. Their successes in local elections has led to them not only winning outright control in a number of authorities, but also holding the balance of power in others. Conservative and Labour politicians may be united in thinking that decision-making has suffered in hung councils, but the Liberal Democrats regard their increased influence as beneficial, resulting in a consensus approach to decisions, more accurately reflecting local public opinion. While some chief executives complain of uncertainty and inability to plan ahead and that their administrative burdens have increased, others regard hung councils as a challenge that enables them to exercise their skills in management.

Access to meetings and related information

Local authorities are now more aware of the need for publicity. They are required by law to afford certain rights to the media and the public. Many, though, are still suspicious of the media and are often concerned about the relative inexperience of, and the depth of knowledge shown by, many civics correspondents. For their part, the media often accuse councils of taking the really important decisions away from the public arena.

Public registers must be kept, showing names and addresses of councillors with their committee membership. Registers must show powers delegated to officers, as explained earlier in this Chapter.

The rights of the media and the public are covered by a number of Acts of Parliament — Public Bodies (Admission to Meetings) Act 1960, Local Government Act 1972, Local Government Planning and Land Act 1980, Local Government (Access to Information) Act 1985 and Local Government Act 1986. The right to attend meetings and see documents of principal local authorities (all local authorities other than parish or community councils) are governed by the 1985 Act.

Under the 1985 Act, the media and public are given automatic access to all council, committee and subcommittee meetings, unless the business is *confidential* or *exempt*.

What can be classified as *confidential* within the meaning of the 1985 Act is fairly limited and covers information supplied by government departments or matters where disclosure is prohibited by statute or the courts. If a matter is *confidential*, then exclusion of the media and public is automatic — the councillors cannot decide for themselves to allow the media and public to stay in the meeting.

What can be classified as *exempt* within the meaning of the 1985 Act is much wider and there is the facility for the councillors to decide for themselves to allow the media and public to stay for an exempt item.

Exempt principally covers personal and commercially sensitive information, matters in the course of negotiation, and issues protected by legal privilege. The officer who put together the agenda will have decided beforehand that an item was likely to result in the disclosure of exempt information and that item will have been listed as such in the agenda. Any report supporting that item will not have been sent to the media or been available for public inspection, in the usual way.

However, the decision to exclude the media and public for the consideration of that item must be formally proposed, seconded and voted upon by the committee itself. It is not sufficient for the resolution just to say that disclosure of the information would be prejudicial to the public interest — it must give a reason, usually referring to the specific paragraph of the Schedule to the Act regarded as authorising exclusion. If the motion to exclude fails, then that item must be taken in public and copies of any supporting report immediately circulated to any media and public then present — so, it should not be assumed that exclusion for the consideration of exempt items is always a foregone conclusion!

Copies of agenda papers and those reports taken during the open part of the meeting must be available at meetings. Councils must not consider any matter unless it has been listed on an agenda open for inspection for at least three days before the meeting. However, in the case of a committee or subcommittee (but not the full council), this prohibition can be removed, but only if the chairman of the meeting rules that the matter is *urgent*, as already explained earlier.

The reports should list any *background papers* which have been used to a material extent in drafting the report. It will usually be up to the officer drafting the report to decide what constitutes a background paper. Background papers are open for public inspection and a charge may be made for providing copies of background papers.

The Department of the Environment has, in the past, advised local authorities against imposing embargoes, even though it used embargoes fairly widely itself. However, those local authorities with a positive attitude to the media will recognise the value in giving the media advance copies of a report, even under an embargo, especially if the matter is complex, so that the media has a better opportunity to prepare its material and, if necessary, seek advance clarification from councillors and officers. Apart from benefiting the media, this kind of arrangement will also benefit the local authority because the chances of more accurate reporting are enhanced.

New Labour — Modernising Local Government

The first New Labour Government Green Paper on *Modernising Local Government — Local Democracy and Community Leadership* included a series of proposals on how authorities might lead and involve their local communities and how they might modernise the way they worked.

Lord Hunt of Tamworth chaired a House of Lords all-party Select Committee on Relations Between Central and Local Government — and the report suggested that local authorities should be free to adopt innovative decision-making arrangements. Such changes required primary legislation and Lord Hunt introduced a Private Member's Bill (the Local Government (Experimental Arrangements) Bill — known as the 'Hunt Bill'). This Bill failed due to political problems in Parliament.

Based on reactions to its Green Paper, the Government produced its White Paper *Modern Local Government: In Touch with the People*, which led to its own Bill: the Local Government (Organisation and Standards) Bill. However, that Bill failed to be enacted before the end of the 1998/1999 Parliamentary Session and was, therefore, lost. In the 1999/2000 Session the Government reintroduced its proposals, this time in the form of the Local Government Bill, which became the LGB 2000.

LGB 2000 — executive models

The LGB 2000 covers two broad issues — internal organisation and ethical standards. The ethical standards element of LGB 2000 is dealt with in the next Chapter *Propriety and Ethics*. For the purposes of internal organisation, the LGB 2000 regards local authority activities as being one of two kinds: 'executive' (service delivery) and 'non-executive' (eg. regulatory, such as granting planning permission).

The executive activities will, under the LGB 2000 models, be undertaken by:

- a Leader (appointed by the authority) and Cabinet (appointed by the authority or the Leader); or
- a directly elected (by the voters) Mayor and Cabinet (appointed by the Mayor); or
- a directly elected Mayor and Council Manager (appointed by the authority).

Depending on the model adopted, executive action can be taken by the elected Mayor, the Cabinet, a committee of the Cabinet, a single member of the Cabinet or an officer of the authority.

The Cabinet (where there is one) is not a committee in the usual technical sense of the word and that means that the Cabinet can meet in private even when taking executive decisions, and the proportionality rules and the access to information provisions do not apply to it. The Cabinet cannot have more than 10 members. Members of the executive will be able to claim pensions, for the first time. The ability of the Cabinet (or the elected Mayor) to meet in private when taking executive decisions has been the cause of understandably adverse comment. For example, the leader of the *Local Government Chronicle* for 11 February 2000 under the headline *'Seeing through new transparency plans'* commented:

> *"The Blair government has demonstrated a cavalier attitude to freedom of information since tearing up then minister David Clark's proposals for legislation in this area. Many local and regional papers are now finding the move towards cabinet government is encouraging a similar culture of secrecy which ministers seem happy to perpetuate. Existing committees may often amount to little more than theatre, but at least the public can get a seat.*

The draft guidance says many decisions will henceforth be taken by individual executive members, while the executive itself can meet in secret. This, we are told, will 'ensure that decisions are transparent and accountable'. More secrecy, viewed through ministerial eyes, means more transparency".

The remaining councillors, outside the Cabinet, deal with the non-executive functions and scrutinising the activities of the executive — and they do this in committees, as previously.

Each Council has to adopt a formal Constitution. The Constitution has to include some basic elements: a description of the adopted executive model and how it is intended to work in practice, including defining the relationships between the executive, non-executive and scrutiny arms of the council and between those arms and the council itself; the Standing Orders; the Schemes of Delegation (of executive powers); and the authority's local Code of Conduct for councillors and officers.

LGB 2000 — implementation

Before adopting an LGB 2000 model, each local authority has to undertake a widespread two-stage consultation exercise. Where a directly elected Mayor is proposed, there has to be a referendum. Regardless of the authority's preference, a referendum for an elected Mayor can be demanded by 5% of the voters and the authority has to abide by the result of the referendum. There has to be a gap of five years between one referendum and the next and only people currently on the electoral register can count towards the 5% (although the Secretary of State has the power to set a lower percentage).

The first stage of the consultation exercise involves an explanation of the three models, although the authority is not allowed to steer the consultees to respond in a particular way — a bit difficult for an authority which decided to operate a new Cabinet and Leader model in advance of the LGB 2000.

The second stage of the consultation process relates to the particular model preferred by the authority. The detail on which consultation takes place is, effectively, the proposed formal Constitution which the authority intends to adopt. Those 'proposals' are also submitted to the Secretary of State, although apparently not for approval.

The Secretary of State has very wide powers, including the power to direct an authority or class of authorities to hold a referendum for an elected Mayor. This whole process is likely to take several years, although the Secretary of State expressed the wish that all authorities would have started their consultation processes within six to nine months of the LGB 2000 coming into effect. Because of the Secretary of State's powers of direction and the Government's determination that local government shall be 'modernised', the existing committee system for executive decision-making is now doomed.

Facilities at meetings

When meetings are open, the local authority must provide **reasonable** accommodation for media and public. Most local authorities will do their best to accommodate the media and public, if interest in a particular meeting is high — if necessary by shifting the meeting to a larger room, if available, or arranging a PA broadcast to an adjacent overflow room, if they have enough warning.

Lord Widgery, the then Lord Chief Justice, said that if a committee chose to meet in a very small room and turned round and said the public could not be admitted because there was no room, it would be acting in bad faith and it would not be beyond the long arm of the court. He said: *"The committee must in the first instance so organise its affairs as to recognise its obligation to the public"*. It has been held, however, that if, because of widespread public interest, there is not enough room for both media and public, the media may be admitted and the public excluded. But a committee has no power to admit the public while excluding the media.

Reporters must be given as far as is practicable, reasonable facilities in which to work at a council or committee meeting. There is no statutory right for taking photographs or for filming the meeting.

Parish and community council meetings

The rights to attend and see documents of parish or community councils is significantly different from principal councils since they are governed by the 1960 and 1972 Acts, rather than the 1985 Act.

The media and public have the right to attend full council and committee meetings but *not* subcommittee meetings. They may be excluded only if a resolution to exclude them is proposed, seconded and passed. The grounds for such a resolution are if the members believe "publicity would be prejudicial to the public interest" or "because of the confidential nature of the items to be discussed' — in other words, much more a matter of subjective personal opinion.

Media and the public have the right to see agendas and minutes. There are no rights as far as other documents and reports are concerned — councils may make these available as "they see fit or think necessary".

General facilities to be provided for media and public are the same as explained above for principal local authorities.

Media and information services

Many local authorities, particularly larger ones, recognised the need for better publicity and have done more than they had to do by law. They accepted the Bains Report recommendations and appointed press and information officers and public relations officers. In addition, many produce their own newspapers or information handouts.

The job of the public relations officer is to keep the media and public informed and to promote the work of their authority. The good ones will not stop at just issuing press releases: they will stress the positive side of the authority's work, act as a source of inspiration, suggest and inspire human interest stories, and put inquiring journalists in touch with the technical experts who can answer their questions.

Although press officers are the obvious source of information about an authority, they are not the only source and they should not be expected to supply a party political view of an issue. Chief officers can also be approached, if a technical explanation of any issue is needed. There is no reason why journalists cannot approach elected mayors, group or council leaders, chairmen, spokesmen and individual councillors, where a party political view would be useful in understanding why an issue is being raised. Indeed, journalists may find that individual councillors will take the initiative in approaching them! When dealing with press officers, chief officers and councillors, much more will be achieved by journalists if there is mutual trust.

Limits on information which can be supplied

The distinction between the authority as a body and the individual councillor is important. As a result of the Widdicombe Report, the Local Government Act 1986 prohibited the authority from publishing anything designed to affect public support for a political party or anyone identified with a political party.

The existing powers of local authorities under the Local Government Act 1972 and the Local Government (Scotland) Act 1973 to provide information were later restricted to providing information concerning the authority itself — not about matters relating to local government generally. In 1988, the Secretary of State issued a code of recommended practice covering style, distribution, cost and other matters relating to publicity by authorities.

Every authority, including joint boards, joint committees and parish and community councils, must keep separate accounts of expenditure on publicity.

General information

In addition to the rights of access to meetings and related information explained above, principal councils have a duty to make certain other information available to their electorate. The government made it clear that the same rights should be afforded to the media.

This information includes:

- three days' notice of meetings open to the press;
- agendas and minutes of council meetings;
- register of planning applications;
- record of payments to councillors;

- statutory register of members' interests;
- local government commissioners' (ombudsmen's) reports of a complaint of maladministration by the authority;
- the annual accounts;
- the annual audit (including the right to inspect certain documents);
- performance indicators;
- a number of statutory plans, including the Best Value Performance Plan;
- general financial information;
- the annual report.

The last two items deserve looking at in more detail. The Department of the Environment (as it then was) issued codes of practice relating to both. The first related to information which should be sent out with the annual Council Tax demands — the code suggested that the accompanying material should give details about the way the charge is made up and the reasons for any change from the previous year.

Council tax demands are issued by unitary councils, London borough councils, metropolitan borough councils and shire district/borough councils in a two-tier area. It is common for shire district/borough councils to point out, in any accompanying material, that a large percentage of the charge is devoted to services supplied by other authorities — for example, education, social services and roads by the county council and police and fire and rescue services by any relevant statutory authorities.

On the annual report, which outlines the work of the authority in the year under review, the code suggested that the annual report should make it possible for Council Taxpayers to judge the efficiency of their own local authority by comparison with similar authorities by providing comparative statistics. Many in local government argued that such statistics could be, at best, misleading and at worst highly contentious. The rule is to use comparisons but to be careful because conditions in one authority are seldom the same as elsewhere. The statistics can, however, be a broad guide to areas worthy of further examination.

Annual reports, like the standard of services, vary enormously from authority to authority. Some councils spend a lot of money publishing glossy, highly professional reports; others do it on a very low budget. Many argue that the limited interest of the public in local government does not justify such expenditure. Despite these reservations, the annual report can provide useful stories for local newspapers.

Provision of services through third parties

Under the former, Conservative, Government, the role of local government changed in recent years towards it being an **enabler**; not simply a **direct provider of services**.

The term *'enabling authority'* came into use to describe the premise that local government should only do for itself those things which the private sector was either unable or unwilling to do — restricting its role to enabling others to do that work. The government believed that where services were provided by a local authority directly, then wherever possible they should be subject to the competition of the market place and, if a local authority could not compete on price, the contract should be awarded to others.

The idea of using private contractors to carry out part of the local authority's work is not new and will continue now that CCT has been replaced by Best Value. There has always been a mixed provision of services; for example, many authorities have used private practice lawyers, architects and surveyors to supply professional services which the authority does not possess in-house. Another example is major construction work undertaken by private contractors after a voluntary competitive tendering (VCT) exercise.

Compulsory Competitive Tendering

What was new was the introduction of compulsion. The Local Government, Planning and Land Act 1980 first introduced Compulsory Competitive Tendering (CCT) to a limited range of 'blue collar' jobs, mainly in building maintenance and construction work. Authorities who wished to continue to do this work for themselves established Direct Labour Organisations (DLOs) to do so.

The Local Government Act 1988 extended the concept to a wider range of services, including refuse collection, cleaning buildings, street cleansing, grounds maintenance, catering for schools, care homes and other establishments, and the repair and maintenance of vehicles. Authorities who wished to continue to supply these services themselves established Direct Service Organisations (DSOs) to do so.

There was a further extension in the Local Government Act 1992 to cover housing management and the more problematical area of professional and support services — some of which impinged on the core activities of the authority and for which CCT might not be as straightforward or as appropriate as the government thought. In recognition of these difficulties, consultations were undertaken by the government on the feasibility of its proposals for professional and support services and changes had to be made.

A *de minimis* (too small to be worth including in the scheme) threshold was agreed below which CCT would not be required — which meant that many shire districts did not have to expose their professional or support services to CCT. One proposal was abandoned altogether (corporate and administrative services) and others modified quite significantly (resulting in 30% of personnel services, 35% of financial services, 45% of legal services, 65% of construction and property-related services and 70% of IT/IS services being subject to CCT). The government also accepted the point that the cheapest price should not be the only criterion in judging CCT bids for professional services — quality of service came into the equation as well.

The same Act also introduced the concept of *internal trading accounts* for professional services, either as a first step towards CCT or for introducing a more commercial approach in those services which would not be the subject of CCT.

While the 1992 Act CCT proposals were being the subject of consultation, the Conservative Government was also engaged in its review of the structure of local government. It was pointed out that the two processes, CCT and creating new the authorities, could not sensibly be done at the same time — a point which the government eventually accepted. The result of this was that the introduction of the 1992 Act CCT regime was postponed in those areas affected by local government review — in effect giving the affected authorities a chance to settle down after reorganisation before having to undertake the CCT exercise.

CCT practical considerations

Having described the development of CCT, it is useful to discuss a few aspects of its implementation. The Regulations laid down by the government to cover the CCT process developed and became more restrictive (in terms of what a local authority could continue to do for itself) after the introduction of CCT under the 1980 Act.

DLOs/DSOs were required to operate under some significant limitations: their ability to tender for other work outside their authority's area was restricted; their accounts had to be separate from the authority's accounts; they had to produce an annual report; and they were obliged to make a 6% return on capital. These burdens applied whether or not the economy was in recession and many DLOs/DSOs complained that this favoured the private contractor who did not suffer such rigorous control.

If a DLO/DSO failed to make its 6% return, the Secretary of State could require the contract to be re-tendered. The Secretary of State could also prohibit the DLO/DSO from bidding for the work at all.

The initial CCT process itself was subject to scrutiny by the Secretary of State, who could intervene and require the CCT process to be run again if he was satisfied that there had been a contravention of the regulations. One example of this was 'anti-competitive' behaviour, where the Secretary of State believed that the local authority had tried to impose conditions in the tender which might put off private contractors from tendering. Disappointed tenderers sometimes complained to the Secretary of State when the CCT contract had been awarded to the in-house organisation and, if he was satisfied that there had been 'anti-competitive behaviour', he required the CCT exercise to be repeated.

One of the factors which had a significant effect on the CCT process was the Transfer of Undertakings (Protection of Employment) Regulations 1981 (TUPE). TUPE was introduced in order to comply with the European Acquired Rights Directive and is a good example of the increasing European influence on UK law. The implications of

TUPE are still from time to time the subject of litigation in the UK and European Courts and the precise position is still uncertain, even after many years of litigation. In order to provide a clearer framework for Best Value (which replaced CCT on 2 January 2000 as a result of the Local Government Act 1999), the New Labour Government announced its intention to legislate to amend TUPE in the interests of greater certainty and clarity, and to consult on its proposals during summer 2000.

Put extremely simply, TUPE can mean that when a business is transferred as a going concern, the existing workforce must also transfer at its current rates of pay and conditions of service, including pension arrangements. Such a result would not be very attractive for a private contractor who might see less opportunity to operate a contract profitably if he had to continue paying the existing workforce at its existing rates of pay. Originally, the Secretary of State took the view that TUPE did not apply to CCT because local authorities were not businesses trying to make a profit and any attempt by a local authority to apply TUPE would be regarded by him as 'anti-competitive' behaviour. As a consequence of subsequent litigation, the then Secretary of State had to change his view — local authorities were then allowed to express their opinion about whether or not TUPE applied, leaving the risk with the private contractor in framing his bid. In July 1999, the New Labour Government issued a statement to the effect that public/private partnerships and tendering exercises would thereafter be conducted on the basis that TUPE would apply, unless there were genuinely exceptional reasons for a different view.

If the DLO/DSO won the contract, the regulations also required there to be a clear division at councillor and officer level between the contracting and client rôles within the authority — the 'client/contractor split'.

When CCT was first introduced, many feared that competition would mean the death knell of direct service provision by local authorities, especially given the plethora of regulations applied by the government to achieve its view of a 'level playing field'. In practice, that fear proved to be over-pessimistic. The majority of contracts were awarded to in-house organisations, probably due to the lack of experience by the private sector and, therefore, the absence of any real market at that stage of the development of CCT. The private sector then gained experience of local authority requirements and many firms set about recruiting former local government officers to join them with a view to winning contracts when they came up for renewal.

CCT knock-on effects

The introduction of the CCT process had the positive effect that many in-house organisations became more adept at matching their services to what the client actually wanted — cutting out unnecessary activity in the process.

Authorities may have had more than one DSO for different services and there was a growing practice to group them into a contract services division, under the direction of a contracts services manager with the status of a senior chief officer. This had advantages of emphasising the client/contractor split in responsibilities and introducing higher level professional management. Some of these new chief officers were recruited from the private sector while others were promoted within local government. They all had one common feature, an entrepreneurial approach. While DSOs had to comply with public sector rules of probity, they usually had a much greater degree of freedom than conventional departments (including their own section of financial regulations), including, in some cases, the freedom to seek support services from outside the local authority.

When support services such as legal, finance and personnel were provided from within the authority, they were regulated by a *Service Level Agreement* (SLA). Although the SLA could not, as a matter of law, be a formal contract (the local authority cannot really contract with itself), it would usually have had the appearance of one and may have been regarded as such. The SLA between the central support department and the DSO set out the detail of the service to be provided, the costs to be recharged and procedures — possibly even penalties for defaults. This again brought a much greater clarity into relationships and put the DSO in the same position as if they were a private sector contractor.

SLAs have also spread from DSOs to become a common feature throughout an authority, regulating work between central support and other departments.

There was a tendency for many authorities to reduce the number of their chief officers and departments through amalgamations, partly to reflect the *enabling authority* concept (less direct service delivery, possibly through CCT) but also as part of a move to decentralise central support functions to service departments. This decentralisation was partly a response to the rigours of CCT but was also thought to provide a leaner, more effective, administrative core, thus reducing the authority's overheads. Successive financial squeezes accelerated this trend.

This shift in emphasis towards being client-oriented provided the foundation for New Labour's replacement of CCT, Best Value.

CCT is dead, long live Best Value

Many people in local government hoped that the advent of the New Labour Government would put a swift and immediate end to CCT and, in particular, the planned extension of it to new unitary authorities, where the implementation of some aspects of CCT had been postponed — probably led to that hope by the resolutions passed at the 1995 Labour Party Conference. If those people were looking for immediate clear and decisive action in that direction, then they were disappointed — they had to wait until 2 January 2000 before CCT was abolished and replaced by *Best Value*.

The second New Labour Green Paper — *Modernising Local Government — Improving Local Services through Best Value* proposed that there should be a statutory duty on local authorities "to obtain best value by securing economic, efficient and effective services". Quality of services would matter as well as their cost. Although there would be no compulsion to put services out to tender, there would be no presumption that services should be delivered directly, if more efficient and effective means were available. Competition would still perform an important role. The government 'would not hesitate to intervene' if authorities were reluctant to put right performance failure.

The Green Paper listed the 12 'provisional' principles underlying *Best Value*. Local authorities would be expected to produce a Local Performance Plan which would list the authority's objectives and performance measures; performance and efficiency targets; and a programme of fundamental performance reviews. There would be a system of independent audit/inspection and certification, with the Secretary of State intervening as necessary. The Local Government Act 1999 (LGA 1999) gave statutory effect to these proposals.

For some years local authorities' performance was judged against a set of Audit Commission performance indicators (ACPI); the LGA 1999 introduced a further set of Best Value performance indicators (BVPI), specifically related to Best Value. BVPIs were of two types: Best Value corporate health and Best Value service delivery. Best Value corporate health relates to the performance of the authority as an institution and involves 18 BVPIs in four groups: customers and the community; management of resources; staff development; and partnership working. Best Value service delivery is, as the name suggests, about standards in actual service delivery — in five service areas: education; social services; housing and related services; environmental services; and cultural and related services. Each of these service areas is examined under five groups: strategic objectives; cost/efficiency; service delivery outcomes; quality; and fair access.

Each authority has to undertake a programme of service reviews — the programme content and timing is up to the authority, within a five-year cycle, and reviews must examine the enduring and essential role of fair and open competition in achieving Best Value.

The whole exercise is pulled together in the Best Value Performance Plan (BVPP) which has to be published on 31 March each year, with the first BVPPs being published on 31 March 2000. The DETR guidance on BVPPs suggested that they should contain: a summary of the authority's objectives and current performance, compared with previous years; a summary of the authority's approach to efficiency and improvement; a description of the review programme and the key results of completed reviews; a description of future performance targets and plans of action; comments upon any audit and inspection reports; a description of consultation processes; and a summary of the authority's finances. The BVPP is audited each year by the authority's auditor, with the outcome of the audit being published by 30 June.

The Secretary of State has powers to intervene in any authority which is demonstrably failing, although unless there is a serious failure or an urgent need for intervention, the authority will be given an opportunity to improve first.

IDeA and Beacons

While the New Labour Government was developing its Best Value replacement for CCT, local government was taking its own action in the search for quality performance amongst local authorities. The Local Government Association (LGA) had been reviewing the future of the existing Local Government Management Board (LGMB) for some time. In July 1998, the LGA decided to wind up the LGMB and split its work between two new arm's-length Agencies: the *Improvement and Development Agency* (IDeA) (training and management practice) and the *Employers' Agency* (national negotiations on pay and conditions). The IDeA initiative was aimed at peer-group reviews and self-assessment and was endorsed by the Government. Some months later, in February 2000, the Convention of Scottish Local Authorities (COSLA) decided that activities similar to those undertaken by IDeA would, in Scotland, not require an arm's length organisation but would, instead, be handled within COSLA itself.

The IDeA's role quickly developed. Twelve pilot councils, under the supervision of IDeA and with support from the DETR and the Audit Commission, took part in the development of models for self-assessment and external review which could be used in the future.

In January 1999, the Liberal Democrats (eight months after they gained control of Liverpool and in frustration at their inability to effect change) requested authority-wide help from IDeA to reverse years of poor service delivery at the highest Council Tax outside London — the request was triggered by an adverse Ofsted inspection. The IDeA team included chief executives from other authorities and spent a week carrying out a 'diagnostic health check' — in effect, a 'pre-hit squad' to avoid Government intervention.

In February 1999, the Government announced its Beacon Councils scheme, developed by the DETR in partnership with the IDeA. The idea behind the scheme involved beacon status being awarded to up to 40 councils in the first year, so that others could learn from them. Each type of authority would be represented in the successful applicants — in the event, 42 of the 211 applicant authorities were chosen in January 2000 by the government's advisory panel. Councils could apply for beacon status for one or two of their services, where they felt that they had a proven track record in: community safety, education, housing, modernising planning, modern service delivery; social services and sustainable development. The incentive for authorities to win beacon status was that in the 'longer term' they would be able to test out new freedoms and flexibilities. Beacon councils would be involved in hosting open days (up to six each year), secondments, mentoring, conferences, road shows and publications — all aimed at spreading best practice to other authorities. The second round was announced in February 2000 with different themes.

The IDeA's priority areas of activity include: supporting improvement; beacon councils; Best Value; best practice; and councillor, manager and workforce development.

Citizen's Charter

An increasing number of local authorities are producing their own versions of a citizen's charter either for the whole authority or for an individual service. These often point out rights to information and standards of service and can be useful for measuring performance, or lack of it.

The Conservative Government gave itself powers under the Local Government Act 1992 to require the publication of a wide range of information. This was seen as implementing that government's own citizen's charter and they used the Audit Commission to ensure publication.

The Local Government Finance Act 1992 imposed a duty on authorities to consult representatives of non-domestic ratepayers (the uniform business rate) on their expenditure proposals, including capital expenditure. They have to do this before they fix their precept or Council Tax, even though the non-domestic ratepayer now has no direct interest in the level of the local precept or Council Tax.

4 Propriety and Ethics

Members' allowances — pecuniary interests — registers of interests — National Code of Conduct — non-pecuniary interests — external audit — surcharge — Nolan Report — Local Government Bill

Members' allowances

The Local Government Act 1972 introduced the concept of attendance allowances to cover 'approved duties', as a means of payment for councillors on principal authorities (that is all councils other than parish councils and community councils). Under the Local Government and Housing Act 1989, the Government moved towards implementing the call of the Widdicombe Report for a change in the way allowances were administered. The members' allowances regime is covered by regulations made in 1995 (although they are due to change), the main features of which are:

- an authority which wishes to pay allowances must make a scheme, describing the allowances, which has to be published;
- allowances can include a basic allowance, attendance allowance, financial loss allowance, special responsibility allowance and travelling and subsistence allowances;
- there is no longer any overall cash limit on the total allowances paid, nor is there any restriction on the relative proportions of the different allowances;
- all councillors can claim a basic allowance, regardless of the number of meetings they attend, at a rate fixed by the council;
- *attendance allowance* can be claimed by councillors for *approved duty* — attendance at formal meetings within the council and other duties approved by the council from a range of duties prescribed by the government;
- *special responsibility allowances* can be claimed by senior councillors — such as leader of the council, group lenders, committee chairmen or spokesmen — at rates fixed by the council;
- *financial loss allowances* can be claimed by people who are not councillors (eg. co-opted members) and who carry out approved duties;
- *travelling and subsistence allowances* are payable within maximum rates laid down by the government.

There is an increasing trend amongst authorities to abandon attendance allowances in favour of an enhanced basic allowance for all councillors and increased special responsibility allowances for the senior councillors. The Local Government Bill (LGB 2000) made provision for the Secretary of State not only to change the existing allowances regime but also to introduce pensions for councillors. On the issue of allowances, the LGB 2000 provides for the abolition of attendance allowances, the payment of allowances for carers and the appointment of an independent allowances panel in each authority to recommend local schemes of allowances and award pensions. The last point was the source of controversy due to the suggestion that only the councillors acting as part of the executive in one of the LGB 2000 models would be eligible for a pension — the backbenchers would be left out in the cold. The Government has yet (April 2000) to announce contribution rates for these pensions.

Before 1995, the local authority had to make available for public inspection the amounts of the allowances paid to its councillors in the previous financial year, leaving it to the media to make the effort to obtain the information. From 1995 onwards, the local authority has to send this information to the local media. The amounts of allowances claimed by individual members tends to excite some interest!

Misconduct in local government

One of the commonest of many misinformed criticisms of local government is that people only go into it for what they can get out of it — Chapter 2 attempted to explain why people decide to become councillors.

Of course, misconduct does sometimes happen, in local government as in other walks of life — there are about 450 local authorities with about 20,000 councillors and this means that there are bound to be more problems than, say, with 659 MPs. But problems are relatively rare and subject to severe penalties — penalties which are much more severe than those applied to MPs. Although there have been few cases of corruption in recent years, they tend to attract enormous publicity.

Declaration of pecuniary interest

Under the Local Government Act 1972, whenever a councillor is present at a meeting where he or she has a pecuniary interest, direct or indirect, in any contract, proposed contract or other matter which is the subject of consideration, he or she:

- must disclose that pecuniary interest as soon as possible after the start of the meeting; and
- must not speak or vote on the matter; and
- will probably have to leave the room, as well, for that item, if the council's standing orders require this to be done — failure to do this may also constitute maladministration.

Failure to comply with this requirement is a criminal offence. The Chief Executive has a duty to report to the police any cases where it is thought members may not have declared a pecuniary interest when they should have.

A *pecuniary interest* is one which involves pecuniary (financial) advantage or disadvantage to the councillor. If the pecuniary interest is that of the councillor himself or herself, then that is described as a **direct** pecuniary interest. However, pecuniary interests of certain other people, with whom the councillor has some specified connection, are also caught — these are called the **indirect** pecuniary interests of the councillor. Indirect pecuniary interests caught by the legislation are:

- pecuniary interest of a spouse of the councillor, but only if the spouse is living with that councillor, and only if that interest is known to the councillor;
- pecuniary interest of a partner or employer of the councillor;
- pecuniary interest of a limited company in which the councillor has shares above a specified level.

The first bullet point above is an interesting one in modern times, where informal partnership, rather than formal marriage, is now a fairly common form of adult relationship. A pecuniary interest of a partner living with the councillor will, however, probably be regarded by the Ombudsman as a **non-pecuniary interest,** as described later.

There are, however, exceptions which can enable the councillor with some sort of theoretical pecuniary interest to take part in the decision-making process:

- the item is about the payment of members' (including chairmen's) allowances;
- the councillor is a member of, or employed by, any **public** body (indirect pecuniary interest only);
- the councillor's interest is as a ratepayer or inhabitant of the area or as a consumer of water;
- the item is about the terms on which the right to participate in any service (including the supply of goods) is offered to the public;
- the councillor's shareholding in a company is less than one percent of the company's issued share capital or less than £5,000 nominal value (whichever is the less — indirect pecuniary interest only);
- the councillor's pecuniary interest is *"so remote or insignificant that it cannot reasonably be regarded as likely to influence"* the councillor in any debate or voting on the issue.

Some of these exceptions are subjective, rather than objective, and it is not always clear whether or not a councillor has a declarable pecuniary interest in a matter. In such cases, councillors can take advice from the Chief Executive, Monitoring Officer or one of the authority's legal officers. But officers can only advise, since they can never be fully aware of the councillor's personal interests. Councillors, in the light of this advice, must decide whether or not there is a declarable pecuniary interest — the legal responsibility (and the penalty if they make a mistake) rests with them.

In some cases, the Secretary of State can issue either a **general** or **specific** *dispensation* enabling councillors with declared pecuniary interests to take part in debates and, depending on the circumstances, to vote. An example of a general dispensation is that issued in 1973 by the Secretary of State which authorised councillors who are tenants of unfurnished accommodation to take part in debates on, and vote on, matters relating to council housing policy, other than in relation to their own tenancy. On other issues, a specific dispensation to vote, as well as speak, will only be granted if the political balance of the council is critically affected by the councillor being unable to vote; but, even then, a dispensation to vote will not be granted if the councillor's pecuniary interest is very direct (say, the councillor owns a piece of land involved).

There is an additional provision (section 106 of the Local Government Finance Act 1992) which is often overlooked by councillors and which can land them in trouble if they do. If a councillor is two or more months in arrears with their Council Tax and the issue under discussion is likely to affect the calculation of the Council Tax, then they must declare the fact that they are in arrears and must not vote, but they can remain in the meeting and take part in the discussion. This particular provision has greater significance for the annual revenue budget meeting.

Registers of interests

The Local Government Act 1972 also included provision for a statutory register kept by the Proper Officer (the officer designated for keeping the register) in which councillors can record certain kinds of interests (employment, partnership, and tenancy of self and/or spouse), if they wished to do so. In other words, it is voluntary. The register is open to inspection by other councillors, but not the public.

The Local Government and Housing Act 1989 introduced a further (this time, compulsory) statutory register in which councillors must declare certain kinds of interest (employment, office, trade, profession or vocation; sponsorship; contracts; land; licences; corporate tenancies; and interests in securities). That register is open to public inspection. Entries must be made within four weeks of taking office and amended within four weeks of any change. Failure to register or making a false or misleading entry is a criminal offence. The new provisions are now to be found in the LGB 2000.

An authority may also decide to keep a further non-statutory and voluntary register on issues such as membership of bodies. Such a register, if it exists at all, will not be open to public inspection.

The National Code of Conduct

In 1974, the then Prime Minister's Committee on Conduct in Local Government recommended that the statutory provisions concerning pecuniary interest should be supplemented by a Code of Conduct. The first Code, issued in 1975 under a government circular was commended to local authorities — it was essentially a voluntary arrangement, but it introduced the concept of *non-pecuniary interest.*

The process was taken further by the Local Government and Housing Act 1989. The Code was reissued in a revised form in 1990. This version of the Code was given formal statutory status and councillors are now obliged, when signing their declaration of acceptance of office, to undertake to be guided by the Code. Although the 1990 Code was clearer than the 1975 version, it still causes difficulties in interpretation. This Code will be replaced, as explained later, sometime in 2000 as a consequence of the LGB 2000.

The Code explains that interests which are not pecuniary can be just as important as those that are.

Non-pecuniary interests

The Code outlines some general obligations on the councillor. The councillor's overriding duty is to the whole community, including people who didn't vote for the councillor. The councillor should never do anything which could not be justified to the public. It is not enough to avoid actual impropriety, the councillor should, at all times, avoid any occasion for suspicion or any appearance of improper conduct.

The Code suggests that non-pecuniary interests *"include those of your family and friends as well as those arising through membership of, or association with, clubs, societies and other organisations such as freemasons, trade unions and voluntary bodies".*

The ambit of the Code extends beyond the formal committee structure: *"you must apply the principles about disclosure of interests to your dealings with council officers and to your unofficial relations with other councillors (at party group meetings or other informal occasions) no less scrupulously than at formal meetings of the council, its committees and subcommittees".*

A councillor who believes that he or she has a non-pecuniary interest has to go through a multi-stage objective self-testing process to decide what to do about it. The councillor has to evaluate the nature of the non-pecuniary interest, on the basis of what other people might reasonably think about it. The councillor has to decide whether the interest is 'private or personal', then whether it is 'significant', and finally whether it is 'clear and substantial'.

An interest is 'private or personal' where others would think that the councillor is, or may be, using his or her position to promote a **private or personal** interest, rather than forwarding the **general public interest.** Interests of family and friends are caught, as are interests through membership of clubs, societies and other organisations. If the interest **is** private or personal, the councillor is next obliged to consider whether it is 'significant'.

What constitutes a 'significant' interest is not defined. The opposite, 'insignificant', non-pecuniary interest is one which the councillor shares with other members of the public generally as ratepayers, Council Tax payers or inhabitants of the area. Such non-significant interests need not be declared and, if the context is a meeting, the councillor can remain in the meeting, can speak and can vote.

However, if the non-pecuniary interest is 'significant' the councillor has to decide whether it is also 'clear and substantial' — to determine how to behave. The interest is 'clear and substantial' if members of the public, knowing the facts of the situation, would reasonably think that the councillor **might** be influenced by it. The emphasis on 'might' is in the Code.

If the 'personal or private' and 'significant' interest is **not** also 'clear and substantial', then the councillor must disclose it (because it is 'significant') but can remain in the meeting, take part in the discussion and vote.

If the 'personal or private' and 'significant' interest **is** 'clear and substantial', then the councillor must declare it and withdraw from the meeting.

Self-dispensation

Under the statutory arrangements for pecuniary interests, as already explained, the Secretary of State can give a dispensation, to enable an affected councillor to remain in the meeting, speak and possibly vote.

With the Code and non-pecuniary interests, the position is different and, depending on the circumstances, the affected councillor can grant himself or herself a dispensation — called *self-dispensation*, even though he or she has a 'clear and substantial' interest. The Code cautions councillors about the use of self-dispensation. The Code suggests strongly that the councillor take advice from the chairman of the council **and** from the appropriate senior officer (usually the monitoring officer).

Only **two** circumstances are envisaged by the Code as appropriate for self-dispensation:

- at least half of the council/committee would similarly have to withdraw; and
- withdrawal, together with that of the other affected councillors, would upset the political balance of the council/committee to such an extent that the decision is likely to be affected.

The Code suggests that the councillor consult the group leader about political balance issues; that the councillor explore the possibility of pairing to maintain the political balance (and therefore avoid the need for self-dispensation); and that the councillor should explain, at the beginning of the meeting, why he or she thinks that the criteria for self-dispensation are satisfied — this gives the council/committee the chance to decide whether or not to proceed with the councillor present.

Even if the criteria are satisfied, the Code advises the councillor **not** to pursue self-dispensation, if the public would regard the councillor's interest as so close that he or she could not put the interest out of his or her mind.

Maladministration — naming the councillor

Different sanctions apply to a councillor who has acted in breach of the Code. Unlike non-compliance with the statutory provisions relating to pecuniary interests, non-compliance with the Code is not a criminal offence. Instead, non-compliance with the Code results, on investigation by the Local Ombudsman (see the Chapter on *External Relations and Controls*), with a finding of maladministration. The irony is that the finding of maladministration is against the local authority as a whole, rather than against the individual councillor who is guilty of the breach.

However, that position has, to some extent, been addressed by the way in which the Ombudsman now publicises the finding of maladministration. The usual rule followed by the Ombudsman is that the people involved in an investigation, whether complainant, officer or councillor, remain anonymous in the Ombudsman's formal report. However, where the maladministration involves breach of the Code by an individual councillor, that councillor can be named in the report. It used to be the case that the Ombudsman could only name the guilty councillor if the Ombudsman felt it was right to do so; the position has now been turned around, so that the Ombudsman is now obliged to name the councillor, unless it would be unfair to do so.

However, that is the present limit to the sanctions which can be applied to a councillor who is guilty of breaching the Code. A guilty councillor cannot be suspended or removed from membership of the council (otherwise than at the next elections!), although they may find themselves removed from committee/subcommittee memberships in the meantime, provided the council acts fairly and follows the correct procedure to achieve that result. The LGB 2000 provisions outlined at the end of this Chapter address this issue.

External audit

The picture in relation to Propriety is completed by outlining the provisions relating to *surcharge*, arising from an external audit investigation. The process followed in auditing local authority accounts is described in the Chapter on *External Relations and Controls*.

Up to 1974, district auditors were entitled to disallow items in the accounts which they considered to be illegal. If they considered that particular councillors or officers were responsible for that illegal expenditure, then they could *surcharge* those councillors and officers.

As a result of the Local Government Act 1972 and the Local Government Finance Act 1982, the power of surcharge by the auditor no longer exists, although the word 'surcharge' is still often used to describe the powers available to the auditor and to the court — and the word 'surcharge' was used in the LGB 2000 when abolishing the right of the auditor (rather than the court) to recover unlawful expenditure from an individual councillor.

Under the Audit Commission Act 1998, if it appears to an external auditor that *'an item of account is contrary to law'* the auditor may apply to the court for a declaration along those lines. The external auditor will either be a partner in a large firm of private practice accountants or the arms-length District Audit Service of the Audit Commission. The Secretary of State has power to 'sanction' such expenditure, thus removing the illegality. However, this power will only be used where the local authority has acted mistakenly and in good faith.

If the court agrees with the auditor and makes a declaration, it may also go further and order those responsible (including former, as well as current, councillors and officers) to repay all or part of the sum involved to the local authority concerned. Councillors and former councillors can be disqualified from membership of any local authority for a specific period where the amount which is declared by the court to be contrary to law exceeds £2,000.

The court cannot order repayment or disqualify a councillor if it is satisfied that the person concerned acted reasonably or in the belief that the expenditure was lawful. In deciding the amount to be repaid, the court must have regard to all the circumstances of the case, including the means and ability to pay of the persons concerned.

Prior to the LGB 2000, in addition to the power to apply to a court for a declaration, if the external auditor believed either that *"a person has failed to bring into account any sum which should have been included"* or that *"a loss or deficiency has been incurred by the wilful misconduct of any person"*, the auditor could issue a certificate stating the amount due from that person. If the certificate exceeded £2,000 then any councillor named in the certificate was automatically disqualified. Any person who was aggrieved by such a certificate could appeal against the decision to the High Court (or the county court if less than £5,000 is involved). This was the course of action followed by the external auditors in Lambeth and Liverpool when losses and deficiencies were certified during 1985 arising from the wilful misconduct of certain councillors in each authority, in refusing to fix the rate by the due date. The external auditor for Westminster City Council followed this procedure in the 'designated homes' case.

This power of 'surcharge' was repealed by the LGB 2000. As a *quid pro quo,* the LGB 2000 introduced a new system of *Advisory Notices*. Where the auditor believes that the authority has or is about to reach a decision to incur unlawful expenditure, or is about to take a course of action which would be unlawful and cause a loss or deficiency, or is about to make an unlawful entry in its accounts, then the auditor can issue an advisory notice to the authority. The effect of such a notice is to put a temporary freeze on the authority's actions and open up a dialogue between the authority and the auditor.

The Nolan Report

In 1994, the then Prime Minister established the *Committee on Standards in Public Life,* under the chairmanship of Lord Nolan (this committee is now known as the *Neill Committee*, after its present chairman Lord Neill). The Committee's third report, produced in June 1997, looked at aspects of conduct in local government. The third Nolan Report suggested that the key reason for lack of clarity about standards in local government was mainly due to the fact that responsibility for the maintenance of standards had moved away from local government.

Nolan believed that the answer lay in making a new start on an ethical framework for local government, taking the best of what already existed, but placing leading responsibility with local government itself. Compare this philosophy with the Green Paper proposals and the LGB 2000 described later.

The Nolan Report put forward its *Seven Principles of Public Life:*

- *Selflessness* — holders of public office should take decisions solely in the public interest. They should not do so in order to gain financial or other material benefits for themselves, their family, or their friends;
- *Integrity* — holders of public office should not place themselves under any financial or other obligation to outside individuals or organisations that might influence them in the performance of their official duties;
- *Objectivity* — in carrying out public business, including making public appointments, awarding contracts, or recommending individuals for rewards and benefits, holders of public office should make choices on merit;
- *Accountability* — holders of public office are accountable for their decisions and actions to the public and must submit themselves to whatever scrutiny is appropriate to their office;
- *Openness* — holders of public office should be as open as possible about all the decisions and actions that they take. They should give reasons for their decisions and restrict information only when the wider public interest clearly demands;
- *Honesty* — holders of public office have a duty to declare any private interests relating to their public duties and to take steps to resolve any conflicts arising in a way that protects the public interest;

- *Leadership* — holders of public office should promote and support these principles by leadership and example.

Against this background, Nolan proposed:

- a clear code of conduct for councillors developed by each individual council within a framework approved by Parliament;
- that each council should have a Standards Committee to deal with matters of propriety and to have powers to recommend to the full council that errant members should be disciplined;
- the creation of new Local Government Tribunals to act as independent arbiters on matters relating to councils' codes of conduct and to hear appeals from councillors and others;
- the involvement of the courts in imposing penalties for misconduct, to replace the surcharge;
- following consultation, the creation of a new statutory offence of Misuse of Public Office.

New Labour — Modernising Local Government

The Home Office is, at the time of writing this (April 2000), still thinking about what to say about the suggestion by Nolan that there should be a new offence of Misuse of Public Office! Certainly, there is no provision for it in the LGB 2000, which is where one might expect to find it.

As for the rest of the Nolan Report, the New Labour Government's response was contained in the last of the *Modernising Local Government* Green Papers to be published — on a new ethical framework for local government. That Green Paper went further than Nolan in some respects. The suggestions in the Green Paper were:

- each local authority would produce its own code of conduct for councillors, following a model developed by the local authority associations under 'guidance' from the minister and subject to final approval by the minister;
- a parallel code of conduct for officers would be produced in the same way;
- there would be a new, wider, compulsory register for councillors to declare those interests *"which might reasonably be thought by others to influence his or her work as a councillor"*. There would be a 'catch-all' final item on the register to pick up membership of organisations *"such as the freemasons"*;
- failure to declare non-pecuniary interests would not be a criminal offence (the *status quo*); but would, in future, make the councillor subject to punishment under the new disciplinary procedure;

- each local authority would have to appoint a standards committee, possibly including non-councillors, to encourage compliance with the codes, but any complaint investigations would be limited to the most trivial complaints;
- there would be a number of regional standards boards, consisting of people nominated by the local authority associations but approved by the minister;
- any significant complaints would be immediately referred to the regional board for investigation, hearing and decision. The councillor could be suspended during the investigation and the sanctions open to the regional board would include censure, suspension or disqualification;
- the decisions of the regional board would be open to appeal to a national standards panel or subject to judicial review by the courts, at the behest of the councillor or the original complainant;
- once all of these disciplinary processes were in place, and following the necessary legislation to create a new offence of Misuse of Public Office (or something similar), the Government *"would be minded to abolish the surcharge regime"*.

Local Government Bill

The new ethical framework appears in the LGB 2000 (and in its lost predecessor, the Local Government (Organisation and Standards) Bill) and the process is even more centralised than that envisaged by either the Green Paper or Nolan. The Secretary of State, after appropriate consultation, is given the power to issue a new Code which each newly-elected councillor has to sign up to when accepting office — failure to do so within two months results in the new councillor losing his or her seat. Each local authority is expected to adopt its own local Code which must, at least, contain the mandatory provisions of the national Code. At the time of writing, April 2000, the new national Code does not exist, so it is not possible to gauge the extent to which the Green Paper proposals have been translated into the final national Code.

Each authority has to establish a Standards Committee of at least three people, of whom one must not be a councillor or officer of that, or any other, authority. The role of the Standards Committee is to: advise the authority on the adoption of its local Code; monitor the Code's operation; train the councillors on compliance with it; and consider any reports arising from an investigation by an ethical standards officer employed by the national Standards Board. Where the authority has adopted one of the LGB 2000 models of internal organisation, the elected Mayor or the executive

Leader cannot be members of a Standards Committee and any other member of the executive who is a member of a Standards Committee may not chair it.

Formal investigation of complaints is not undertaken by the authority but through the national (not regional) Standards Board. There are two Standards Boards — one for England and the other for Wales (Bwrdd Safonau Cymru) — appointed by the Secretary of State/National Assembly for Wales. There are also two national Adjudication Panels, similarly appointed, from which specially appointed Case Tribunals are appointed by the President of the Panel. The Board appoints ethical standards officers to investigate complaints about councillors' failure to comply with the Code and produce a report, if thought to be warranted as a result of the investigation. The report of the ethical standards officer has to be copied to the authority's Monitoring Officer and referred to the President of the relevant Panel for consideration by a specially appointed Case Tribunal. If the Case Tribunal determines that there has been a failure to comply with the Code and that the nature of the failure justifies it, the Case Tribunal can decide that the councillor should be suspended for up to one year or disqualified from being a councillor for up to five years. The Case Tribunal's conclusions are then reported to the authority's Standards Committee.

5 Elections

The franchise — qualifications for election — terms of office — electoral review — proposals for change

Background

Prior to 1974, local government elections used to be held throughout the first week of May. The Local Government Act 1972 changed that: elections are now held on the first Thursday in May, unless the Home Secretary fixes another day. The Act provided for the first time that all councillors of all principal councils in England and Wales (except, of course, the City of London, which democracy continues to pass by) should be directly elected. Gone are the aldermen, who used to be elected by councillors of councils.

Electoral cycles

All councillors, except those elected at by-elections, are elected for four years, but the election cycle for the different types of authority varies:

- *County councils:* elections are held every four years, with the whole council retiring at the same time. Counties are divided into electoral divisions which return one councillor each. Elections were held in 1993, 1997 and so on.
- *London borough councils:* elections are held every four years with the whole council retiring at the same time. The boroughs are divided into wards each returning between one and three councillors. Elections were held in 1994, 1998 and so on.
- *Metropolitan borough councils:* these are divided into wards, with between one and three councillors representing each ward. Elections are held in three years out of the four, with one third of the council (one councillor from each ward) retiring each time. There are no elections in these areas in those years where, in other parts of the country, county council elections are held. Elections were held in 1990, 1991, 1992 and then in 1994. There were no elections in 1993, 1997 and so on.
- *Shire district/borough councils in two-tier areas:* these have the same type of representation as metropolitan borough councils, but

these authorities can choose whether to have one-third of the council retiring in three years out of four, as in metropolitan borough councils, or the whole council retiring at the same time. Where they opt for the one-third system, the calendar is the same as for metropolitan borough councils; where the whole council retires together, elections are held midway between those of counties; 1991, 1995 and so on.

- *Unitary authorities:* these have the same type of representation as shire district/borough councils, but special arrangements are made where a hybrid solution (one or more unitary authorities and a smaller residual county council) is adopted for a county area. The statutory order creating the new unitary authority may state that the first elections for the new unitary authority will be for a term of office of less than four years, to avoid future clashes with the county council elections.
- *Parish and community councils:* elections are held every four years, with the whole council retiring at the same time, 1991, 1995 and so on. There have to be at least five councillors of a parish council, the actual number being fixed by the district council. Where parishes and communities are divided into wards, separate elections are held for each ward. Where there are no wards, then there is one election for the whole council.

However, the position may now change as a consequence of the Local Government Bill, which is outlined in the last section of this Chapter.

By-elections

Whenever a by-election is held — when a councillor dies, resigns or is disqualified from membership — in any type of local authority, the person elected serves out the time of the person originally elected for the seat. But, if a councillor resigns or dies after the September of the year prior to an election the following May, the seat remains vacant until that election.

Qualification to stand for election

Anyone can stand for election to a local authority, provided that, on the day of nomination and poll, they:

- are a British, other Commonwealth, Republic of Ireland or other EU State citizen; *and*
- are properly nominated; *and*
- are **21** years old, *and*

- can prove one of the following specified connections with the area:
  1) — are (and remain thereafter) a local government elector for the local authority area; *or*
  2) — have, for the whole of the preceding 12 months, occupied, as owner or tenant, land or other premises in that area; *or*
  3) — have had, for the whole of the preceding 12 months, their principal or only place of work in that area; *or*
  4) — have, for the whole of the preceding 12 months, resided in that area; *or*
  5) — have, (in the case of a councillor of a parish *or* community council) for the whole of the preceding 12 months, lived in the parish or community, or within three miles of it; *and*
- 6) are not disqualified.

Disqualification from standing for election

Prospective candidates who meet the qualification requirements will still be barred from seeking election if they:

- have been adjudged bankrupt or made a composition or arrangement with their creditors; or
- have, in the five years before the election, while a councillor of any local authority, been ordered by the court, upon a certificate of the district auditor, to repay more than £2,000 in respect of any loss or deficiency; or
- have in the five years before the election, received a sentence of imprisonment (whether suspended or not) for three months or more without the option of a fine; or
- have been held by an election court to have committed a corrupt or illegal practice:
  — within that local authority area and personally guilty, 10 years before the election; *or*
  — if within that local authority area and guilty by their agent, three years before the election; *or*
  — if outside that local authority area and personally guilty, five years before the election.

In addition, paid officers cannot be councillors of their employing authority. Teachers cannot be councillors of the local education authority which maintains the school in which they work, but may, however, be co-opted on to that local education authority's education committee (if one exists).

The Local Government and Housing Act 1989 disqualified a paid officer of one local authority from being a councillor of any other local authority if that officer was in a 'politically restricted post'. What constitutes a 'politically restricted post' was explained in the Chapter on *Councillors and Officers.*

Entitlement to vote

Only those people whose name is on the register of electors, which is maintained by the electoral registration officer, may vote. To be eligible for inclusion on the electoral register, a person must:

- be at least 18 years old or attain that age during the 12 month period covered by the register (however, such a person may only vote if they have attained 18 by the date of the poll); *and*
- be a British or other Commonwealth or Irish Republic or other EU citizen; *and*
- have a qualification based on normal residence; or have a service qualification, a qualification as a merchant seaman, or a declaration as a voluntary mental patient.

There are exceptions. Peers (regardless of whether they have been retained in the House of Lords by the House of Lords Act 1999) and other EU State citizens can vote (and stand) in local elections, but not in Parliamentary elections. The following people cannot vote in local elections:

- foreign nationals (other than those entitled to be registered);
- some patients detained under mental health legislation;
- convicted people detained in a penal or mental institution (but not people on remand, since they have not been convicted); and
- people convicted within the previous five years of corrupt or illegal election practices.

Overseas and Absent voters

Certain British citizens living abroad do not have the right to vote in local government elections — although they can vote in Westminster, Scottish Parliament, Welsh Assembly and European Parliament elections and, for that reason, their names appear on the electoral register. An outline of this appears in the *Who can vote* section of Chapter 8 *Elections* in the companion book, *Essential Central Government.*

Holidaymakers are allowed an absent vote in local government and national elections, following regulations approved on 24 June 1986 giving effect to the provisions of the Representation of the People Act 1985 to extend the franchise. If a voter expects to be absent from the local government area on polling day, he or she can apply for an Absent Vote. Under the Representation of the People Act 1985 an Absent Vote is allowed at a particular election if the electoral registration officer is *"satisfied that the applicant's circumstances on the date of the poll will be or are likely to be such that he cannot reasonably be expected to vote in person"*.

There is a special exemption for electors who are taken ill prior to the poll. Their applications can be accepted up to the sixth day before the election.

Electoral register

Every unitary authority, London borough council, metropolitan borough council, and shire district/borough (but not the county council) in a two-tier area, has to appoint an electoral registration officer. The principal task of that officer is the compilation of the electoral register.

This involves sending an electoral registration form, completion of which is compulsory, to every home in the area. Copies of the electoral register may be sold at a prescribed fee per thousand names. The key place and date for registration used to be place of residence on 10 October each year. The draft register was open for public inspection until 16 December, during which period people could apply to the Registration Officer to have mistakes (usually not appearing on the register at all) corrected. After that, the register came into effect usually on the following 16 February, although the date could change if there was a General Election. People changing address could not be registered at their new address until the register was next updated and published.

That all changed as a result of the Representation of the People Bill (RPB 2000). The RPB 2000 introduced a new system of registration where entitlement to vote is not tied to residence on one specific date during the year. The electoral registration officer still carries out an annual canvass (on 15 October with a view to publication on 1 December) but it is now possible for someone to have their name added to the register — so-called 'rolling registration' — at the beginning of a month. Because the register can now be altered on a monthly basis, the old system of objection and correction between 10 October and 16 December is no longer necessary. The register cannot (except as a result of a formal appeal) be altered for the purposes of any particular election once the final date for nominations has passed.

Election procedure

The notice of election must be published at least 25 days before the election. Nomination papers for candidates must be handed in, by noon, 19 days before the election (all nomination papers must bear the candidate's name and those of a proposer and seconder and eight other people eligible to vote in the area); a list of the candidates nominated must be published by noon on the 17th day before the election; withdrawal of candidature must be made no later than 16 days before the election; and notice of appointment of polling or counting agents must be made by five days before the election.

Each local authority has to appoint a *Returning Officer* (usually the Chief Executive) to be responsible for conduct of the election. The Returning Officer:

- appoints presiding officers and poll clerks to attend each polling station;
- supervises the counting of votes;
- rules on whether ballot papers have been spoiled; and
- publishes the results.

Polling stations are open from 8am to 9pm for local elections; for Parliamentary elections, the hours are 7am to 10pm.

When a person (or their proxy, if they have opted for that form of voting) turns up at the polling station to vote, their name is checked against the register by the presiding officer/poll clerk. If their name is on the register and they have not been given a postal vote to use in that election, they (or their proxy) are given a ballot paper. If their name is not on the register, for whatever reason, or they have previously been given a postal vote, they will be refused a ballot paper. Postal votes cannot be given in at the polling station — they must be delivered to the proper place, in accordance with the instructions on postal voting.

The votes are counted in the 'counting place' — either in a building convenient to the electoral division in rural areas; or in a centrally located building in the more densely populated urban areas. The count is not open to the public, but the candidates and a fixed number of observers nominated by them are able to witness the count and raise any queries with the supervising returning officer.

Any dubious ballot papers (where the voter's intention is not clear; or the voter might be identified from what they have written on the ballot paper; or the official mark is missing) are considered by the returning officer in consultation with the candidates and decisions made by the returning officer as to their validity. The nightmare scenario for a returning officer is a very close count, where the difference between the leading candidates is less than the number of dubious ballot papers!

There are legal limits setting the maximum amount that can be spent by candidates on their election expenses. Exceeding these limits constitutes an election offence. The candidate's agent must send to the returning officer a return of the candidate's expenses — failure to do this is also an election offence.

Any disappointed candidate can, if they have grounds for doing so, challenge the result of an election by going to court with an *election petition* against the returning officer. There may be a challenge on the basis: that the original nomination papers were invalid in some way; that the decisions made by the returning officer during the election (especially disallowing ballot papers as being invalid) were incorrect; or that there has been an election offence.

Boundary and Electoral Review

The Local Government Commission for England mentioned in the Chapter 1 *Structure and Functions* has other responsibilities in addition to the structural review with which it was preoccupied. The Commission also assumed responsibilities from the former Boundary Commission for England — local authority boundary and electoral review — including town and parish councils.

The Commission has a duty to conduct periodic reviews to correct imbalances in the electorate of local government areas. The Commission issued a consultation document with a suggested programme of reviews. The Commission went further by raising wider issues, including: a minimum and maximum size of councils; single or multi-councillor wards; and the merits of whole-council or by-thirds elections. Some of these suggestions, if endorsed, required legislation to effect the change. The New Labour *Modernising Local Government* Green Paper *Local Democracy and Community Leadership*, raised similar issues — these have been addressed in the Political Parties, Elections and Referendums Bill, which also transferred the responsibilities of the Boundary Commissions to a new Electoral Commission. An outline of the other provisions of the Political Parties, Elections and Referendums Bill appears in Chapter 8 *Elections* in the companion book *Essential Central Government*. The issues about election dates, methods of voting and multi-councillor electoral divisions were addressed in the Representation of the People Bill, which is outlined in the last section of this Chapter.

European Union

One of the consequences of the Maastricht Treaty is that, as of 1996, EU nationals also have the right to stand and vote in local elections in the UK.

New Labour — Modernising Local Government

The New Labour Green Paper *Modernising Local Government — Local Democracy and Community Leadership* contained a section dealing with modernising local electoral arrangements.

The turn-out in local elections in the UK, compared with other countries, is not high — indeed, in the EU league table, the UK (40%) is in bottom place. The Green Paper discussed what the reasons for this might be, which were thought to be deep-seated and could only be addressed in the longer term.

Regardless of turn-out, it is estimated that between 2 and 4 million people are absent from the electoral register, which, after all, is supposed to be compulsory. One of the reasons for this may be the introduction of the Poll Tax (Community Charge) by Mrs Thatcher, which resulted in many people deciding to refuse to appear on the electoral register in order to evade the Poll Tax. When the Poll Tax was abolished a few years later, perhaps many of those people saw little incentive to rejoin the electoral register.

The suggestions in the Green Paper included:

- maximising voting — but by encouragement through publicity, rather than by compulsion;
- anonymous registration for those who are reluctant for their name to appear on the register;
- a rolling register — to be amended at anytime, not just once a year;
- taking the polling station to the voter — where there are large numbers of people — for example at workplace, college, or supermarket (this was tried as an experiment at two Tesco supermarkets in the May 1998 Croydon LBC elections);
- voting over a longer period, including the previous few days;
- extending the availability of absent voting;
- electronic voting; and
- annual elections — not annual election for each councillor, but annual elections for a proportion of each council (presumably extending the by-thirds system to all councils).

The reasons for a poor turn-out in the local government elections are, as the government admits, complex. It is just possible that people will not feel inclined to vote if they believe that their vote is wasted — as it probably would be in a solid Labour or Conservative or Liberal Democrat electoral division. Interesting, then, that the Green Paper omitted one proposal that might have increased voter turn-out — some form of proportional representation which might encourage more people to vote. In addition, the steady drain of powers away from local government to central government and quangos would not have escaped the notice of most people, who might have begun to wonder whether local government really mattered anymore. Perhaps this drain had also been responsible for the decline in the number of reporters and correspondents dedicated to local government in the local, regional and national media — with the result that most local government stories appearing in the national media are written from a London perspective. Presumably the new Electoral Commission created by the Political Parties, Elections and Referendums Bill will try to drum up enthusiasm for elections, given that one of its rôles is "promoting participation and understanding of our democratic systems of government".

Representation of the People Bill

At the time of writing this (April 2000), the Bill has not made it to the Statute Book to become the Representation of the People Act 2000. The Bill disenfranchises people held in mental institutions as a result of criminal activity but, apart from that, makes no other change to the franchise. What the Bill does seek to achieve is to simplify the way in which residence is determined, including people in mental institutions (except those there because of criminal activity), people remanded in custody and homeless people, where a new concept of 'local connection' is introduced to determine where such people, living away from their former place of residence, can be registered for voting purposes. The Bill also introduces changes aimed at making it easier for people with disabilities to vote.

At present, the electoral register can be sold to anyone willing to pay the charge — mostly commercial organisations. In future, as a consequence of the Bill, the electoral register will be maintained in two versions — one being the full version which will be open to public inspection and used for elections but of which copies can only be supplied to people prescribed by regulations (either free or at a charge); and the other being an edited version excluding the names of those people who do not wish to have their names included in it — this edited version can be sold to anyone.

The more interesting provisions in the Bill relate to pilot schemes. In relation to pilot schemes for the local government elections in May 2000, just over 40 local authorities volunteered to take part in pilot studies running and evaluating different voting arrangements. These pilots are authorised by the Bill. The pilots include: electronic voting; total postal voting; voting spread over a number of days; and voting on Saturdays. Similarly, in the elections for the Greater London Authority, voters were able to cast their votes over a number of days, in order to increase the chances of a reasonable turnout. The experience gained in these pilots may then result in permanent changes to the voting arrangements not only in local elections but also in elections for Westminster, Scottish Parliament, National Assembly for Wales, and the European Parliament.

Local Government Bill

In relation to dates for local elections, the Local Government Bill envisages three options, all involving councillors holding office for four years but with elections being held at different intervals — option one involves the whole council being elected at the same time; option two involves one-half of the council being elected every two years; option three involves one-third of the council being elected in three out of four years. Comparison with the first section of this Chapter will reveal that option two is new. In addition, the Secretary of State is given the power to rearrange the election cycle of individual authorities and, if appropriate, introduce the idea of multi-councillor electoral divisions in shire county councils.

6 External Relations and Controls

Relations between local and central government — the local authority associations — ultra vires — judicial controls — legislative controls — administrative controls — the Ombudsman — financial controls — the Audit Commission

Relations between local and central government

Not everyone will agree with or accept the analysis which follows, but it should at the very least provide the stimulus for a debate. It must be the case that central government is right to exercise some control over local government, but the key questions are about the extent of the control which is really necessary, the way in which that control is used and the tone of the language used by central government towards local government.

The local government of today is markedly different from that of the 1960s. In those days, there were, of course, administrative controls over the way local government worked and the *ultra vires* principles applied then, as now.

But, the main difference was that each local authority was able to determine, for itself, the level of services it should supply (usually directly), its **revenue** expenditure and fix the level of its local revenue tax, the rates. In those days, the percentage of local authority revenue expenditure funded by general grant from central government was about 60% to 65%, so percentage increases in the rates to meet a particular level of additional expenditure were not as great as they are now, with central government revenue support now running at something in the region of 80%.

If the local authority was spending more on local services than the local ratepayers wanted, then they made their displeasure known through the ballot box at the next elections.

However, as total local government revenue expenditure rose in absolute terms and as a proportion of the national GDP, central government naturally, and quite rightly, sought to exert greater influence and, then, control over local government activity, in the national financial interest.

This increase in control really began with a Labour government, when Labour was last in office at national level — particularly the middle to late 1970s. The national inflationary pressures at that time would not have helped the situation. The phrase 'the party's over', in the context of local government revenue expenditure, was uttered by a Labour Secretary of State. The Labour government at that time, for those people with long enough memories, could reasonably be regarded as essentially 'centralist' in its approach to local government.

The change to a Conservative Government in 1979 brought a hardening of central government's attitude towards local government. As more and more responsibilities were given to local government, they were not accompanied by a demonstrable increase in resources — instead, the government took refuge in "appropriate provision will be made in the Rate Support Grant [as it then was] settlement" — an assertion difficult to prove or disprove.

There then followed a period where additional responsibilities and initiatives were usually funded through 'top-slicing' (and reducing) the local government **general** grant and then obliging authorities to compete (often spending valuable time in doing so) for the top-sliced grant as a **specific** grant determined by the government — local discretion being replaced by central direction. Examples of this include the Urban Programme and its successor, the Single Regeneration Budget.

The process was accelerated by the introduction of the Poll Tax (Community Charge) by the Thatcher government. The paradox here was that one of the objectives of the Poll Tax was stated to be to reinforce local accountability for the level of local taxation through the ballot box at the local elections, since the Poll Tax bore directly on the individual voter. However, ironically, the crude revenue budget capping regime which accompanied the introduction of the Poll Tax, effectively removed that local accountability, because it was the government which now controlled the overall level of each local authority's revenue budget.

While this was going on, powers and duties were being transferred away from local government (with a majority of local authorities no longer under Conservative control) towards a collection of non-elected, non-democratically accountable bodies (quangos), often appointed by government ministers. Examples of this process include: Training and Enterprise Councils (TECs); FE and Sixth Form Colleges; housing associations; housing action trusts; and the Careers Service. The resources associated with the transferred activities were also moved away from local government. The Local Government Chronicle of 19 July 1996 carried a news item, *'More in quangos than councils'*:

> *"Members of Britain's 'unaccountable' quangos outnumber elected council councillors by nearly three to one. A Democratic Audit report published this week reveals that there are between 66,000 and 73,500 people who run quangos responsible for billions of pounds of public money. Almost all of them are appointed by the government or are self-appointing".*

Not everything went entirely the government's way. When CCT was first introduced, there were existing private contractors ready and able to take over manual services such as refuse collection and cleaning, if the local authority's in-house service failed to win the competition. However, the position was different for the non-manual services which the government attempted to privatise later. The intended massive transfer of professional service delivery to the private sector through CCT largely failed, despite the best efforts of the government to skew 'the level playing field' in favour of the private sector. This was largely due to uncertainty over the future legal and commercial impact of TUPE on any transferred activity and to the absence of a real market because the relevant private sector was not, at that time, properly prepared to create it.

Towards the end of the Conservative administration, relations between central and local government became even less cordial — with government ministers seemingly less inclined to disguise their true antipathy towards local government. Central government increased its ability to intervene by setting up its Offices for the Regions — although presented as a step towards devolved central government, the arrangement enables control and supervision of local government to be exercised much more closely than hitherto.

The advent of the New Labour Government promised a sea-change in central government/local government relations, especially since, by this time, the number of Conservative controlled local authorities was in single figures. Against that background, it would not have been unreasonable to have supposed that central government might now be more inclined to trust local government to behave responsibly.

Initially, the signs were encouraging — the language emerging from central government was moderate and palliative, with words such as 'partnership' being used by government ministers in joint meetings with local government leaders. However, the expected early abolition of CCT and budget capping failed to materialise; and there has been no early return of services from quangos to directly-elected local authorities.

Indeed, in some respects, although the language used might appear to be different, it has, in certain areas, been difficult to discern any real difference between the local government policies of the New Labour Government and those of its predecessor.

The New Labour Government published six Green Papers to do with *Modernising Local Government.* Some local authorities, when they found the time and resources to do so, introduced innovative management practices and mechanisms for public consultation and participation, to the extent permitted by law — although others did not feel the need to alter their way of doing things. It would obviously be useful for there to be some modernisation of the legislative framework within which local government is expected to work, but it is instructive to look at the detailed suggestions, beyond the rhetoric, in those Green Papers and the way they are presented.

Each of the Green Papers suggests that its aim is for greater flexibility, new ways of working and some measure of greater freedom — but, in every case, the suggestions are backed up with prescriptive mechanisms giving ministers even more control over what local government does on a day-to-day basis and greater opportunity to intervene if they are not satisfied.

Even the *Guardian* was moved in its leader of 8 April 1998 *'Reforming town halls — but Whitehall still rules'* to comment:

> *"Is the colonial power ready to retreat? For 18 years local government suffered tighter controls and ever more centralisation under Conservative rule. The imperial centre removed local council powers, capped their taxing capabilities, and transferred £30 billion of services to unelected quango control. All these moves were opposed by Labour which presented itself as the defender of local democracy. But battered and bruised local councillors remained suspicious of what would happen once office was won. They now have their answer. ... Whitehall may now use nicer words — 'democratic renewal' — but imperialism still reigns".*

The *Local Government Chronicle* leader of 9 April 1998, commenting on the Green Paper on Ethics, was headed *'Ethics plans betray Labour lack of trust'* and said:

> *"Although no-one is going to condemn external scrutiny, bringing the [regional standards] boards in so early on an investigation is bound to raise further questions about the government's confidence in councils. This reinforces the impression left by the meagre financial freedoms offered in the finance green papers last week".*

In fact, the proposals in the Local Government Bill (LGB 2000) are even more centralist in their approach. In the same issue of the *Chronicle*, Professors Jones and Stewart were commenting on the earlier Green Paper on *Best Value:*

> *"One aspect of the consultation paper worries us deeply. There is a basic contradiction between the statement 'the government considers that the judgement about whether best value is being achieved is ultimately one for local people to make' and the proposals for central government interventions, which imply that it is ultimately for central government to make... The two statements are contradictory. The government claims these powers 'reinforce' local accountability. In reality they replace it".*

Each authority now has to produce an annual Best Value Performance Plan in compliance with 'guidance' issued by the Government, which is audited by the external auditor.

So, is it too pessimistic to wonder whether local government can really be regarded as such any longer — or has the time come to recognise a new reality and regard it as 'local administration', even though local authorities may still be directly-elected bodies and still exercise some discretion at local level? On the other hand, perhaps local government has only ever been (and can only ever be) a devolved form of aspects of central government.

The Local Authority Associations

Local government needs a single voice for its negotiations and contact with central government. For many years that was lacking, as the different types of principal local authority tended to have their own association representing them — the *Association of Metropolitan Authorities* (AMA), the *Association of County Councils* (ACC) and the *Association of District Councils* (ADC). At times, those local authority associations did not see eye to eye, a weakness which central government was able to exploit — a state of affairs which could not continue if local government was to have an effective relationship with central government.

In April 1997, the new *Local Government Association* (LGA) was formed, representing over 500 local authorities with a total population of 50 million people in England and Wales and with total annual budgets in excess of £65 billion. The transition to a single association from three separate associations with different agenda was not easy and there are still instances of internal disagreements reflecting old allegiances — which, it is hoped, will disappear over time. Occasionally, individual local authorities will decide to leave, or join, the LGA if they disagree with LGA policies. Those non-member local authorities will not expect (nor would they receive) special access to government ministers alongside the LGA.

Special arrangements exist for Wales, recognising its constitutional position as a nation in its own right. The *Welsh Local Government Association* (WLGA), established in 1996, although now an integral part of the LGA, is regarded as having autonomy for all local government matters in Wales and in its dealings with the Welsh Assembly.

The position in Scotland is different again. Relations with the Scottish Executive are handled by the *Convention of Scottish Local Authorities* (COSLA), established in 1975, of which all Scottish local authorities are members.

The equivalent organisation in Northern Ireland is the *Association of Local Authorities in Northern Ireland.*

For those local authorities which are not principal local authorities (parish and community councils), their interests are covered by the *National Association of Local Councils* (NALC), founded in 1947. The objectives of the NALC are different from the other local authority associations: it provides a source of training and procedural, legal and other advice to parish and community councils, many of which cannot afford to employ suitably qualified officers to provide that advice and support for themselves. The *Association of Larger Local Councils* was founded in 1981 with the aim of securing a greater range of functions for the larger parish and community councils.

The need for external control

The first section of this Chapter contained provocative views intended to stimulate a debate on only one aspect of external control. What is beyond debate is the notion that it is necessary for local government, like any other form of government, to be subject to external controls to protect the individual from the abuse of power at local level and to ensure that local government acts reasonably consistently across the country and in the financial national interest.

Those controls can be judicial, legislative, administrative or financial, and involve the courts, the Ombudsman, ministers and the Audit Commission. The most important, truly external, controls are judicial (exercised by the courts, whose jurisdiction is extremely wide and whose judgements are enforceable) and legislative (exercised by Parliament). The Ombudsman also works as an external control, but there are limits on the issues which the Ombudsman can investigate and the Ombudsman cannot force the local authority to take action to remedy the maladministration. Although control by ministers and through the Audit Commission are also significant, it should be remembered that they share one common feature with local government — they are all part of the Executive.

All of these aspects are considered in turn, starting with judicial control.

Judicial control

To understand the mechanisms of judicial control (or *judicial review*), it is first necessary to understand how judicial control comes into play. There are three distinct but related aspects to judicial control:

- does the local authority possess the necessary legal power to pursue its course of action?
- even if it has the necessary power, are its reasons for pursuing that course of action good and proper?
- even if it has the power and its reasons are good and proper, is it following a correct and fair process?

The answer to any of these questions, if it is 'no', will provide the basis for the court to intervene and, if appropriate, put a stop to the local authority's actions.

A creature of statute

As already explained, local authorities owe their existence to statute — unlike a private individual, a local authority (as a corporate body) can only do something if there is a specific statutory provision which authorises or permits the local authority to do it. If something is within the local authority's powers, it is *intra vires*; if the authority does not have the necessary statutory power, then it will be acting *ultra vires* (beyond *(ultra)* its powers *(vires)*) and, therefore, unlawfully, if it proceeds.

Although there are now many cases on the issue of *ultra vires*, the best example is still the 1981 case involving the GLC 'Fair fares' policy. When the (old) Labour Party gained control of the GLC in May 1981, one of its first actions was to implement its manifesto commitment to introduce heavily subsidised fares on London Transport. Obviously this would involve a huge loss of income and to balance its revenue budget the GLC issued a *supplementary precept* on all the London borough councils as collection authorities, to raise the additional money from the ratepayers. That course of action is no longer possible, because, as explained in the Chapter on *Finance,* supplementary precepts are now only lawful if they are for less, rather than more, money. The Conservative-controlled Bromley London Borough Council applied for judicial review of the GLC's actions, on the grounds that they were *ultra vires*. Although initially unsuccessful in the High Court, Bromley persevered and succeeded in the Court of Appeal and the House of Lords. The GLC had to abandon its scheme.

Over the years, the common law (law developed through the courts) has extended the idea of corporate power to include additional, but **subsidiary**, power which is reasonably necessary to permit the corporate body to achieve its mainstream objectives.

This common law position was reflected in the statutes covering local government and, in its current form, is section 111 of the Local Government Act 1972. That provision authorises a local authority to do anything (whether or not involving the expenditure, borrowing or lending of money or the acquisition or disposal of rights) which is *"calculated to facilitate, or is conducive or incidental to, the discharge of any of its functions"*.

However, section 111 can only be used where the local authority can point to another specific statutory power enabling it take action, to which the action under scrutiny is truly 'incidental'. In the 1991 Hammersmith LBC interest swaps case, Lord Templeton ruled that powers are not 'incidental' only because they are 'convenient, desirable or profitable'.

Local government lawyers have to be careful to avoid placing too wide an interpretation on section 111. For some time, the Audit Commission was taking the position that section 111 was not as wide as some local authorities thought. In the 1992 North Tyneside severance payments case, the Court of Appeal agreed and ruled that severance payments made in excess of the statutory provisions were *ultra vires* and did not come within the ambit of section 111. In 1994, Credit Suisse also discovered this to its cost, when it failed to persuade the court to order the enforcement of financial guarantees given earlier by Allerdale District Council to support a time-share company set up by the council — those guarantees were *ultra vires* and, therefore, unenforceable. Nor can the 'incidental' powers in section 111 be used to avoid restrictions on the exercise of the main statutory power.

The same limitation is also placed on what used to be called 'the free twopenny rate power' — section 137 of the 1972 Act. This power enables the local authority to spend an amount per head of population (currently £2.50 for county councils and district/borough councils in a two-tier area; £5 for unitary authorities, metropolitan borough and London borough councils; and £3.50 for parish/community councils) on anything for the direct benefit of their area, provided that the benefit received is commensurate with the expenditure. Separate accounts need to be kept for this expenditure and the power cannot be used to circumvent any restrictions on the use of powers granted by other Acts. There are also restrictions on the way in which this discretionary money can be used for publicity — the Local Government Act 1986 Act forbids expenditure on any material which sets out to affect public support for a political party, or anyone identified with a political party.

If a local authority wishes to extend its powers, it must get a local Bill through Parliament. These are also known as Private Bills, and the meaning of this and the procedures involved are explained in *Essential Central Government*. This method of increasing the powers of a local authority, either generally or for a specific purpose, was fairly common (especially amongst the municipal corporations) until the 1960s. Since that time enthusiasm for this process has waned, because it became clear that Parliament was increasingly reluctant to adjust local government powers otherwise than through general legislation.

To complete the picture, it should be said that during the last debate about local government structure, leading to the 1992 rolling programme, the issue was raised (by the local authority associations and some prominent academics) of a 'power of general competence' to avoid the limitations of section 111 and enable local government the freedom to pursue innovative policies and practices for the benefit of the local area. That debate on that particular issue failed to produce any result.

The New Labour Green Paper *Modernising Local Government — Local Democracy and Community Leadership* floated the idea of a *'new framework'* under which *"local communities through their councils could have greater responsibility for their own affairs"*. It was said that under this new framework, with Parliamentary approval, *"new powers and dispensations from existing legislation could be given to local authorities to meet local priorities and aspirations"*. When one looked beyond the rhetoric, it had to be said that the mechanism suggested in the Green Paper on how this might be achieved in practice would result in greater, not less, government control over local government innovation. The Local Government Bill included a power for the promotion of economic, social or environmental well-being.

Local Government Bill

The Bill creates a new power, subject to conditions and controls vested in the Secretary of State. Authorities will have the power to do anything which they consider is likely to promote or improve the economic, social or environmental well-being of all or part of their area, and in doing so they must have regard to the achievement of sustainable development in the UK. Under this new power, an authority can incur expenditure, give financial assistance, enter into arrangements and agreements, and provide staff, goods, services or accommodation.

The limitations on this new power are that it cannot be used to circumvent restrictions on other powers and the authority raise money solely for the power. In addition, the Secretary of State can prohibit authorities from using the power in any particular way and authorities must, in any event, follow the 'guidance' issued by the Secretary of State. In addition, authorities will be expected to prepare a Strategy under which they propose to use the new power, following yet more 'guidance' from the Secretary of State. The Secretary of State has the power to modify existing legislation which appears to inhibit local authorities from achieving their objectives under the LGA 2000 — although in what circumstance that might happen are, as yet, unclear.

Wednesbury principles

So, even if the necessary power exists, what are the local authority's real reasons for taking the action? Lawyers and courts prefer to have regard to precedents (decisions taken in previous cases) to follow a reasonably consistent line in decision-making. One aspect of judicial control provides a good example of this, since the case setting out the guiding principles was decided in 1947 — *Associated Provincial Picture Houses Ltd v Wednesbury Corporation* to give it its Sunday title — or the *Wednesbury* case, for short.

The *Wednesbury* case was about licensing cinema performances on a Sunday and whether children should be able to attend (how times change!). In this case the local authority won the argument, but the principles used to decide it have henceforth been described as the *Wednesbury* principles in the many judicial review cases which have followed it.

Even though a local authority may possess the necessary legal power, the court will still intervene if the decision is so unreasonable that no reasonable council could have reached it, *"taking into account all relevant considerations and disregarding all irrelevant considerations"*. The courts now sometimes refer to *Wednesbury* unreasonableness as 'irrationality'.

One example of this is where Derbyshire County Council decided in 1990 to remove all of its adverts from the *Times Educational Supplement*, because it disagreed with what Times Newspapers were then doing. This was regarded by the courts as *Wednesbury* unreasonable, because the real reason had nothing to do with the cost effectiveness of advertising for teaching staff. More recent examples can be found in the various cases (notably Somerset County Council in 1994) where local authorities have attempted to ban hunting from their, publicly owned, land. In those cases, the attempts had to be abandoned after court intervention.

Is the process fair and correct?

Even if the power exists and the reasons satisfy the *Wednesbury* test, the final question relates to the process by which the decision was taken. For most of the time, local authorities are acting 'administratively', rather than 'quasi-judicially' and they do not have to follow any specific procedure in reaching their decisions. However, there are exceptions and care has to be exercised.

If there is some statutory provision or external or internal code or set of rules which requires the decision to be taken in a particular way or following a set procedure, then failure to follow that procedure will lay the local authority open to judicial review.

On some occasions (like dealing with any form of appeal or licensing application), the local authority may, indeed, be acting 'quasi-judicially' and then the local authority has to adopt a procedure which satisfies the *Rules of Natural Justice* — hear both sides fairly and do not act in a biased way.

Even where there is no specific statutory provision and the local authority is acting 'administratively', the local authority can sometimes come unstuck in the courts about the way it has gone about making the decision, especially one affecting individuals in the community. This aspect provides a good example of the common law (that decided by the courts) being developed and adjusted to meet the expectations of modern society. Over the past 15 years, the courts have developed a legal concept known as 'the legitimate expectation of consultation' — this has resulted in a local authority having to go through a sometimes elaborate and lengthy consultation process, with a wide range of people, if it wishes, say, to close a school or a children's home or an elderly persons' care home. The consultation process must be a genuine one: at a formative stage in the decision-making process; a clear explanation of the proposal and any options; a reasonable time to comment; and a genuine willingness to consider comments and change the proposal.

Mechanisms for judicial intervention

The most common form of judicial intervention and control is where an aggrieved individual applies for *judicial review* of the local authority's decision. The number of judicial review cases has increased significantly in the last few years. In this type of action, as the name suggests, the court reviews the local authority's decision (applying the issues highlighted in the previous three sections) and, if it disagrees with the local authority's action or the way it was decided, the court will quash the decision and tell the local authority to try again or to do better next time. Depending on the nature of the local authority's decision and the fault found by the court, the local authority may be able to have another try at the decision or it may be forced to abandon its intended course of action altogether.

Judicial review actions usually result in one or more specific types of order, depending on the nature of the case and the 'relief' sought from the court.

Where the local authority has refused to comply with some statutory duty, the court, if convinced by the applicant's arguments, will issue an order of *Mandamus,* which orders the local authority to carry out the duty. Mandamus cannot, however, be used to compel a local authority to carry out something which is merely permissive or discretionary.

Two other judicial remedies against local authorities are *Prohibition* and *Certiorari,* which can be used against them when they act, or are proposing to act, without jurisdiction, or are in breach of the Rules of Natural Justice.

Declarations and *Injunctions* are further legal remedies against local authorities. An action for either enables the legality of an act or decision of a local authority to be tested in the courts. A declaratory judgement is a finding by the court on a question of law or rights — declaring what the law actually means; an injunction is used to stop a local authority doing something, or requiring it to do something.

An individual who wishes to take out an injunction against a local authority must ask the Attorney General to take the action. That is why many of the judicial review cases are cited as R v [local authority] *ex parte* [individual].

Individuals may also take civil action against local authorities for a 'tort' (civil wrong) such as negligence. Local authorities may be held to be responsible for any action, or lack of action, by them or people in their employ. The liability of an employer for the torts of an employee is called 'vicarious liability'.

Legislative control

Almost every piece of legislation passed by Parliament affects local authorities in some way, either adding to or taking away from their powers. Private Bills sponsored by local authorities are, of course, subject to rejection or amendment by Parliament.

Control over local government has increased greatly in the last decade. Legislation has been introduced giving the government power to prohibit excessive Poll Tax and Council Tax increases and to control local authority budgets. Other controls limit the use of capital receipts, prohibit political advertising and seek to control the way that a local authority conducts its business. Much of the detailed control mechanisms are to be found in subordinate, delegated, legislation (statutory instruments made by ministers, but subject to Parliamentary approval). Although these controls might be regarded as administrative, because they are exercised by ministers (the Executive), nonetheless it was Parliament (the Legislature) which created them.

There are three types of Act — mandatory, adoptive or permissive. A *Mandatory Act* compels a local authority to take certain action, like selling council houses under the Housing Act 1980. This is a particularly good example as it provoked a lot of opposition from Labour-controlled local housing authorities.

An *Adoptive Act* is one which gives a local authority power to carry out a function but which needs a resolution by the local authority to adopt the Act before it applies.

A *Permissive Act* is one which gives a local authority discretion over taking on new powers, generally minor ones.

Administrative control

This is exercised by central government departments, who are generally concerned with seeing that minimum standards of service are maintained throughout the country. Ministers and departments do not have overall detailed control of the work of local authorities (yet), but a number of Acts make provision for supervisory powers, which can be exercised through circulars or directives. Powers may exist to enable a minister to act if an authority is not discharging a function properly.

For instance, the Local Authority Social Services Act 1970 laid down that *"local authorities shall, in the exercise of their social services functions, including the exercise of any discretion conferred by any relevant enactment, act under the general guidance of the Secretary of State"*.

Some Government departments have inspectorates: eg. the Social Services Inspectorate and Ofsted. Central Government departments also have the power in relation to some services, notably the police and fire (the Home Office), to inspect and ensure operational efficiency. Other legislation requires local authorities to submit schemes for the development of services, like those that they were required to bring forward for the introduction of a comprehensive system of education.

With the arrival of the Best Value regime there has been a significant increase in the number of plans which local authorities now have to produce and submit to the Secretary of State. Apart from the Best Value Performance Plan itself, others include: Annual Library Plan, Children's Services Plan, Community Care Plan, Community Strategy, Crime and Disorder Reduction Strategy, Development Plan, Early Years Development Plan, Education Development Plan, Local Transport Plan, Youth Justice Plan, Housing Investment Programme Plans, Local Agenda 21 Strategy, Lifelong Learning Development Plan and Admission Arrangements for maintained schools. All of these plans provide an opportunity for Government direction of local policy and intervention for non-compliance. In addition, there is a growing concern in local government that these plans will be used by Government as a means of allocating RSG (see the next Chapter on *Finance*).

In rare cases, ministers can intervene in local authority business if the local authority is considered to be acting illegally or failing to carry out a statutory duty or government policy. For example, the then Secretary of State for the Environment considered that a number of local authorities had been too slow in processing council house sales following the introduction of the duty to sell them under the Housing Act 1980. In particular, he singled out the City of Norwich and gave notice that he would take over administration of the council house sales there. The city council sought an order in the High Court quashing this intention, but this was rejected, a decision later confirmed by the Court of Appeal. The Secretary of State then sent a civil servant to oversee council house sales in Norwich.

The previous big revolt by a Labour-controlled local authority was in 1972 when Clay Cross Urban District Council refused to raise council house rents as required by the Housing Finance Act 1972. The councillors of the Clay Cross UDC were surcharged and disqualified from membership, and the Secretary of State sent in 'Commissioners', who were civil servants, to act on his behalf at the council's expense.

The opportunities for intervention by Government (the development of the so-called 'hit squads' under the previous Conservative administration provides one example) show signs of continuing to increase under the New Labour Government. The word 'intervene' appeared in several places in the *Modernising Local Government* Green Papers and the subsequent legislation increased the scope for central control. The Ofsted inspection process has now been extended to LEAs, as well as individual schools. For example, in the case of the London Boroughs of Hackney and Islington, the DfEE removed responsibility for schools and passed it to private companies — an approach more to be expected of a Conservative Government.

Local authorities can exercise a subordinate legislative function by making by-laws. A by-law is a local regulation governing such matters as the use of a municipal park or library. 'Model by-laws' are suggested by the relevant government department but each authority can frame its own, subject to the approval of the department. By-laws which depart significantly from the 'model by-laws' are seldom approved.

Ministers can act in a 'quasi-judicial' manner, acting as arbiters in disputes between local authorities and individuals. This occurs most commonly in planning, where individuals may appeal to the minister against a decision of the local planning authority. The appeal is handled by an inspector appointed by the minister (holding an inquiry, if necessary) and the inspector's observations are considered by the minister, before the minister makes a final decision.

Where a local authority needs to acquire land and buildings to enable it to carry out a particular project, the local authority can make a compulsory purchase order (CPO) authorising it to acquire the land and buildings compulsorily if the owners are unwilling to sell or are dragging their feet in negotiations. The CPO needs to be confirmed by the relevant minister before it can come into effect and where there is any significant objection, a local inquiry will be held by an inspector appointed by the minister.

Local Government Ombudsmen

The *Commissioners for Local Administration* (local ombudsmen) were established by the Local Government Act 1974. There are three in England, and one each for Wales, Scotland and Northern Ireland.

The ombudsmen can investigate administrative decisions, but not policy decisions, of a principal local authority (not a parish/community council), police authority, or national park authority. But they cannot investigate: subjects that affect the majority of the inhabitants; contractual matters; personnel matters; a number of educational matters involving schools; or anything in which a person has the remedy of an **appeal** to the courts or to a minister.

The ombudsmen are interested in 'maladministration', which is not defined in the 1974 Act. However, the ombudsmen have provided their own view of what can amount to maladministration:

- taking too long to take action;
- not following any internal or external rules or the law;
- breaking promises;
- giving wrong information; or
- not taking decisions in the correct way.

Anyone wishing to complain about maladministration by one of the authorities mentioned above may make a direct approach to the ombudsman. When an ombudsman receives a complaint there is usually informal contact with the local authority's chief executive before making a decision on whether or not to investigate. Once a decision to investigate has been taken, an authority has 14 days to provide its formal comments. An investigating officer will then interview the complainant and then study all relevant records and interview relevant councillors and officers. The Ombudsman has the same powers as a High Court Judge to order the production of documents and witnesses. All investigations are private.

Sometimes, as the formal investigation proceeds, the ombudsman may informally suggest to the local authority that if it adopts a particular course of action, that will be regarded as a 'local settlement' and the formal investigation can thereupon be discontinued. However, that may not always be possible and, then, the investigation is concluded with a formal report.

There are three findings open to an ombudsman when making the formal report:

- no maladministration;
- maladministration but no injustice; or
- maladministration causing injustice.

The report may recommend how the matter should be put right, including apologies, compensation and changes in procedures

The report will not usually identify individuals. However, if the ombudsman believes that there has been maladministration involving a councillor, or that the councillor's conduct has breached the National Code of Conduct, then the ombudsman must identify, by name, the individual councillor concerned, unless he or she is of the opinion that it would be an injustice to do so.

One copy of the ombudsman's report goes to the complainant, one to the authority complained about, and one to any other person named in the report. The authority must make the report available for public inspection — it has to advertise this in the local press. Copies of the report are also made available to the media by the ombudsman (unless the ombudsman rules the matter should be kept private, which is rare).

If the report criticises a local authority, it has to consider the report within three months and tell the ombudsman the action it has taken or how it proposes to put the matter right. A decision not to take any action on the report can only be taken by the full council. If the local authority fails to make what the ombudsman considers to be a satisfactory response, or decides to take no action, then there is usually a further, second, report from the ombudsman about that and the local authority is required to publish a statement of the ombudsman's views in any two newspapers circulating in the area.

That is the limit of the ombudsman's powers. Unlike the courts, the ombudsman cannot force a local authority to take action. However, in the vast majority of cases, and particularly in view of the adverse publicity, agreement between the ombudsman and the local authority is usually reached. The ombudsmen produce their own annual reports and any local authority which has particularly disappointed an ombudsman will have a guaranteed place in that year's 'rogues gallery'.

The total costs of the Commission for Local Administration are met by local authorities, pro rata to their population.

Financial control

Financial controls were increased by the Local Government Finance Act 1982, which removed the power to levy supplementary rates or precepts. Although the 1982 Act forbade a local authority to increase its rate or precept during the year, it did allow a substitute rate or precept, but only at a lower figure.

Further controls came with the Rate Act 1984, which gave the Secretary of State for the Environment power to limit the rates levied by specified authorities (or for all authorities after Parliamentary approval). This power has been extended to the Council Tax and the budgets of all local authorities. In addition, the government controls money from the uniform business rate and borrowing, as well as the use of capital receipts (see the Chapter on *Finance*).

The Audit Commission is another example of financial control — but one which has had its remit extended beyond the purely financial into the realms of effective management.

Audit Commission

The Secretary of State can specify how authorities keep accounts, how they publish them, and public inspection rights. The accounts of all local authorities are subject to intensive **internal** and **external** auditing. Internal audit is carried out by a division of the treasurer's department. The Local Government Finance Act 1982 set up the Audit Commission to oversee external auditing.

The Audit Commission has taken over responsibility for the district audit service from the Secretary of State for the Environment and the Welsh Office and the District Audit Service is now an arm's length contracting organisation within the Audit Commission. Commission members are appointed by the government from local government and from the private sector. The Commission has the power to appoint auditors to every local authority in England and Wales, either from the District Audit Service or from 'approved' auditors in the private sector. One of the responsibilities of the Commission is to produce, for Parliamentary approval, the Code of Audit Practice required by the Local Government Finance Act 1982, which all external auditors are obliged to follow.

An officer or councillor of a local authority can be required to give information or explanation to the Commission or anyone authorised by it. Failure to comply can lead to summary conviction and a fine not exceeding £200, and to an additional fine not exceeding £20 for each day the offence continues.

The statutory annual audit

The auditor can require the production of all documents and information from the local authority and its officers and councillors. Obstruction of the auditor is a criminal offence.

Before each year's final audit a local authority must make available, for public inspection for 15 working days, the 'books, accounts and vouchers' (note: not **all** documents) relating to the year of account. The times and place where these will be available for inspection must be advertised and the advertisement must include a summary of the public's rights, together with the name and address of the auditor.

A local government elector for the area may question the auditor about any matter relating to the accounts and may make written objections to the accounts. A copy of any written objection is sent to the local authority. The auditor must be available at all reasonable times to receive information from any interested person and, where appropriate, should remind informants of their right to object to any item in the accounts.

If the auditor believes that a matter raised by a local government elector is very urgent, the auditor may suggest that the elector apply to the Audit Commission for an extraordinary audit. The auditor may take the initiative and report to the Audit Commission that an extraordinary audit is desirable. Finally, the Secretary of State may decide that such an audit would be in the public interest.

Once the audit is underway, the auditor must take note of all questions put by electors, reach conclusions on any objections (if necessary, after holding a formal or informal investigation or hearing) and express an opinion on the statements of accounts.

The Public Interest Report

The auditor must also issue a report 'in the public interest' if a matter of sufficient importance comes to their attention which, in their opinion, cannot be dealt with adequately by some other method. The Code of Audit Practice suggests that it might be appropriate for an auditor to consider issuing a 'public interest' report in the following circumstances:

- delayed preparation of the accounts;
- excessive or inadequate balances or prospective deficits;
- lack of action on previous reports of the auditor;
- fraud;
- objections received at the audit.

The Local Government Act 1992 provides that an auditor's 'public interest' report or written recommendation must be considered by the local authority to which it is addressed within four months of it being sent to that authority. There is provision for the period to be extended 'if it is reasonable to allow more time'.

The meeting at which the report is to be discussed must be publicised in a local newspaper for at least seven days before the meeting and will normally be open to the public unless they are excluded on any of the statutory grounds — 'confidential' or 'exempt' information (see the Chapter on *Decision-making, Information and Quality).*

A copy of the decisions made must be sent to the auditor and the Audit Commission and a summary published in local newspapers. The Audit Commission may itself publish information about contravention by local authorities of their obligations regarding performance standards, auditors' reports and accounts.

The Three Es and the Management Letter

In addition to the usual audit to ensure financial probity, the auditor is required to ensure that the authority has made proper arrangements for securing 'economy, efficiency and effective use of resources' — usually referred to as 'the three Es'. The Audit Commission also promotes work on value for money and efficiency studies, including comparative studies of performance. This part of its work has been extended considerably in recent years. The Audit Commission may, each year, produce an outline programme of reviews of national interest, which can be supplemented at local level.

In addition to formal statutory audit reports mentioned so far, the Code of Audit Practice also advocates the auditor to use a non-statutory 'management letter'. According to the Code, this is a letter *"addressed to members which will give a summary of the audit activities and details of the significant matters which have arisen from all aspects of the audit"* — in other words, issues which have emerged over the year which the auditor feels might merit the local authority's attention but which are not so significant that formal action is needed.

What this means in practice is that the external auditor will decide to examine certain aspects of the local authority's operations from this '3Es' point of view, rather than to verify probity. Quite often, the utility of these reviews (and the results which they produce) is not immediately evident to the local authority concerned, which has to meet the auditor's costs.

7 Finance

Local revenue budgeting at national and local level — Rates — Community Charge (Poll Tax) — Council Tax — uniform business rate — the local budget process — budget control — revenue grants — capital borrowing — capital receipts — capital grants — EU funding — private partnerships — capping and passporting

A key political issue

Finance dominates the local government scene. There is usually a money angle to every major local government story, and the fiercest political debates in council chambers and committee rooms are, more often than not, about competing priorities for finite resources.

In a time of tight public expenditure, local government finance is more important than ever, because it is a dominant feature of relations between central and local government. Local government accounts for more than £50 **billion** (1998/99) of public expenditure, so it is not an insignificant issue on the national scene.

The way in which central government calculates local authority entitlement to the general government grant is a constant source of debate at national, as well as local, level. Because the overall public expenditure pot is regarded as finite, any change in the national grant calculation methodology inevitably produces winners and losers, compared with previous years. The more cynical observers suspect that any adjustment in the methodology is not totally unconnected with any forthcoming local government elections.

The winning local authorities are hardly likely to complain, but the losing local authorities will — often wanting to send delegations of senior councillors and chief officers, accompanied by the local MPs, to see the Minister to explain their local difficulties and ask for a more generous (or 'fairer') grant settlement than they have been told to expect. Since the Government announced its intention to set local government finance controls three years ahead, it has declined to accept delegations of this type.

The difficulty is that the stage at which these delegations take place (if they do) is almost too late — the overall amount for local government general grant is regarded by the Government as finite; each local authority will have had a preliminary notification of how much to expect in the form of general grant; if the settlement is adjusted further to accommodate a particular lobbying local authority, then the losers at that stage (they may have regarded themselves as winners up to that point) will feel aggrieved.

There will inevitably be contingency sums throughout the Government's budget, so if it really wishes to, the government could probably meet the concerns of the lobbying authorities, without any knock-on effects on other local authorities in that year. However, in reality, Government usually stands its ground, if only because, if it doesn't, next year there will be even more lobbying local authorities. So, the success rate of these delegations is not very high — but one imagines that the local councillors believe that they should be seen to be doing **something**, to prepare the local population for the hard decisions which will need to follow to produce a balanced budget.

At the local level, once the overall position is known, the nature of the argument shifts to one about distribution of the finite resources within the local authority. The arguments will be about the central administration as against the service departments, with the service departments usually doing better, if only because what they do impacts more directly on the public. The argument will be further refined as between the various service committees, each of which will be urged by their related chief officers to put its plate up for the most it can get from the council.

It is during this process of argument that it can sometimes be interesting to observe the dynamics of the process and, in particular, the behaviour of individual councillors. One can occasionally see a councillor adopting a particular service-oriented stance when he or she is speaking as a member of a service committee and, later in the process, adopting a different (and sometimes inconsistent) stance when speaking as a member of a central committee. It is usually the job of the Policy and Resources Committee to try to pull it all together, as best it can, so as to present a reasonably coherent picture to the full council. It does not always succeed, so the resources debates at full council can be lively. Under the new executive models introduced under LGA 2000, the job of constructing the budget for approval by the council will fall on the elected Mayor or the Cabinet — service committees, and the Policy and Resources Committee, will soon be things of the past. A more detailed description of the budget process is given in a later section in this Chapter.

How can central government and local government both be right?

The annual local government spending discussions take place at national level between representatives of government departments (civil servants and, as appropriate, government ministers) and representatives of the local government associations (officers and, as appropriate, senior councillor representatives). There is a series of departmentally-based meetings looking at each department's spending assumptions and the whole process is pulled together later, at a centrally-based meeting. Apart from departmental civil servants at these meetings, there is always a civil servant from the Treasury and the power and influence which the Treasury exerts over the whole process then becomes evident.

During the last few years of the Conservative Government, when the Revenue Support Grant (RSG) settlement was being discussed at national level, the disagreements between central and local government about what was the real position became more confusing.

Central government often asserted that there would be a 'real-terms' increase in local government expenditure for the forthcoming year because of the RSG settlement. For its part, local government was saying that existing services would have to be cut, often drastically, to achieve a balanced budget. How could they both be right?

The answer lies in the fact that the two sides were approaching the issue from completely different bases.

Central government works out its view of total local government expenditure using its own macro-economic figures which have no direct connection with what is actually being spent on the ground by individual local authorities; the disparity between the government's largely theoretical figures and actual levels of expenditure can worsen over time; the assumptions about inflation built into the government's view may be significantly more optimistic than the inflation which local authorities are actually experiencing; the government may not 'fully fund' additional expenditure which is decided at national level, but paid for at local level — for example, teachers' pay; and allowances in the government's figures for 'efficiency gains' can, in reality, amount to non-specific reductions. All of these factors can produce the result that central government can claim that the RSG settlement is better than it really is.

On the other hand, the focus at local level is entirely driven by real (rather than notional) demands for service and the resources actually available to the local authority to meet those needs from within a balanced budget for each financial year. Central government revenue support (RSG plus specific grants plus UBR), running at about 80% of expenditure, produces two main effects. Firstly, any difference between the central government notional figures and the local real figures is increased in relative terms, because the proportion of the total expenditure coming from central government is so high. Secondly, even if a local authority had the freedom to increase the Council Tax to make up the difference between the central government notional position and reality, the gearing effect of the 80% level (4:1) would make the Council Tax rises relatively large. Local authorities do not, of course, have complete freedom to do this, because of the capping regime, crude or otherwise.

This is why many local authorities will find themselves having to cut services in order to balance their budget within a capping limit, at a time when central government is saying that this is unnecessary.

One short-term solution is to use the revenue balances (cash accumulated as a working reserve from savings and underspendings in previous years) to mitigate the increase in Council Tax. That assumes, of course, that the balances have not already been used up in previous years for this same purpose.

The use of the revenue balances in this way is often one of the more contentious aspects of the budget debate at the council meeting. Even then, cuts may still have to be made, because there may not be enough in the revenue balances to bridge the RSG shortfall and leave sufficient for a working contingency for the proper financial management of the local authority. Where a local authority runs down its revenue balances so that they are at a very low level, it may well find itself receiving criticism about this from the external auditor in the next 'Management Letter' or, even, in a 'Public Interest Report'.

Any announcements of extra money by central government should be treated with caution. A very illuminating account of how central government, especially under New Labour, massages its figures appeared in the *Guardian* of 7 March 2000 under the headline: *'Blunkett's magic tricks and the £19bn boost for education that doesn't exist'.*

Revenue and capital

It is important to understand the difference between revenue expenditure and capital expenditure, since, although the difference is an accounting one, nevertheless they are dealt with differently in the local government and central government context.

Revenue (or current) expenditure is, essentially, money spent on the day-to-day running costs of the local authority, producing a short-term benefit only in the same financial year. A major part of revenue expenditure is on employees' pay, since local government is labour-intensive. Other examples of significant revenue expenditure are: the leasing, repair and maintenance of land and buildings and the purchase and leasing of goods and services from third parties. The money used for revenue expenditure is raised from a combination of government grants, Council Tax, the uniform business rate, income raised from rents and charges for services, and revenue reserves. The budget process is done on a year-by-year basis and the council's financial year runs from 1 April to 31 March.

Capital expenditure is, essentially, money spent on major capital projects, such as the acquisition of land and the construction of buildings and roads, and on major items of equipment — providing a benefit beyond the current financial year. The money used for capital expenditure of this type is either borrowed, or raised by selling assets (capital receipts), or raised through one-off partnership deals with the private sector, or through the Private Finance Initiative (PFI), or supplied through a capital grant. Capital programmes are usually planned three to five years ahead, because many large projects take some time to be completed and are often paid for over more than one financial year.

Money borrowed long-term for capital purposes cannot be used for revenue purposes. It can, at times, be difficult to know, in relation to relatively small items, which side of the revenue/capital dividing line they fall. For that reason, money raised for revenue purposes can be used for capital purposes, but only on relatively small items and then only in compliance with any constraints laid down by central government.

Raising the revenue at local level

The Council Tax is raised at local level from domestic Council Taxpayers by the collection authorities issuing the necessary demand for payment. Collection authorities are unitary authorities, London borough councils, metropolitan borough councils and shire district/borough councils in two-tier areas.

In shire district/borough areas, the demand will not only include the Council Tax levied by the district/borough council for itself, but also the *precept* issued by the county council for the Council Tax which it needs for the services which it provides.

Council tax demands will also include a precept issued by the parish or community council, where one exists.

In addition, Council Tax demands will include the precept issued by the local Police Authority for its purposes and, where one exists, a similar precept issued by the Combined Fire, or Fire and Civil Defence, Authority. Similarly, in metropolitan county areas and in those counties which are now entirely covered by unitary authorities, precepts will be issued by a variety of statutory joint boards or bodies for police, fire and civil defence and public transport.

Thus, the demand for the Council Tax payment issued by the collection authority will probably contain additional demands originating from one or more precepting authorities. Where the collection authority is a shire district/ borough council, the amount of the county council's precept will be significantly larger (because it runs expensive services such as education and social services) than the collection authority's own tax requirement. Most shire district/borough councils make sure that the local taxpayers understand this.

Three different systems for raising revenue in 10 years

There have been three different systems for raising revenue at local level during the last 10 years — and the change from one system to another, at a time of financial restraint, brought disruption to local government which it could have done without. Although many collection authorities experienced problems with collecting the Community Charge (because of its nature), it is to the great credit of local government that the changes themselves were made without many really major problems.

The three systems were: the Rates (to 1990); the Community Charge (Poll Tax) (1990 to 1993); and the Council Tax (1993 onwards).

Up to April 1990, Rates, a tax based on the value of property owned, or occupied, were the backbone of local taxation. Rates covered both domestic and non-domestic property. Rates had continued in varying forms since 1601, and most countries have some form of property tax.

In April 1990, the Poll Tax was introduced — a tax on individuals, rather than on property ('poll' means 'head'). This was a tax payable, in relation to domestic property, by all adults over the age of 18 years, with some relief for those on low incomes and in special classes. It was thought that this would stop the public criticism of Rates as being an unfair tax. It did not work, being an administrative nightmare and highly unpopular because it was also unfair, but in different ways from the Rates. Commercial property was covered by the new uniform business rate.

In April 1993, the Council Tax was introduced to replace the Poll Tax — it is a combination of the old Rates system with a small Poll Tax element. The uniform business rate continues. The Council Tax, like any form of taxation, will inevitably be the subject of much criticism and some good stories.

The advantages and disadvantages of a rating system

The advantages were:

- It was administratively cheap to collect and a predictable source of income — helping accurate budgeting.
- It was difficult to avoid paying Rates. Unlike people, property is immobile.
- It was a simple and well-understood form of local taxation.

The disadvantages were:

- Only about 25% of the local electorate received a bill and although others, for example, lodgers paid indirectly, they did not have a sense of directly holding the local authority to account through the ballot box.
- Rates paid on property did not take account of the use made of services or of the ability to pay. In the context of domestic Rates, the often-quoted example was of two identical properties — one occupied by a retired couple on a fixed income, the other by a wage-earning family of four. Both paid the same Rates.
- Any sizeable improvement to a property could mean that, on a future revaluation, the Rates would rise significantly and this could act as a disincentive to house improvements.

The Community Charge (Poll Tax)

It is still important to have an understanding of the Poll Tax as its repercussions, both political and administrative, will continue for some time due to its deep unpopularity. When it was introduced, it was seen as bringing into the scope of local taxation a number of people who had previously escaped the net of local taxation; for example, young adults still living at home and lodgers. Moreover, the idea of each individual receiving a bill, instead of one bill for a household as in the Rates system, was thought to increase accountability and emphasise the cost of local services.

The problem was that people move about and, particularly in dense urban areas, with large floating populations, it is extremely difficult to keep track of them without imposing rigorous bureaucratic controls that would be unacceptable to the public. Furthermore, people had to register for the Poll Tax and not everybody took kindly to filling in a form which would result in them receiving a bill from the council. There was a strong political campaign against the Poll Tax. Collection problems left some councils unable to collect much more than half the sums due. These factors made the pressure for a change overwhelming.

The first response of the government was to increase substantially government grant, so as to allow a gross reduction of £140 in Poll Tax bills. This was paid for by a 2.5% increase in VAT. The result was that only about 14% of local expenditure was financed by the Poll Tax, compared with 21% by the uniform business rate. This might have worked if it had been introduced at the same time as the tax, because it is a well known maxim that any change in local taxation has to be smoothed for almost all the payers, not just the few covered by transitional schemes, if it is to be successful. It is the headline figure of the tax, not the actual amounts that individuals might have to pay, that attracts attention. As it was, the change was far too late and did little to calm public unrest and nothing to ease the administrative problems. The continuing pressure led to the Poll Tax being replaced by the Council Tax.

The Council Tax

The Council Tax combines elements of the Rates and the Poll Tax. Indeed it was conceived as having a 50% *property* element and a 50% *personal* element. The tax has a range of discounts, exemptions and reductions, which reflect the hybrid nature of this tax.

The personal element of the tax is based on the assumption that two adults occupy the property. The most common discount is 25% for single person households, derived from the fact that 50% of the personal element is 25% of the total. The tax is not increased if more than two adults occupy the property.

When calculating the size of the household, some residents can be 'disregarded'; for example, severely mentally impaired people, carers and students (including student nurses) do not count. This means that they become invisible for the purpose of counting the number of persons in a household, so its size for the purposes of the Council Tax may be reduced to a single person and therefore initiate the 25% discount.

There is a 'reductions for disabilities' scheme which reduces the banding of houses in bands B to H, if they have been adapted or extended to meet the needs of a disabled person. The purpose of this is to remove any unfairness which might otherwise be caused by such a house being put in a higher band and the owners having to pay more Council Tax, because of the added value of the adaptations/extensions.

Owners of unoccupied dwellings receive a discount of 50%, effectively excused from the personal element of the tax. But even this provision can cause problems. In Wales, local authorities have a discretion to charge more than the standard 50% for second or holiday homes in rural areas, due to concerns about the creation of 'ghost villages' consisting of houses which are empty for most of the year. Apart from the adverse impact on local community life, this 50% concession is generally thought to have driven up local house prices to a level which the local people can no longer afford. The problem is starting to appear in other parts of the country and South Lakeland District Council raised the issue in May 1998 with a view to promoting legislation (through its own Parliamentary Bill, if necessary) giving it the same powers as Welsh authorities.

There is a range of exempt dwellings, mostly different kinds of unoccupied dwellings — for example, where the owner has moved into hospital or residential care. Various limited kinds of occupied dwellings are also exempt — for example, a hall of residence provided predominantly for student accommodation.

There is also a Council Tax benefits scheme for those people on low incomes.

There was a transitional relief for those who would have suffered large increases as a result of the change from the Poll Tax, although by 1996 virtually nobody continued to qualify for this transitional relief.

To appreciate the arguments about the Council Tax it is necessary to consider the advantages and disadvantages of a rating system based on property values.

The Council Tax differences from Rates

The Council Tax system's valuation differs from the old domestic rating system in two main regards — it is based on capital, not rental, values, with a reference date of 1 April 1991, and, instead of properties being individually valued, they are placed into one of eight valuation bands. For the purposes of billing, there is a set ratio between the different bands, with band D being the datum point.

band	values in England (£)	values in Wales (£)	ratio
A	up to 40,000	up to 30,000	6/9
B	40,001-52,000	30,001-39,000	7/9
C	52,001-68,000	39,001-51,000	8/9

D	68,001-88,000	51,001-66,000	1
E	88,001-120,000	66,001-90,000	11/9
F	120,001-160,000	90,001-120,000	13/9
G	160,001-320,000	120,001-240,000	15/9
H	over 320,000	over 240,000	2

The bands are deliberately broad so that they cover a range of property values — and the width of the bands gets larger as the value of the property increases. The aim of the bands being set up in this way was two-fold: firstly, to avoid the need for frequent property revaluation, as the property market fluctuated; secondly, to aim for people in broadly similar houses within a particular local authority's area paying similar Council Tax bills. There are different bands for England and Wales, reflecting the national differences in property values in the two countries.

The number of houses falling within the tax bands varies across the country, since property values vary geographically. For example, across the whole country, 25% of homes fall in the lowest band, band A; in the north-east, the proportion rises to 60%.

The Commissioners of the Inland Revenue, now through the Valuation Office Agency, allocate properties to valuation bands under the direction of the Secretary of State. Initially, there was a large number of appeals against the bands allocated to properties, because the valuations were based on 1991 values and did not take account of the drop in house prices caused by the recession before the introduction of the tax. But that factor is not a ground for an appeal.

The aim of the ratio mentioned earlier, with its datum point being band D, is to define the steps in the actual tax bills from band to band. People in the higher bands pay more Council Tax that those in the lower bands, but not pro rata to the difference in property value. The ratios can be changed by the Secretary of State.

The calculation of the rate of Council Tax is:

$$\frac{\text{(the amount the authority intends to spend)} - \text{(non-Council Tax revenue)}}{\text{Council Tax base}}$$

Uniform Business Rate (non-domestic Rates)

Uniform Business Rates, introduced with the Poll Tax in 1990, have continued with the Council Tax. They are a property tax paid by occupiers of commercial and industrial property; but they are no longer a **local** tax. The pooled nature of the Uniform Business Rate is intended to protect businesses and local authorities from the wide disparities in the values of local Rate bases.

The Uniform Business Rates are set by central government but gathered by the collection authorities, who then hand over the proceeds to central government. The government then redistributes the money from the central pool to local authorities in proportion to their adult population.

Some non-domestic properties such as churches or agricultural land or buildings are exempt and charitable buildings can receive a reduction.

Properties are valued and given a Rateable Value by the Valuation Office Agency, based on what the property could have been let for in 1993. The Secretary of State may prescribe other dates. There is a right of appeal. The government then sets, each year, the national multiplier (the rate in the pound), with separate rates for England and Wales, and this is levied on the Rateable Value. For example, a shopkeeper with a Rateable Value of £4,000 and a national multiplier of 50p will pay 4,000 x 50p, that is, £2,000. Many non-domestic ratepayers faced massive increases because the previous revaluation of their premises had taken place in 1973.

The budget process at local level

The local council's financial year runs from 1 April to 31 March. As already explained, the money used for revenue expenditure is raised from a combination of government grants, Council Tax, the uniform business rate and income raised from rents and charges for services. Short-term borrowing is also used, because cash flow does not always match expenditure. The revenue budget process can only be an annual process, because of uncertainties surrounding the amount of central government grant and any capping limits.

Capital programmes are usually planned three to five years ahead, but the capital programme will be rolled forward one more year as part of the revenue budget process, because the revenue budget will need to contain provision for meeting the interest payments on long-term capital borrowing — usually referred to as the 'revenue implications of the capital programme'. The revenue budget will also need to contain a *minimum revenue provision* to repay any outstanding borrowing debt — 2% of council housing debt; 4% of debt for other purposes.

Local authorities continue to run their financial processes in the traditional way of drawing up a budget, deciding financial priorities and culminating in a meeting to decide the level of local taxation — the Council Tax. However, they now start the process early in the previous financial year and because of 'capping' or the threat of such action, often have to make major reductions in services (sometimes at the last minute) to comply with overall revenue expenditure limits set by central government.

The budget meeting to set the charges for the financial year ahead will take place in February and the process will have taken almost a year to reach this point. The key committee throughout is the policy and resources committee. It usually meets in June or July to decide a broad budget strategy; remember that this will be for the next financial year starting the following April.

The other committees will be asked to draw up revenue and capital estimates according to this broad strategy. This could be, for example, to aim for an overall reduction, or for a standstill or a no-growth budget, or for a planned percentage increase. Sometimes the policy and resources committee will ask committees to draw up plans based upon a whole range of such options, and not until later on in the year, perhaps even at the final budget meeting, will one of these strategies be decided.

The committees will therefore draw up their plans, with capital and revenue being separated. Throughout the process, numerous estimates will be given as to how much the various options will cost the community and the effects on services. The committee deliberations are reported back to the policy and resources committee, which might adjust the broad strategy when, in December if they are lucky, the extent of government grant is announced. In January or early February, the committees draw up their final draft estimates for revenue and capital expenditure. These estimates are brought together at a policy and resources committee meeting in January/February. This meeting will determine contingency levels (to cover inflation, pay awards and unforeseen expenditure) and estimate the level of cash balances.

Finally, the policy and resources committee will recommend to the full council at a special meeting in February, the levels of existing and any new services and the Council Tax required to finance them. This is likely to be approved, although probably with some modifications and often after a highly political debate. The budget meeting is an unusual one with a limited agenda, specifically to approve the estimates and set the Council Tax. The leader of the council and the leaders of the opposition parties (or where a council is 'hung', the group spokesmen) make longer than usual prepared speeches.

The revenue budget, and the level of the precept or Council Tax, has to be fixed by a specific date. If necessary, the budget meeting may need to be adjourned for a short period of days to a later day, if irreconcilable differences emerge at the first meeting. The legal duty to fix the precept or tax means that, if necessary, the budget meeting will continue into the small hours to achieve some sort of decision.

The Rates Act 1984 introduced the concept of the government 'capping' the expenditure of local authorities, if they spent more than government spending assessments. This placed a limit on what the government regarded as excessive spending by some authorities. The power to 'cap' rests with the Secretary of State for the Environment, Transport and the Regions (and the Secretary of State for Wales) subject to Parliamentary approval.

The Local Government Finance Act 1988 made similar 'capping' provisions for the Poll Tax and the Local Government Finance Act 1992 extended it to the Council Tax. The new provisions provide for the Secretary of State to designate authorities where in his opinion the budget requirement is excessive or there is an excessive increase between the budget for one year and the next. A key figure in the process now is a council's standard spending assessment (SSA) — as the capping criteria invariably use it as a benchmark. The Secretary of State will then notify the authority concerned of the total for their budget and they may make representations or may accept the position. Consequential reductions in the amount of the Council Tax will have to be made to balance the budget within the capping limit.

Revenue budget control

Once estimates have council approval, they become the spending programmes of the individual committees. The budget is the prime system of management control. It is possible during the financial year for a committee to transfer money from one budget heading to another — this is known as *virement* and is generally subject to individual committee or full council approval, although officers may have limited virement powers delegated to them.

If a committee wishes to exceed its authorised budget, it must apply to the policy and resources committee and, possibly, the full council for a *supplementary estimate*. The money is usually found from balances, savings or underspendings. The Local Government Finance Act 1982 removed the right of a local authority to increase its precept or tax during the financial year by levying a *supplementary precept* or tax. The local authority may, however, introduce a lower *substitute precept* or tax.

It is usual, around October/November time, to review each committee's performance against its original budget provision — usually called the 'revised estimates' stage. It may well be that closer (and more often) control than this is used, where budgetary control has been less than effective in the past or the budget head is politically sensitive.

The process of revising the estimates can give rise to virement requests, if service committees discover that they are underspending on some budget items and they would like to redirect those unused resources elsewhere in their budget where there are unmet pressures. It needs to be understood that it is about this time of year that thoughts are already turning to next year's budget and the likely SSA settlement. If the omens are bad, the central committee/full council may not be inclined to approve virement requests, to ensure that the local authority's cash balances are increased to give greater room for manoeuvre in framing next year's budget.

Government revenue grants

Central government gives grants to local authorities which now amount in total to about 80% of local government expenditure, if the uniform business rate distribution is included. Revenue grants from central government come in two main forms:

- *general grants* — to pay for general running costs;
- *specific grants* — to help pay for specific revenue or capital

schemes; for example, the Mental Illness Specific Grant paid by the Department of Health to improve community-based provision for mentally ill people under the Care in the Community scheme.

Revenue grants are given for the following reasons:

- to achieve a specific purpose — for example, the reduction of Council Tax;
- to help poor areas, where the Council Tax base would not be sufficient to raise the necessary level of Council Tax to meet local needs;
- to reduce the cost of a service which is either spread unevenly across the country or which is of benefit to the nation as a whole as well as to the inhabitants in the local authority's area — for example, coastal defence or police;
- to help fund a service when the government has laid down specific requirements — for example, the fire service.

The Revenue Support Grant

The major grant introduced in 1990 is called the *Revenue Support Grant* (RSG) and is a general grant, replacing the earlier *Rate Support Grant*. The RSG is meant to adjust for the different levels of need in different areas with different resource bases. If the RSG system worked as intended, then for a given standard level of service, the Council Tax should be the same throughout the country.

In practice it does not work like that. Its distribution is based on a complex formula, calculated annually, which produces a figure which represents what the government thinks it will cost to provide a national level of service per adult in each local authority area. This is called the *Standard Spending Assessment* (SSA). The system is by no means perfect and has come in for increasing criticism:

- annual calculations complicate and sometimes delay the budget process at local level;
- at times, it is difficult to fathom why some criteria have been used to calculate the various elements of the SSA;
- the capping regime has progressively distorted spending patterns to such an extent that they can no longer be regarded as reliable indicators of need;
- the data often used is from the 1991 census.

If all local authorities were to spend at SSA level, then, in theory, the Council Tax would be the same all over the country, and the government works out what this level would be.

The amount which each local authority actually receives in RSG is then calculated on the difference between its SSA and the amount that it will receive from the national uniform business rate plus its assumed income from a standard level of Council Tax. The shortfall between the SSA and calculated income will, therefore, be the level of RSG which the local authority will receive.

Rents, fees and charges

Local government charges for many services — council house rents, leisure services, collection of trade refuse, car parking, and so on. This is becoming a greater source of revenue because it is directly linked to the use made of the services. Often, increases in charges are greater than the rate of inflation, but this is one way in which the RSG/reality gap mentioned earlier can be bridged. Many charging schemes have remission arrangements, so that only those people who can afford to do so actually pay the full charge.

Capital expenditure

This is spending on items which will last a long time — land, roads, buildings, major items of equipment and so on. Estimates (usually called the 'capital programme') for such expenditure are drawn up separately from the revenue estimates and will look some years into the future.

The local authority has to fund the approved capital programme, using one of the methods outlined below:

- borrowing within credit approvals;
- usable capital receipts;
- capital grants from central government; for example, Transport Supplementary Grant (TSG);
- entering into a joint venture or partnership with the private sector; for example, under the Private Finance Initiative (PFI); or
- contributions from revenue sources.

Capital borrowing

From April 1990, the government made a major change in the way it controls capital expenditure — by switching to a system that controls **borrowings** rather than **expenditure**. An authority's capital borrowing is limited by:

- its Basic Credit Approval (BCA); plus
- any Supplementary Credit Approvals (SCA); plus
- any grants for specific projects.

Local authorities borrow to fund capital expenditure for a number of reasons: it is fairer that all those who will gain benefit from the item should contribute during its lifetime, rather than those who were in the area when it was acquired; it makes economic sense at time of inflation to pay back with devalued money. However, when interest rates are high, borrowing can be an expensive (but probably the only) option.

Local authorities can borrow from the public and private sectors: the Public Works Loan Board (PWLB); the general money market; the financial institutions in the City of London; the Stock Exchange, where authorities may float stock but this is now very rare, as is the issuing of local bonds to small investors; and the European Union.

Although the terminology used often describes the government's approval of the local authority's capital programme as a 'capital allocation', in reality, it is no more than permission for the local authority to borrow the money, and pay the costs of doing so, itself.

The Basic Credit Approval (BCA) is an aggregate figure arrived at through different government departments who issue Annual Capital Guidelines (ACG) relevant to their area of activity. Those departments will have different approaches to deciding what levels of borrowing to approve. Some ACGs will be determined largely by need (social services in relation to the number of elderly people in the area); some will be determined by assessment of efficiency and effectiveness (part of the Housing Investment Programme (HIP)); and some will be determined by success in a competition (Capital Challenge Fund for regeneration). A local authority may receive up to five ACGs — housing, education, transport, social services, and 'other services' (for example, libraries and fire service).

A local authority's BCA is reduced by an amount which the government expects that local authority to be able to finance through its usable capital receipts in that year — the *Receipts Taken Into Account* (RTIA). In some years, some local authorities receive a zero BCA because of this. The RTIA system is a mechanism for, in effect, redistributing usable capital receipts — from those local authorities with large usable capital receipts to those with low usable capital receipts. The redistribution is achieved through the government then being able to increase the ACGs/BCA of the 'surplus asset poor' authorities, according to need.

The BCA is intended to be a general borrowing permission (in other words, the local authority can, if it wishes, undertake capital projects which may not have been determining factors in the ACGs — but it will have difficulty in convincing the government to give it an ACG in a later year for the same project). If a BCA is not used fully, any unused part lapses.

Supplementary Credit Approvals (SCA) tend to be linked to specific projects and can only be used for that purpose. Again, individual SCAs are given either according to need or as a result of a competition. There is increasing use of one-off additional programmes for specific purposes (for example, additional spending on schools from the Windfall Tax under the *New Deal for Schools* programme).

Capital receipts

The local authority's capital programme can be increased above the level implied by the BCA and any SCAs by the usable part of any *Capital Receipts*. Capital receipts are the money raised by the disposal of capital assets which are surplus to requirements. Any capital receipts are divided into two parts — the *Usable Part* and the *Reserve Part.*

The *Reserve* part must be set-aside to repay existing borrowing debt, effectively supplementing the *Minimum Revenue Provision* in the revenue budget to repay any outstanding borrowing debt (see the Budget Process section, above). The disadvantage of this set-aside of capital receipts is that it can discourage the disposal of surplus assets.

The *Usable* part can be used to supplement the BCA, enabling local capital resources to be recycled into new capital assets more relevant to present-day needs. The percentage of any capital receipts which are usable is determined by the Secretary of State. The 1998 percentage is 50%, except for council house sales, where the percentage is reduced to 25%. Where the capital receipt is being spent on a similar kind of capital asset (sell old residential care home and build a new residential care home which meets modern registration standards), 100% of the receipt can be used — the 'in-and-out' procedure.

The power of the Secretary of State to vary the percentages is illustrated by a temporary relaxation from 13 November 1992 to 1 January 1994, during which period all new capital receipts received in that period could be used on capital projects. This was designed to give a £1.75 billion boost to the economy.

The capital receipts regime can be adjusted by the Secretary of State in other ways. Many local authorities were sitting on large amounts of *reserve* capital receipts which were more than was required for paying of earlier borrowing. The former Conservative Government was content to see this as a means of depressing local government capital expenditure. The New Labour Government had different ideas and through the *Capital Receipts Initiative* is now issuing additional SCAs to recycle these unused reserve capital receipts into housing and housing-related regeneration schemes.

Capital grants

As the name suggests, these are grants of money, rather than permission to borrow. These grants are for a specific purpose and can only be used for that purpose. Apart from government departments, grants can also come from the public bodies which distribute National Lottery 'good causes' money. The EU is a completely separate source of capital grants.

Projects which are approved for government capital grant purposes are often funded partly by grant and partly by SCA. Examples of this hybrid approach were: Transport Supplementary Grant (TSG) schemes approved as part of the Transport Policies and Programme (TPP), Single Regeneration Budget (SRB) schemes and coastal defence schemes.

European Union sources of finance

Essential Central Government outlines the kinds of regional policies and funds run by the EU. The funds of particular interest to local authorities are: the *European Regional Development Fund* which finances infrastructure projects and industrial investment; the *European Social Fund* which supports training and employment initiatives aimed at young people and unemployed people; and the *Structural Funds* which have a variety of *Objectives*. The European Investment Bank (EIB) can also be a source of finance.

Initially, the government tried to reduce local authority capital allocations to take account of EU money, but there was an increasing resistance by the EU to this action because it meant that, in effect, the money went to the government rather than to the area. In the case of *Structural Fund* grants to assist regeneration of coal mining areas, the government was forced to give ground in order to have the EU money released.

Some local authorities are adept at obtaining EU funding and realise that they will fare better if they maintain an office in Brussels for the purpose of gathering intelligence and lobbying the decision-makers. Local authorities which take this very seriously have their own office; most share an office on a metropolitan or regional basis; and others (those with a better resource base and no declining industry problems) feel that an officer at headquarters, supplemented by an agent in Brussels to gather intelligence, is all that is required.

The European Regional Development Fund, set up in 1975, is a significant source of EU aid for UK local authorities. Its purpose is to correct regional imbalances in the EU. The regional fund is divided up into national quotas. Applications are submitted by national governments — in the UK, the DETR, the Welsh Assembly, Scottish Executive and Northern Ireland Office/Executive select the local authority projects most suitable for submission. The fund can meet up to 45% of the cost of infrastructure projects which contribute to the development of a region.

Help is also available from the *European Social Fund*, which is an employment fund originally established under the Treaty of Rome, to meet the costs of training and retraining in specified categories. Most schemes receiving assistance from this fund are operated by the DfEE but there has been an increase in the number of local authority projects receiving money.

The first two Objectives of the *Structural Funds* are important in the sense that they can give access to substantial resources: promoting economic development in underdeveloped regions (Objective 1) and regenerating regions adversely affected by industrial decline (Objective 2). Objective 1 status is given to a region if its GDP is less than 75% of the EU average. In the UK, two regions have held this status: Merseyside and the Highlands and Islands. During the period 1993/99, Merseyside received £580 million in EU funds because of this status. South Yorkshire's GDP has dropped below the

75% benchmark, so is now eligible for Objective 1 status — however, the basis of EU Structural Funds is under review.

The EU also has regulations regarding advertising and tendering public procurement contracts that are having an increasing effect on local government. For more information on the EU, see the relevant Chapter in *Essential Central Government.*

Capital finance from private sources

There are various ways in which a local authority can undertake capital development, using private sources, rather than through borrowing or capital receipts.

Where development is proposed, the developer will often be quite willing to provide land free of charge (for a new school) or fund (or carry out) capital works (usually road access and traffic management) which would otherwise fall upon the local authority. This approach by the developer is not entirely altruistic — unless the infrastructure is in place, the development cannot take place; the local authority has insufficient capital resources at its disposal to provide the infrastructure; so, the developer supplies the infrastructure to enable the development to proceed and the developer to make a profit (the cost of the infrastructure works will be recouped from the developer's ultimate clients). This is usually called 'planning gain', and can cause unease in some quarters that the developer is, in effect, buying the right to develop from the local authority.

The *Private Finance Initiative* (PFI) was introduced by the Conservative Government to enable the funding of public sector projects by the private sector — this could be viewed as, in effect, another way of privatising aspects of the public sector infrastructure. The use of PFI achieves the effect of apparently reducing public expenditure, since the capital expenditure is regarded as private in the Nation's accounts. New Labour regarded the PFI as a valuable source of finance and saw the further development of public/private partnerships as being consistent with *'Improving Local Services through Best Value'.*

However, the PFI initiative had a troubled start. Those troubles surrounded whether the participating local authorities had the necessary legal powers to enter into arrangements of this kind with the private sector — since they nearly always involved the private sector financiers asking the local authority to give guarantees to underwrite the project. The issues are to do with the concept of *ultra vires* and are discussed in the Chapter on *External Relations and Controls,* especially the paragraphs about section 111 of the Local Government Act 1972. The recent Local Government (Contracts) Act was passed to provide some assurance about the local authorities' legal capacity to enter into partnership agreements with the private sector.

When New Labour came into office they announced their intention to develop a new framework for public/private partnerships, of which PFI would be one component. The extent to which New Labour have embraced PFI can be judged from some news reports during February 2000. Firstly, David Blunkett, Secretary of State for Education and Employment, was reported in the *Financial Times* of 21 February 2000 as confirming that over £1bn was being raised through PFI to rebuild and refurbish 270 rundown schools — with 400 more in the pipeline.

In the *Local Government Chronicle* of 24 February 2000, Manchester City Council was reported as negotiating with six consortia to select the best for a housing PFI partnership to regenerate the Stockport Road and Plymouth Grove Estate under a scheme worth £90m over 30 years. However, the road to PFI riches is not exactly short or easy, as can be seen in North Yorkshire. In the *Yorkshire Post* of 23 February 2000, Accord plc was named as the preferred bidder for a PFI contract with the County Council worth £5.5m to construct new school buildings for over 1,000 pupils. Two of the four schools involved were Church of England schools and it took the best part of three years of negotiations to sort out the legal difficulties caused by this feature for the PFI project.

Lotteries

Profits from lotteries may be used to finance small projects specified in the terms of the lottery. It may also finance revenue expenditure. Lotteries were never a major source of money and fewer councils are now running them. The National Lottery has, presumably, had an adverse impact on local lottery sales.

New Labour — Modernising Local Government

At the end of March 1998, the New Labour Government published three Green Papers from its *Modernising Local Government* series, setting out its proposals (some more welcome and practical than others):

Improving local financial accountability floated the following proposals:

- the Council Tax would be retained in its present form and there would be no revaluation of the 1991 base;
- increased stability in the quantum (amount) and distribution of government grant, and in particular keeping the SSA calculation methodology stable for a period of three years;
- the abolition of crude **universal** capping — to be replaced by reserve selective capping;
- the introduction of local referendums on spending and Council Tax decisions;
- linking annual elections to budget decisions;v local authorities to meet the cost of Council Tax benefit above a specified threshold.

Business Rates proposed the following:

- retain the national non-domestic Business Rate, with pooled revenue, much as now;
- a new power for local authorities to set a supplementary rate at local level, but subject to a complex system of centrally-controlled constraints;
- strengthen links between local authorities and business interests in their area;
- reduce the burden of Business Rates on small businesses.

Capital finance suggested the following:

- changes to the capital allocation process to encourage strategic and corporate planning;
- better asset management by using asset registers, asset management plans, performance indicators and bench-marking;
- improving forward planning, possibly by issuing supplementary credit approvals for more than one year;
- fairer methods of taking into account capital receipts in determining allocations, including changing the RTIA system;
- continuing the development of PFI and other partnerships with the private sector — and clarifying the problems of local authority powers to enter into partnership arrangements.

From crude capping to sophisticated passporting

In a speech to the LGA at the end of December 1999, Hilary Armstrong, Minister for Local Government declared an end to crude capping:

> *"For years, local authorities have asked for greater financial flexibility and more local responsibility through the end of universal Council Tax capping. With this year's local government finance settlement, we have gone an extra mile towards that destination ... The ending of crude and universal capping is a manifesto commitment. That means that it will happen ... But the actions of local authorities will be crucial to determining how we fulfil that pledge ... I expect local authorities to look carefully at their permitted increases, including passporting, and make a careful judgement as to whether they need to make those increases in budget and whether their Council Tax payers can afford them".*

So, not exactly local freedom, but a move in that direction.

Although capping was being phased out, it has to be understood that other methods of control were being phased in. New Labour increased the amount being 'top-sliced' from the **general** revenue support grant, so that they could use it in the form of **specific** grants for expenditure directed by the Government. Although presented by John Prescott as a means of increasing local authority expenditure, 'passporting' actually works in such a way that local authorities are expected to pass on increases in specific service areas, with little or no local discretion.

An example of this was the £50m grant for schools announced by the Government in its RSG settlement in February 1999. The devil was in the detail — when the details were announced in February 2000, Sir Jeremy Beecham (Leader of the LGA) was moved to say:

> *"Councils are being held to ransom. The majority of local authorities already stretch themselves to spend more on education than the Government's designated amount. Now they will have to consider cutbacks in other services or Council Tax rises to meet the Government's criteria. It is a simple smoke and mirrors trick. Through this grant, the government can claim to be spending on education while in reality the cash will come from other services. Government should not dictate how the RSG is spent. Councils should be answerable to their communities for spending decisions".*

An example given by the LGA illustrates the 'smoke and mirrors' trick: In order to qualify for the extra grant, a local authority must maintain the same education budget as the previous year, plus match the increase in the education SSA. So, an authority which received an education SSA of £100m last year but actually spent £110m, and was granted £105m next year, must find £115m — a total of £15m over SSA.

A direct example of this (and the scope for misunderstanding) was reported in the *Local Government Chronicle* of 25 February 2000 under the headline *'Stockton denies DfEE's accusation of withholding funds'*. Mr Blunkett wanted Stockton-on-Tees BC to 'passport' an extra £3.8m to its schools in 2000/2001 and complained when the BC only planned to increase schools expenditure by £2.2m. However, Stockton BC had increased its education budget in 1999/2000 by passing onto schools the benefit of a one-off windfall of £1.6m gained from a business rates revaluation of school properties. The DfEE had incorrectly viewed this one-off £1.6m as part of the base budget. Stockton's Leader complained to Mr Blunkett saying: *"The government has got its sums wrong and it should admit as such"*. It seemed that DfEE officials were embarrassed at what was an elementary statistical error.

In this context, the DfEE's approach is at odds with its own, as revealed in the eye-opening article (which is worth the effort to find and read) which appeared in the *Guardian* of 7 March 2000 under the headline: *'Blunkett's magic tricks and the 19bn boost for education that doesn't exist'*.

'Universal capping' may well be a thing of the past but Government is increasing its grip on local authority budgets in other ways. Concern is being expressed in some quarters that the plethora of plans which authorities now have to produce (Best Value Performance Plan, Annual Library Plan, Children's Services Plan, Community Care Plan, Community Strategy, Crime and Disorder Reduction Strategy, Development Plan, Early Years Development Plan, Education Development Plan, Local Transport Plan, Youth Justice Plan, Housing Investment Programme Plans, Local Agenda 21 Strategy, Lifelong Learning Development Plan) will be used by Government to exert even greater control over local authority budgets. The concern is that the General Grant will continue to be whittled away through 'top-slicing' and the top-sliced resources distributed by central government through an increasing number of Special Grants linked to the Plans, the content of which will have been approved by central government.

8 Housing

The relevant bodies — background commentary — social housing — public housing finance — the right to buy — housing homeless people — maintenance, demolition or improvement of housing — Housing Benefit — private sector — the future

The relevant bodies

In the field of housing, the relevant bodies are:

- Central government departments: the Department of the Environment, Transport and the Regions (DETR); the Scottish Executive and the Welsh Assembly.
- In Northern Ireland: the Northern Ireland Secretary of State/Northern Ireland Executive; the Northern Ireland Housing Executive — with sole responsibility for the provision of social housing.
- Quangos at national level: The Housing Corporation (which now issues its own Circulars), Scottish Homes and Housing for Wales.
- Local housing authorities: unitary authorities, London borough councils, metropolitan borough councils and shire district/borough councils in two-tier areas. In addition, county councils have certain reserve powers to provide housing in place a local housing authority, but these powers can only be exercised with the Secretary of State's approval and are seldom used.
- Quangos at local level: housing associations and social landlords.

Public housing was also provided by Scottish Homes and the Development Board for Rural Wales, but their housing stock has been transferred to alternative social landlords, mostly housing associations.

Historical context

The provision of fit and proper public housing is one of the cornerstones of local government. As explained in the first Chapter, local government emerged in the 19th century in order to meet the public health problems all too evident at that time. Although a wholesome water supply and an effective and safe sewerage system were necessary for greater public health (those used to be local government functions as well), the elimination of overcrowded and poorly constructed housing, and its replacement with housing built to modern standards, was equally important in the fight against disease.

The years between the First and Second World Wars were a period of major public housing activity. A start was made on clearing the worst slums and new housing estates provided in their place, largely in the existing urban areas. In the 1950s and 1960s, once the immediate effects of the Second World War had been dealt with, the development of public housing continued with new emphasis.

The years immediately after the Second World War

The bombed sites within the major cities provided cleared areas for new public housing. The immediate concern in the late 1940s had been to provide instant housing for displaced families at a time when building materials (and, indeed, most things) were in short supply — and so the 'prefab' was developed, a prefabricated specially-designed single-storey compact house which did not use conventional building materials and which could be manufactured off-site and erected quickly. The prefabs were intended to have a limited life — but the standard of their construction was so good and their design so effective that they survived well into the 1970s and examples can be found in building museums today.

At the same time, the growth in the population meant that public housing needed to be provided in several different ways to meet the increasing demand for better quality housing. The view was taken in the 1960s (by central government which then, as now, controlled the capital building programmes) that the only way to deal with the slums was to demolish them and start again. Different attitudes would probably prevail today, so that, with modern techniques and materials, existing communities can be maintained; but the solution chosen then was wholesale clearance.

The 1960s

One feature of the slums was that they were a high density form of housing — so much so, that the only way to accommodate anything like the same number of people on the cleared sites was to build upwards. So, there followed a period of extensive slum clearance programmes, under which local housing authorities used the power of the compulsory purchase order (CPO) on a large scale, to meet central government targets for new housing. The CPO was the only means by which the local housing authorities could assemble the large sites required for redevelopment within a reasonably short time.

The approach of building upwards found expression in the tower blocks of flats which certainly produced housing of a better physical quality than before, but which eventually produced a much poorer style of living from the social point of view. The tower blocks were designed by people who had never lived in a housing environment like that, and never would. Although living in tower-block flats suited some people, the majority of council tenants did not like them and they were unpopular after the novelty had worn off and the social problems of that kind of living environment started to emerge.

The physical characteristics of the new tower blocks also required new construction techniques and local housing authorities were encouraged by central government to use the new system-building processes which were starting to emerge at that time. It was only some years later that problems inherent in some of those system-building processes started to emerge. In some cases, the solution to the combined problem of a tower block built using discredited system-building and the social difficulties associated with that method of housing was to demolish it and start again. The housing built in the place of the tower blocks has been of a more domestic scale which fosters community and neighbourly spirit in a way which the tower block could never do. Most modern public housing (now usually provided through housing associations rather than local housing authorities) is on this domestic scale — two (or at the most three) storey housing on a street pattern with individual gardens.

However, building within, or on the edge of, established urban areas was not enough to meet the demand. So, 'New Towns' were developed in largely rural locations to supply not only housing, but also the social infrastructure needed for an effective community — shops, schools, leisure facilities and employment opportunities. The local authority in the host area was nearly always a rural district council which did not possess the experience or expertise to undertake a project of that size. So, in most cases, a New Town Development Corporation was established under the overall supervision of the New Towns Commission, to produce and then manage the new town. All of the New Town Development Corporations have now been disbanded and their public housing management responsibilities transferred to social landlords.

The more recent years

The Housing Act 1988 represented a major shift in the position of local authorities with regard to the provision of housing. The function of local housing authorities changed from being mass providers of affordable rented housing to operating mainly a strategic and enabling view — that is, helping other agencies to provide housing and advising them as to what type of housing is needed. The Conservative Government wanted to see a move away from large scale local authority provision of housing to a "more pluralist and more market oriented system". The Local Government and Housing Act 1989 stated that local housing authorities were no longer obliged to keep a housing stock at all.

There has been an enormous change in housing provision in recent years, mainly through the big increase in owner occupation and a smaller increase in the private rented sector and local housing association sector; the only sector to have reduced is the local housing authority. Nationally, home ownership now accounts for some 67% of housing. The remaining 33%, in the rented sector, is divided between local housing authorities (19%), housing associations (4%), and private landlords (10%). These proportions vary greatly from area to area.

The proceeds of sale of council houses were not fully recycled into providing new council housing — the Conservative Government drastically reduced the new local authority public sector house building programme. Most new public sector house building was arranged by the government through housing associations funded via the Housing Corporation. In some parts of the country, some of the larger housing associations now manage more houses than many local housing authorities. The effect on local government was compounded by the same government's policy aimed at increasing the number of home owners (and presumably people sympathetic to the ideology of that government), achieved by compelling local housing authorities to sell their public housing stock to sitting tenants at discounted prices.

The move of housing away from local government was extended beyond housing associations by the Housing Act 1996, which created a new category of 'social landlord'. Social landlords include new non-profit making 'housing companies', with local authority and tenant involvement — but not control. The Housing Corporation supervise and register social landlords. These provisions of the 1996 Act had been envisaged in the White Paper *Our Future Homes* and the DoE (as it then was) consultation document *More Choice in the Social Housing Sector.*

Provision of local authority housing

The 1957 Housing Act made it a duty of local housing authorities to consider local housing conditions and the need to provide further housing. The Act gave local housing authorities the power to provide housing by: buying land and building on it; buying houses; or converting or improving houses bought by them. The Housing Act 1985 has now replaced the 1957 Act as the *Principal Housing Act.*

Local housing authorities can also provide land for development by private builders and can give assistance to housing associations, housing co-operatives and social landlords. When local housing authorities build houses and flats to rent, they can also provide or sell furniture to tenants and provide facilities for tenants to do their own laundering and catering. They can also, with the consent of the Secretary of State, provide shops, recreation grounds and other amenities.

Local housing authority tenancies

Local housing authorities have a wide discretion in selecting tenants, although they must give preference to those in insanitary or overcrowded houses, and to large families living under unsatisfactory conditions. All authorities must have an 'allocation scheme', describing how allocations are to be made and the priorities to be applied. Most schemes award points for factors constituting 'housing need' and give priority according to the total of the points scored.

The security of tenure offered by the Housing Acts means that if a local housing authority wishes to terminate a tenancy for any reason, it has to obtain a court order for possession — there are only limited grounds for obtaining such an order; for example, failure to pay rent, allowing the property to deteriorate, or causing a nuisance to neighbours. More recently, the Housing Act 1996 has extended the grounds upon which possession orders can be sought — nuisance or annoyance to visitors in the locality; where a partner has been forced to leave the property due to domestic violence; and where the tenancy was obtained by deception or false statement. Under the 1996 Act, the local housing authority can also apply to the High Court or county court for an injunction against tenants for anti-social behaviour — with the ultimate sanction of arrest and imprisonment for contempt of court for any breach of the injunction. However, the collection of sufficient evidence to convince the court remains a problem — the neighbours often feel too intimidated to volunteer evidence and some local housing authorities are trying to solve that problem by using their own staff as witnesses.

When a tenant dies, the tenancy can pass to the surviving spouse or another member of the family who has been living there for at least 12 months. There can be only one succession tenancy of this type. However, if the council considers that the property is more extensive than is reasonably required by the successor, it may seek a possession order, provided that notice has been served between six and 12 months after the date of the previous tenant's death. The court will order possession if it considers that reasonable and suitable alternative accommodation is available.

Local housing authority tenant rights

The rights of local housing authority tenants are set out in the *Council Tenant's Charter*. Local housing authorities are required to consult tenants on housing management matters that will affect them and to consider representations from tenants before making major decisions.

The Leasehold Reform, Housing and Urban Development Act 1993 also strengthened the right of a local housing authority tenant, to have certain repairs carried at the authority's expense as landlord and the right (when they have to move home) to be paid compensation for improvements which they themselves have made to their homes.

In addition, local housing authority tenants were given, by the 1988 Housing Act, the right to choose an alternative 'approved landlord' (the so-called 'Tenants' Choice' provisions of the Act), with the Housing Corporation playing a key role in this process. Housing associations have been the instrument used where local authority tenants have exercised their right to change their landlord in this way, sometimes, but not always, with the encouragement of the local housing authority. By July 1996, 51 local housing authorities had transferred their housing stock to housing associations, an overall total of 220,000 properties. This provision has now been replaced by the registered social landlord provisions of the 1996 Housing Act.

The Leasehold Reform, Housing and Urban Development Act 1993 extended this right by allowing tenant management organisations (TMOs) to enter into arrangements with their local authority to take over the housing management function themselves, thereby creating an alternative to a housing association take-over. Over 100 of these TMOs are now operational, with more said to be in the pipeline.

Public sector to private sector — the right to buy

The right to buy their home was conferred on council tenants by the Housing Act 1980 (now by the 1985 Act). Similar provisions apply in Scotland and Northern Ireland. A total of 2.1 million homes previously in the local housing authority, housing association and New Town sector were transferred to private ownership between 1980 and 1995; with the continuing annual rate said to be 60,000 since then.

Many councils previously sold houses willingly to tenants but the Conservative Government forced them to do so on a much greater scale — and at a discounted price. This policy was intended to increase house ownership but it also had the effect of reducing the stock of public housing available to meet the needs of people who, for one reason or another, could not arrange for themselves rented accommodation in the private sector.

This caused a political storm, with, principally, Labour local housing authorities objecting to this provision. The right to buy now applies to tenants who have been in residence for at least two years. There are some exceptions to the right to buy: for example, the tenants of sheltered housing for elderly or disabled people cannot exercise the right — since, otherwise, the availability of this specialist form of warden-managed housing would rapidly become fragmented and reduced.

Tenants are entitled to a discount on the market value of the council house, of up to 60%, depending on the previous length of their tenancy. In the case of flats, the

Housing and Planning Act 1989 increased the maximum discount to 70%, presumably because they are less attractive as buying propositions, and put a limit on the future service charges levied by the local authority. In any case, whatever the discount, the selling price must not be below a figure determined by the Secretary of State. This is known as the 'cost floor' rule.

A purchaser of a council house must repay part of the discount (pro rata to the time elapsed since the purchase) if the house is sold within three years.

If the Secretary of State believed that a local housing authority was not meeting its statutory requirement of allowing tenants to buy their property, a Commissioner could be appointed by the Secretary of State to take over these functions. Any costs involved would be charged to the local housing authority. This happened in Norwich.

Council tenants exercising their right to buy were originally able to obtain a mortgage from the local housing authority. However, this has now been replaced by a 'rent to mortgage' scheme, introduced by the Leasehold Reform, Housing and Urban Development Act 1993. The price fixed for the house consists of two elements: the *initial capital payment* and the *deferred financial commitment*. The intention is that repayments for the *capital payment* part will be no greater than current outgoings on rent, although the former tenant would also have to pay the cost of repairs. No interest will accrue on the *deferred financial commitment,* which will become payable on the sale of the house; the death of the purchaser; or by the purchaser making a payment at any time.

Other methods of encouraging the move to home ownership include shared ownership schemes (where the tenant buys a share of a property from a housing association and pays rent for the other share) and the Cash Incentive Scheme (where the tenant is given cash help to buy in the private sector).

Homeless people

Local housing authorities have a statutory duty to provide housing for people who are made **unintentionally** homeless and for those people threatened with homelessness within 28 days. This duty was originally in the Housing (Homeless Persons) Act 1977, but now appears in the Housing Act 1996.

The 1996 Act narrowed the ambit of homelessness by allowing local housing authorities to take into account the availability of accommodation in the UK and **elsewhere** — thus providing some relief to those housing authorities presented with large numbers of illegal immigrants. In general, asylum seekers who did not claim asylum status at the port of their initial arrival in the UK are not eligible — although some asylum seekers are eligible if they satisfy certain conditions. People who have been granted refugee status and others with, for example, exceptional or unconditional leave to remain in the UK, are eligible for assistance. The point is that the entitlement of asylum seekers and refugees to assistance is complex and will depend upon quite detailed individual circumstances. The 1996 Act also introduced a limitation of two years on the length of time for which accommodation was to be provided in certain cases, and a review of all cases after that period.

A code of guidance issued by the Secretary of lays down the priority groups of homeless people for whom the local housing authority must ensure that accommodation (either by itself or by third parties) is available:

- people with dependent children;
- people made homeless by an emergency and disaster (such as flood or fire);
- people vulnerable because of old age, mental or physical handicap or other special reason; and
- pregnant women and their households.

People falling into these categories do not have to be housed immediately in permanent accommodation, but the code of guidance says this should be secured as soon as possible. Local authorities frequently use short-life, or bed and breakfast, or hostel accommodation as an interim measure in the early stages of investigating applications from people who, on the face of it, appear to be eligible for accommodation as priority cases.

Local housing authorities do not have to provide housing permanently for people who have made themselves **intentionally** homeless — some people do this because they want to move from one area to another — or for those who normally live outside the local housing authority's boundaries. But if anyone who is intentionally homeless falls into any of the priority groups listed above, the local housing authority must give advice, assistance and at least temporary accommodation.

If people think they have been wrongly designated as intentionally homeless they can challenge the local authority by taking judicial review proceedings in the courts.

Due to the effects of the recession there has been a big increase in the number of homeless people, as a result of their properties being repossessed by building societies or banks. This has proved to be a major problem for some local housing authorities because their own housing stock has dwindled through sales and very little new building. The cost of temporary bed and breakfast arrangements at a time of a capped revenue budget is a major worry.

There has also been criticism that people identified as homeless, and provided with permanent housing, are effectively jumping the housing queue of people patiently waiting their turn for a council house. One of the provisions in the Housing Act 1996 was introduced to meet this criticism. From January 1997, there is a single route to the allocation of long-term social housing — the local authority housing register.

For those people who are truly homeless — sleeping rough on the streets — the government introduced, in 1990, the *Rough Sleepers Initiative* for central London, providing places in short-term hostels and leased places in 'move-on' accommodation. The Initiative has been extended, from March 1996, to include permanent homes, high-care accommodation and special accommodation for people with drink problems. The Initiative was extended to Bristol in June 1996.

Maintenance of local housing authority stock

Local housing authorities do, of course, have responsibilities for the maintenance of their own rented stock. However, the almost continuous revenue and capital budget constraints on local housing authorities over the last few years has meant that there is a large backlog in council house repairs. Some tenants have been waiting so long for their houses to be repaired that they have taken legal action against their local housing authority landlord to enforce appropriate action.

A national 'repair-it-yourself' scheme for council tenants came into operation in January 1986. This enabled tenants to carry out certain repairs which were the responsibility of the housing authority and to reclaim the cost. However, the procedure is complicated and the 'right to repair' is little used.

The government eventually recognised the problems which had been accumulating in council house repairs through the revenue and capital budget constraints which it had imposed, and so it introduced several measures aimed at redressing the deficiencies. The most run-down estates would be improved through the *Single Regeneration Budget (SRB) Challenge Fund;* and an additional *Estate Renewal Challenge Fund,* usually by subsidising transfer from local housing authorities to other forms of social housing management, such as housing associations.

Another, earlier, measure also involved transferring the housing stock from the local housing authority. The Housing Act 1988 gave the Secretary of State a wide power to designate an area as a *Housing Action Trust Area,* provided that a majority of the tenants, after a secret ballot, wished to opt out of local housing authority ownership and management. In such an area, a quango called a *Housing Action Trust* (HAT), separate from the local housing authority is established, with the aim of: repairing and improving property; providing effective management; ensuring diversity of tenure; and improving social and environmental conditions. The local authority's housing stock is transferred to the HAT, which can also take over some of the local housing authority's other functions in that area. There was initially little interest in the schemes, because the tenants feared large rent increases and because they preferred 'the devil they know', the local housing authority, as their landlord.

Six HATs were set up by April 1994. The first HAT, North Hull, completed its task and was wound up in March 1999. The remaining HATs are Liverpool, Castle Vale (Birmingham) and the London Boroughs of Waltham Forest, Tower Hamlets and Brent (Stonebridge HAT).

Local housing authority finance — Housing Revenue Account

The level of council house rents has been a highly political issue for many years. Before the Housing Finance Act 1972, council house rents were often very low, but the Act forced local housing authorities to increase rents significantly. Some local housing authorities were not too happy about this, especially the Labour-controlled ones. In 1972, Clay Cross Urban District Council refused to raise council house rents as required by the 1972 Act. The councillors of the Clay Cross UDC were surcharged and disqualified from membership, and the Secretary of State sent in Commissioners, who were civil servants, to act on his behalf at the council's expense.

Today, the law says rents should be 'reasonable'. But what is reasonable? It is, of course, a matter for debate, but the courts have held that local housing authorities must keep a reasonable balance between tenants on the one hand and Council Tax payers on the other. The Local Government and Housing Act 1989 requires council rents to have regard to rents in the private sector. This does not mean that they have to be at the same level, but that they should keep the same **relationship**.

Every local housing authority must keep a separate housing account, known as the *Housing Revenue Account* (HRA). In simple terms, this shows the annual cost of providing, maintaining and managing the local authority's housing stock, and the sources of the money to meet the costs involved. In addition, a separate Housing Repairs Account must be kept.

The 1989 Act made substantial changes to housing finance and the operation of the HRA. As well as redefining the items that can be charged or credited to the account, as from 1990-91 it became 'ring-fenced'. This meant that the account must be balanced by rents and government subsidies and cannot be subsidised from the Council Tax. A new system of government subsidies (HRA subsidy) was also introduced and replaced the old subsidies, including those for rent rebates. A total amount is fixed by the government which makes its assumptions about rent levels and expenditure. This total amount is then divided between local housing authorities according to the value of their dwellings and local circumstances. This approach put a stop to the 'open ended' nature of housing subsidies, which were becoming embarrassingly large. This approach, taken with the new rent provisions, made a substantial move towards the HRA becoming self-financing.

Where a local housing authority had rent arrears at 1 April 1990, they had to be written off against the then Community Charge account, to allow the new HRA to have a clear start. After that date, any arrears have to be met from the HRA which means, in effect, from increased rents.

As part of its overall plan to control total local government spending, the government also controls the cost of capital repairs, improvements and mortgages and loan expenditure — for buying land and building houses — by all local housing authorities.

Local housing authorities have to seek approval each year for their proposed housing investment programme (HIP). The government allocation is not a grant, but an approved limit on the amount which they can spend.

In December 1999, the Housing Minister, Nick Raynsford, announced the Government's intention to introduce 'resource accounting' as the basis for the HRA from 2001/2002, making local authority housing finance more transparent and business-like. Resource accounting involves adjusting the way in which the major repairs allowance and stock valuations are calculated and removes rent rebates from the HRA. The problem about such an accounting change is that some councils will gain, while others will lose — giving rise to the possibility of transitional arrangements being needed to soften the blow and give the losers a chance to absorb the impact.

Social Security delivered locally — Housing Benefit

The Housing Benefit scheme offers financial help to council and private tenants who can prove that they cannot afford the rent. Although this is, in essence, a social security function of central government, it is administered by local housing authorities.

Standard Housing Benefit is paid to persons who are working but who have insufficient income to meet their rent, while *Certificated Housing Benefit* is paid to those in receipt of unemployment benefit or income support. Because the government transferred responsibility for this scheme from the Department of Social Security, it pays a subsidy which meets most (at present 95%, but New Labour proposes to reduce this), but not all, of the costs involved.

As of April 1989, local housing authorities were also made responsible for the payment of board and lodgings charges for people living in hostel accommodation.

Alongside the Housing Benefit scheme, local housing authorities have to operate Council Tax Benefit schemes which are administered along similar lines.

Housing associations

Housing associations are voluntary bodies and not part of local government. They are sometimes called the third arm of housing, the other two being local housing authorities (and New Towns) and the private sector. The last Conservative Government saw them as the major providers of new, low cost, properties for rent.

The Housing Corporation was set up, for England, in 1964. The equivalent in Scotland is Scottish Homes and in Wales, Housing for Wales. There is no equivalent body in Northern Ireland, where the provision of public sector housing is the sole responsibility of the Northern Ireland Housing Executive.

One of the main rôles of the Housing Corporation (under the Housing Associations Act 1985) is to keep a register of housing associations. Registration is not compulsory, but unregistered associations have no entitlement to housing association loans and grants. There are some 2,200 registered associations.

The Housing Corporation is controlled by a board whose members are appointed by the Secretary of State. It has powers to discipline any registered housing association which it considers is not operating satisfactorily, and it allocates approved expenditure for programmes agreed between the housing associations and the Corporation.

Housing association activity has increased significantly in recent years. Most housing associations are registered as industrial and provident societies. All have a committee of management elected by the membership of the association. This is voluntary work and although committee members can claim for out-of-pocket expenses, they do not receive any other form of payment.

The size of housing associations varies enormously. Some, with a small number of houses, have no professional staff. Others are large, often formed by amalgamation or take-over, with a substantial workforce. Housing associations are non-profit making. They work closely with local authorities, being particularly useful in specialised areas such as providing sheltered housing for the elderly and those with special needs. They have also given a great deal of assistance in improving older housing in inner city areas.

Housing association tenants have the protection of Tenants' Guarantees issued by the Housing Corporation and Housing for Wales — the equivalent of the Council Tenant's Charter. As a consequence of the Housing Act 1996, there is now the Housing Association Tenants' Ombudsman, giving housing association tenants access to the same kind of external statutorily independent scrutiny enjoyed by their local housing authority counterparts through the Local Government Ombudsman. Similar schemes exist in Scotland and Northern Ireland.

Local housing authorities have the power to make loans or give guarantees to housing associations registered with the Housing Corporation. They normally have the right to nominate 50% of tenants to housing association schemes within their administrative areas. However, where there is partnership in the provision of new housing, a higher percentage of local authority nominations is often agreed.

Social landlords

The concept of social landlords was introduced by the Housing Act 1996, to extend the range of bodies in the social housing field as alternatives to local government. Social landlords are bodies which build and manage social rented housing, including a new type of local not-for-profit 'housing company', involving, but not controlled by, the local housing authority and tenants. Such bodies are intended to take over social housing, mostly thorough large-scale transfers of existing housing stock.

The idea is to open up the social housing sector to new kinds of suitable landlord, supervised and registered with the Housing Corporation, effectively going beyond the housing association approach.

Unfit housing

Quite apart from the provision of new housing, local housing authorities have considerable powers and duties regarding the maintenance and improvement of existing housing. However, most of the work of local housing authorities in respect of the maintenance and improvement of housing which is unfit for human habitation relates to the private sector.

In many cases, action against landlords was taken under the Public Health Acts, principally the Public Health Act 1936. This is one reason why many councils have a combined housing and environmental health department. The activities of a housing department impinge on all the rest of a local housing authority's services, but nowhere so much as environmental health.

The current position is to be found in the Environmental Protection Act 1990 under which local housing authorities have a duty to inspect existing buildings in their area to detect *statutory nuisances*. Statutory nuisances include premises prejudicial to health, as well as nuisances due to smoke, dust, fumes, rubbish and noise. The Act gives local housing authorities the power to secure the elimination of the statutory nuisance.

The Housing Act 1985 also gives considerable powers to deal with houses (which includes flats) that are 'unfit for human habitation'. Matters taken into account in determining whether or not a house is unfit are: state of repair; freedom from damp; natural lighting; ventilation; water supply; and drainage and sanitation.

In the case of **individual** unfit houses, a local housing authority can take action through a repair notice (carry out specified repairs to bring the dwelling up to habitable standard), a closure notice (cease using the dwelling for that purpose) or a demolition notice (demolish the dwelling). Local housing authorities can go further and can buy unfit houses or enter them to carry out the necessary work themselves and recover the cost from the owner. Before making a demolition or closing order, the local housing authority must give the owner a chance to give an undertaking to carry out the required work. When an order is made, the local housing authority has to re-house the occupier, unless alternative suitable accommodation is available, and may have to pay compensation to the occupier for disturbance.

Local housing authorities can also take action against unfit housing on an area, rather than individual, basis. They can undertake, or require to be carried out, improvements to an area, or if improvement is not a practical option at reasonable expense, they can demolish areas of unfit houses.

If the local housing authority believes that demolition is the best option, it can declare an area to be a *clearance area*. Such an area is declared where the houses, and/or the street layout, are considered dangerous to the health of the residents. The local housing authority has powers to acquire, if necessary by CPO, the land and buildings and arrange for their demolition and redevelopment. Before a clearance order can be made, the local housing authority must be in a position to re-house all the tenants and must have sufficient money to carry out the work. This approach has been extended by the Housing, Grants, Construction and Regeneration Act 1996 which enables local housing authorities to pay discretionary relocation grants to people displaced by clearance to help them to buy at least a part share in a new home in the same area.

Renewal areas

The Local Government and Housing Act 1989 provided for a local housing authority to declare an area to be a 'renewal area', where it was satisfied that the living conditions in the area, consisting primarily of housing, were unsatisfactory and that the renewal area approach was the most appropriate way of dealing with those conditions. The renewal area replaced the previous methods of taking action through Housing Action Areas and General Improvement Areas. The declared status of a renewal area usually last for 10 years, but can be terminated sooner.

There are conditions specified by the Secretary of State which must be satisfied before a renewal area can be declared: a minimum of 300 dwellings; a minimum 75% of the dwellings must be privately owned; and a minimum of 30% of the inhabitants must be in receipt of various social security benefits.

Once a renewal area has been declared, the local housing authority can acquire land by agreement or CPO and can provide new housing, improve existing housing, and dispose of improved or unimproved property to a suitable third party for future management. The local housing authority can carry out the works itself or provide grants, loans or guarantees to suitable third parties, including housing associations.

Grants for the improvement of private sector housing

These days, greater effort is made to avoid the disruption to existing communities caused by wholesale clearance of substandard housing — instead, if at all possible, grants are paid to bring the housing up to a reasonable standard. However, for some areas, wholesale clearance is still the only sensible solution.

Under the Housing, Grants, Construction and Regeneration Act 1996 (HGCR Act 1996), local housing authorities have the power to make grants for the purpose of securing the improvement of properties. Grants are now means-tested and some are *discretionary* (a council can give them if it has the money available) and some are *mandatory* (a council must give them to anyone who meets the requirements). The 1996 Act modified the earlier system of mandatory grants for the provision of 'standard amenities', because the level of mandatory grant demand could no longer be afforded. The only grant which remains mandatory is the *Disabled Facilities Grant*; all other grants are now discretionary.

There are now three types of grant payable, subject to limits prescribed by the Secretary of State:

- *Renovation Grant* for the improvement or repair of a dwelling or the provision of dwellings by the conversion of a house or other building;
- *Disabled Facilities Grant* for providing facilities for a disabled person in that person's home or in the common parts of a building containing that home;
- *HMO Grant* for the improvement of a house in multiple occupation (HMO) or the provision of such a house by the conversion of a house or other building.

Renovation Grants are discretionary and can be applied for by an owner or tenant who has lived in the dwelling for at least 3 years. These grants can only be paid for specific purposes such as: repairs to satisfy a statutory notice, the provision of basic facilities, adequate space heating and insulation and means of escape in case of fire.

Disabled Facilities Grants are mandatory and can be applied for by an owner or tenant. There is no minimum prior residence qualification requirement, but the expectation is that the disabled person will be resident in the dwelling for at least five years "or such shorter period as his health or other circumstances permit". Grants are payable for specific purposes such as: access to and within the dwelling, facilities for sleeping, cooking and washing, and measures for the safety of the disabled person.

HMO Grants are discretionary and are dealt with in a way similar to renovation grants.

Group repair schemes

The HGCR Act 1996 introduced the concept of group repair schemes. These are schemes prepared by the local housing authority (subject to the approval of the Secretary of State), for the purpose of carrying out external repairs to buildings included in the scheme or to make them stable or both. There are qualification requirements laid down by the Secretary of State which a building must satisfy before it can be included. Owners and tenants of buildings can apply to participate in the scheme. Works under the scheme can only be carried out if the participant agrees, because the participant has to contribute to the costs involved; up to 100% in some cases. There are conditions covering the repayment of any grant if the property is sold within five years or the nature of its occupation changes.

Home repair assistance

The HGCR Act 1996 also provided for a special kind of grant which may be paid where none of the other grants under that Act are payable — the *Home Repair Assistance Grant.*

The grant is only payable to owners and tenants who have lived in the dwelling for at least three years, although there are exceptions to this: for elderly, disabled or infirm people; for fire escape or protection works; or if the dwelling is in a renewal area. Applicants or their partner must be in receipt of a range of social security benefits. The arrangements are extended to people living on houseboats or mobile homes.

Houses in multiple occupation and overcrowding

The Housing Act 1985 gives local housing authorities the power to make a scheme requiring persons having control of an HMO to apply for registration by the authority. Registration can be refused or granted subject to conditions, including restrictions on the number of people who can be accommodated in the HMO. The local housing authority can require the reduction in the number of residents by serving an *Occupancy Direction* on the person in control of the HMO. Alternatively, the authority can serve an *Overcrowding Notice* fixing the maximum number of people who can be accommodated in each room or prohibiting the admission of new residents. The authority can also require the carrying out of works to make the HMO fit for the number of residents in it. Failure to register or comply with the various notices constitutes a criminal offence.

Private rented sector

The proportion of houses which are privately rented has declined dramatically in the last 30 years, although the trend has reversed slightly in the last few years. About 10% of houses are now privately rented, compared with 50% some 30 years ago and 8.6% in the late 1980s.

There are many reasons for this decline: the rise in owner occupation, slum clearance programmes, more council housing and the impact of rent control. In addition, legislation introduced by successive governments to protect tenants from exploitation and harassment may have discouraged some private landlords. Some people have argued the controls should be relaxed to allow the private landlord to return.

One of the declared aims of the Housing Act 1988 was the revitalisation of the private rented sector which it was hoped would be achieved through a reduction in rent controls and in statutory protection for all new private sector tenants (including housing association tenants) as of 1 April 1989. The recent slight reversal in the downward trend of the private rented sector is, presumably, due to this factor. The government introduced the Housing Act 1996 aimed at helping small landlords by simplifying the paperwork for assured shorthold tenancies (see later) and speeding action on rent arrears.

Rent assessment

Rent officers are appointed by the DETR to administer the Rent Acts and to explain them to the public. Previously the Rent Officer Service operated through 77 separate units based in local authorities — in two-tier areas, county councils were generally responsible for the service under agency arrangements, with support staff being appointed by them. However, in October 1999 its responsibilities were taken over by The *Rent Service* (TRS), a new executive agency of the DETR. Tenancies of most privately rented accommodation were *Protected Tenants,* with rents controlled and registered by Rent Officers and fixed for a period of two years, under the Rent Act 1977. There were also provisions giving Protected Tenants security of tenure.

However, the Housing Act 1980 introduced two new forms of tenancy, to supplement the existing *Protected* and *Statutory* forms of tenancy — the *Assured Tenancy* and the *Shorthold Tenancy*. After the commencement of the 1980 Act, no new protected tenancies could be created. The process of deregulation was continued by the Housing Act 1988 which introduced the *Assured Shorthold Tenancy.* The difference between an Assured Tenancy and an Assured Shorthold Tenancy was in the security of tenure which the tenant enjoyed. The technical procedure for setting up Assured Shorthold Tenancies proved difficult for some landlords, so the Housing Act 1996 took the process further. After the 1996 Act came into effect, all Assured Tenancies were automatically deemed to be Assured Shorthold Tenancies, unless certain exceptions applied; and the requirement for an initial fixed-term of 6 months was removed.

Apart from the introduction of market rents, several other key differences came with the introduction of Assured Shorthold tenancies:

- unlike lettings on Protected tenancies, the 1988 Act does not preclude the charging of premiums on Assured and Assured Shorthold Tenancies;
- rights of succession are significantly weaker, with Assured Shorthold tenants having no succession rights at all;
- the landlord's ability to regain possession is increased — in fact, once the requisite notice has been served by the landlord, possession is automatic and can be obtained through an accelerated paper procedure in the county court.

Is there a future for council housing?

The effects of the policies of previous Conservative Governments in stopping reinvestment by local housing authorities has finally taken its toll. In the *Financial Times* of 22 February 2000, a piece speculated that council housing as we know it may well have disappeared within ten years. The reason given for this was the £20bn cost of the backlog of repairs and maintenance in England, with little or no prospect of housing authorities being able to raise the necessary resources either locally or through the Government. This state of affairs had driven 25 local housing authorities to apply to transfer 300,000 council houses during 2001 to non-profit making social landlords, as the only means of solving their problem.

Jim Coulter, chief executive of the National Housing Federation was reported as saying: *"At this rate of progress, council housing as we currently understand it will have ceased to exist within a decade. It is clear that the State is getting out of the direct provision of housing and housing finance"*. For his part, John Perry, policy director of the Chartered Institute of Housing was reported as saying that council housing was *"at a turning point. Unless the government gives a clear indication soon of how the investment backlog will be tackled, councils and tenants are likely to vote with their feet"*. The real problem for the Government will be whether the private sector has the capacity or inclination to supply the necessary finance.

9 Education

Relevant bodies — Secretary of State — LEAs — governors — teachers — Ofsted and quality— TECs — types of educational institutions — organisation of the education system — surplus places — parental choice — National Curriculum — religious education — special educational needs — local management of schools — independent schools

The relevant bodies

In the field of education, the relevant bodies are:

- Central government departments: the Department for Education and Employment (DfEE) and its Secretary of State; the Scottish Executive; the Welsh Assembly; and the Northern Ireland Secretary/Executive.
- Quangos at national level, such as Ofsted and the Qualifications and Curriculum Authority.
- Local education authorities (LEAs): unitary authorities, London borough councils, metropolitan borough councils, county councils in two-tier areas and the Corporation of the City of London.
- Quangos at local level, such as the governing bodies of FE Colleges and the SACRE for religious education.
- The governing bodies of LEA-maintained schools at local level.

The devolved institutions in Scotland and Wales (and Northern Ireland?) have arrangements of their own — indeed, Scotland has always had a different education system, even before devolution. For the sake of simplicity, the remainder of this Chapter deals only with England — there may be similar arrangements in Scotland, Wales and Northern Ireland, details of which can be obtained from the relevant devolved institution.

The education system in England can be described in more than one way. After the historical context has been set, the approach adopted in this Chapter is to describe the main bodies involved in making the system work, then the various institutions involved and, finally, the various phases of education.

Historical commentary — up to the Education Act 1944

Before the reign of Victoria, educational facilities existed in sporadic parts of the country but were only available for the privileged few whose parents could afford to pay the fees at the schools or for the lucky few who lived in a town where a local wealthy benefactor had decided to endow a school.

Many of the small rural village primary schools which are still in operation today are 'voluntary' schools, but they did not start that way. They were originally provided by the local landowner or vicar who donated the land to a body of school trustees, under special statutory arrangements in the School Sites Act 1841 which encouraged such altruism. The statutory arrangements included a provision that the land and buildings would revert to the descendants of the original donor or to the present-day vicar, if the school ceased to be used as such. Site reversions under the School Sites Acts are still happening today, when small village schools are closed.

Schools of this type were primary or 'elementary' — nobody envisaged widespread secondary education in those days — and usually consisted of a single classroom for the full age range of 'scholars' and, sometimes, an associated teacher's house. Attendance at these schools was not always free — where fees were paid, they tended to be paid weekly at a fairly modest level and were used to pay for the schoolteacher employed by the school trustees. These schools have evolved into the voluntary schools which are an important component of the present-day system of LEA maintained schools. The point to make here is that there was no overall plan at that time for the provision of schools — they were set up because the local landowner or vicar felt it appropriate to do so, not because some other body planned it that way.

The first significant attempt at a more planned approach to school provision came with the Elementary Education Act 1870, which set up school boards in areas where there was a shortage of schools. Their members were directly elected and they could levy a rate (a similar system operates in parts of the US and Canada today) to meet the costs of building and maintaining new schools.

In 1901, the school boards were abolished by an Education Act which made elementary schools the responsibility of the county councils. If they wished, the county councils could also provide financial assistance to such secondary schools as then existed. The Education Act 1918 abolished fees in the elementary schools, raised the school leaving age to 14 and allowed LEAs to provide nursery schools for children under five years old.

The basis of the present education system — despite the changes brought about by some of the more recent Acts — was established by the Education Act 1944. The Secretary of State for Education was made responsible for education in England and Wales (now the Secretary of State for Wales and the Welsh Assembly have responsibility for education in that country). He was required *"to secure the effective execution by local authorities, under his control and direction, of national policy for providing a varied and comprehensive educational service in the area".*

Thus, the overall responsibility for the education service rested in Whitehall, with the 1944 Act making LEAs responsible for actually running and planning the schools in their area. LEAs were directly responsible — under national direction — for schools in the State or 'maintained' sector. It was this Act which set up the present system of primary, secondary and further education; made provision for child welfare and for children with disabilities; abolished fees in secondary schools; and raised the school leaving age to 15 (it went up to 16 in September 1972).

The comprehensive selection battle

Secondary education, and how the secondary schools should be organised, was the cause of much political argument in the 1960s and 1970s — over the issue of 'selecting' children at the age of 11. Children, at the point of their entry into the secondary stage of their education, had to sit a selection test — the '11-plus examination' — and their performance in this test determined whether they went to a 'grammar' school or to a 'secondary modern' school or to a 'technical' school.

In 1965, the then Labour government called for LEAs to make plans for converting their existing secondary schools into 'comprehensive' schools, which would take all children of secondary school age, thus eliminating selection at the age of eleven. In 1970, Margaret Thatcher, then Conservative Secretary of State for Education and Science told LEAs that they were no longer bound to do this. Labour returned to power in 1974 and their Education Act of 1976 required LEAs to submit schemes to introduce comprehensive education, if any of their schools were still selective. Then the Conservatives returned to power in 1979 and their Education Act 1979 repealed that part of the 1976 Act relating to the compulsion over comprehensive education. Hence, there are still grammar schools and selection tests in some parts of the country. As will be seen in a later section, New Labour have now embraced a form of 'selection' which they find acceptable.

The Education Reform Act 1988 and beyond

The late 80s also saw fundamental changes in the organisation and management of the education system — all aimed at a significant reduction in the role of the LEA, through the Education Reform Act 1988. The local community, particularly parents and businessmen, were encouraged to take part in running their local school; the rights of parents were strengthened; and governing bodies were expected to take over much more responsibility for the day-to-day running of their school.

Schools — that is, the governors and parents of a school — could choose to 'opt out' of the control of their LEA, and be funded, as a 'grant-maintained' (GM) school, directly by central government, which then recharged the cost to the LEA. The *National Curriculum* was introduced, with regular assessment of the performance of children. Further education and sixth form colleges were taken out of LEA control and transferred to a new further education sector funded directly by central government, through quangos — the *Further* and *Higher Education Funding Councils*. The Education Reform Act 1988 imposed a timetable and set out the changes that had to be made. However, the Act allowed LEAs discretion to move faster and to make wider changes than it prescribed. Therefore, across the country, there were variations according to the enthusiasm of individual LEAs for the changes.

If anyone doubted that there was a deliberate government policy of reducing the powers of LEAs, they had only to look at the Education Act 1993 (now the 1996 Act). This Act gave the Secretary of State the duty of promoting the education of the people of England and Wales, without mentioning the role of LEAs at all — a prophetic contrast with the equivalent 'LEA/central government partnership' provision which used to be in the Education Act 1944, described earlier. New, unelected quangos, the Funding Agency for Schools and the Schools Funding Council for Wales appeared (they have since disappeared). Where the number of GM schools in a LEA area reached certain levels, the Funding Agency would share, and could take over altogether, the school system planning and financing role of the LEA.

The Department for Education (DfE) was merged with the Department of Employment, to form a single Department for Education and Employment (DfEE). The employment responsibilities of this department are described in *Essential Central Government*. Because of the plethora of Education Acts since the 1944 Act, the statutory position was pulled together in a consolidation Act — the Education Act 1996, which ran to 583 sections and 40 schedules. However, that did not mark the end of legislative activity because an Education Act 1997 appeared but this only had 58 sections and 8 schedules. This was the last piece of Conservative Government legislation in the field of education. As soon as they came into office, New Labour produced the Education (Schools) Act 1997, bringing to an end the Assisted Places Scheme. The School Standards and Framework Act 1998 made significant changes to the education system (see the later section on the Act) and New Labour issued a number of consultative documents aimed at strengthening links between the DfEE and individual institutions, cutting out the LEAs.

The Secretary of State and the DfEE

The Secretary of State for Education and Employment is responsible for education in England. The DfEE is both the principal adviser on national policy and the principal agent for seeing that that policy is carried out by the range of bodies, including LEAs and school governing bodies, responsible for the various aspects of the education service.

Apart from determining disputes between the various bodies now involved in the education process, the Secretary of State can intervene to prevent the unreasonable use of power and can act in default where a particular body is failing to carry out its statutory responsibilities. The Secretary of State can also intervene where no properly constituted governing body exists. In the context of school places, the Secretary of State can direct LEAs and others to produce proposals to remove surplus places or to increase provision.

The amount of contact and communication between the DfEE and LEAs has diminished over recent years, largely due to the diffusion of educational responsibilities over a number of bodies, only one of which is the LEA.

Under the Education Act 1996, the Secretary of State may collect and publish information from all schools, including independent ones, which is relevant to parental choice — usually called 'league tables'. The information is published annually for each locality and includes public examination and national curriculum test results, truancy rates and the first destination of school leavers. The first publication in autumn 1992 (the power was introduced by the Education (Schools) Act 1992) caused quite a furore and attracted considerable interest. There were some mistakes which tended to spoil the effect the government hoped to achieve. However, despite the reservations of educational professionals about league tables, the response since 1992 shows that parents and public are interested in them and are increasingly used by the Secretary of State. The reservations included concerns about demographic factors and the uphill task facing schools with large numbers of 'disadvantaged' pupils in improving GCSE examination performance. However, even with these reservations league tables will continue to be a source of information as the process is refined and each year's figures are published.

Intervention and control by the Secretary of State, as a means of raising standards in schools, has increased significantly under New Labour. The process started with the *Fresh Start* initiative. Where a school fails an Ofsted inspection (see the later section on Ofsted and quality), it is placed under 'Special Measures' until its performance improved. If performance did not improve sufficiently during the following two years, the school would be closed and reopened (a 'fresh start') with new management and teaching staff. By March 2000, nine schools had been required to make such a 'fresh start'.

The Secretary of State then switched the emphasis to GCSE passes as recorded in the league tables. Speaking at an NUT conference on 1 March 2000, the Secretary of State, David Blunkett, stated that he wanted LEAs to consider a 'Fresh Start' for any school where less than 15% of its pupils had achieved 5 or more GCSE passes at Grade C or higher for the previous three years. With one eye on the 'demographic factors' point referred to above, in making his announcement, Mr Blunkett insisted that *"schools with the poorest GCSE results are found in leafy suburbs as well as in inner cities"*. He illustrated his point by mentioning that one under-performing school had only 6% of its pupils in receipt of free school meals (the usual indicator of disadvantage), less than one-third of the national average. On that basis, 100 schools were in the running for a 'Fresh Start'. The front runner was Gillingham Community College in Medway — not one of its 1999 GCSE entrants had attained a pass at Grade C or better.

At the same time, Mr Blunkett also suggested a much broader approach to general improvement in examination passes. He insisted that each school should ensure that at least 20% of its pupils achieved five or more such passes within four years. This benchmark would be raised to 25% by 2006. If that benchmark had been applied to the 1999 results, over 500 schools would have failed to meet it. Other initiatives would be the appointment of 'Superheads' to supervise a group of under-performing schools and the twinning of good and poor schools to raise standards. The Government's plans received a setback when three of its new 'Superheads' resigned in the space of two weeks later in March 2000.

As might be expected, views on Mr Blunkett's remarks were mixed. In the *Times* of 1 March 2000, the LGA was reported as saying that *"teachers were working hard to overcome pupils' social disadvantages and should be supported, not publicly humiliated"*. In the same piece, David Hart, General Secretary of the National Association of Head Teachers (NAHT) *"questioned the wisdom of the fresh start approach. 'I think that the Government needs to back off, because this will not motivate schools'"*. The views of the Secretary of State had to be rapidly toned down by others such as OFSTED, to limit the damage to morale likely to be caused by his remarks. It remains to be seen whether this new approach is any better at raising standards in schools.

Local education authorities

Education is the most expensive service provided by local government, but its relative size has diminished over recent years through the removal of various responsibilities from LEAs — and the influence of the LEA over what remains was further diminished by delegation of budgets to governors through local management of schools (LMS).

The statutory duty on an LEA to appoint an Education Committee was lifted by the Education Act 1993. However, most LEAs continue to appoint an Education Committee, which in turn may set up a number of subcommittees. The Education Committee will usually include people other than councillors — and must include representatives of the churches associated with the local voluntary schools; other people, such as teachers, usually feature on education committees, but they are optional. New Labour put forward proposals that representatives of parents should also be appointed to Education Committees. The way in which education is handled within the local education authority structure will change markedly as a result of the introduction of the executive models envisaged by the Local Government Bill referred to in an earlier Chapter.

Similarly, until recently, every LEA had to appoint a chief education officer (they have a variety of titles). Up to 1974, the Secretary of State had the power to veto any name on a short list of candidates for a chief education officer post. After 1974, the appointment could be made without consulting the Secretary of State. Now, LEAs are no longer obliged to appoint a chief education officer, although almost all LEAs still do so, because of the importance of the service for the LEA.

The principal responsibility of an LEA is to provide and maintain premises for primary and secondary education, and to provide certain adult further education and youth services. The LEA must also provide funding to the governors of the LMS schools, and ensure that all schools are following the National Curriculum. Therefore, although in many matters of day-to-day detail, LEAs have lost power, they still play a significant part in the local administration of a national education system.

However, the LEA role continues to be increasingly subordinate to the Secretary of State. The School Standards and Framework Act 1998 introduced a requirement for every LEA to prepare an Education Development Plan (EDP), setting out the LEA's proposals for developing the provision of education in its area by raising standards and improving performance in schools. The EDP has to be submitted to the Secretary of State for approval.

Governors

The LEA makes, after consultation with governing bodies, the Instruments and Articles of Government for each school which it maintains. The Instrument of Government sets out the composition of the governing body and how its meetings are to be conducted; the Instrument is amended if the number of pupils alters significantly, since the number of pupils on the school roll determine the size and composition of the governing body. The Articles of Government define the powers of the governing body and the headteacher and the extent of delegation from the LEA.

The transfer of responsibilities from LEAs to governors, through LMS, obviously made governing bodies much more important. The Education Act 1986 also changed the composition of governing bodies to reduce the representation of the LEA and to create more places for parents and the local business communities. Head teachers can also choose be a member of their school's governing body.

Prior to the School Standards and Framework Act 1998 (SSFA 1998), the size of the governing body depended upon the number of pupils in the school, but the governing body was always composed of four groups — parents, LEA, teacher and co-opted.

The number of parents and LEA representatives was always the same and co-opted governors were always the largest single group. For example, for a county school with 300 to 599 pupils, there would be four parents (elected by the parents), four LEA representatives, one teacher (elected by the staff) and five co-opted governors.

In a voluntary controlled or aided school there were usually 'foundation' governors, representing the church or other body associated with the school. In some areas, too, district and parish councils inherited a seat on the governing body of some schools. In each case, the co-opted membership was correspondingly reduced.

The composition of school governing bodies was changed by the SSFA 1998 — increasing the number of parents on school governing bodies. The SSFA 1998 also re-categorised schools as community, foundation, voluntary aided, voluntary controlled, community special and foundation special schools. These changes are described in more detail in a later section of this Chapter.

The LEA, however, still maintains a close involvement with each school through its nominees, who are appointed for a four-year term. LEAs sometimes advertise for people willing to become governors as their nominees and since final selection may well be on a party-political basis, the process can sometimes be controversial.

Parent governors are, however, elected for a four year term by the parents of registered pupils at the school. Teacher governors are also elected for a four year term by and from the teachers at the school. Parent governors whose children leave the school can remain on the body for the remainder of the four year term; teachers who leave, cannot remain.

Co-opted governors are chosen by the other governors, who must ensure that the local business community is adequately represented. Sometimes the local district or parish council also has a right to appoint governors, and if so, the number of co-opted governors is correspondingly reduced.

Despite the wider responsibilities of governors, they still look to their LEA for guidance and advice, though the degree of control by an LEA has been much diminished. The LEAs will still retain links with governors, for whom, for example, training courses will be run. The governors also have to provide their LEA with regular information about their spending, and can seek help and advice. In the last resort, the LEA can step in and withdraw the LMS powers, although the LEA would be expected to restore LMS status to the governors as soon as possible.

As they have to make important managerial decisions, governors need to be accountable and they are obliged to report to their parents through an annual report and meeting. The annual meeting is an important event in the school calendar. All parents of registered pupils must be invited, and the head teacher has the right to attend, whether a governor or not. The governors are responsible for conducting the meeting and they may choose to invite others, including the press, but there is no right of press attendance. The meeting is to discuss the governors' annual report to parents, and resolutions can be passed, provided that there are 20% of parents present. The resolutions have to be considered by the governors or passed to the LEA if the subject matter is its responsibility — and a report must be made on the issue the following year.

Governors also now have a role in the discipline of the school, although the primary statutory responsibility is the head teacher's. The governors have the power to draw up a statement of general principles, and the head teacher must take these into account when reaching decisions on individual pupils. Only the head teacher has the power to exclude a pupil, but the governors and the LEA have to be informed. The governors can direct the head teacher to reinstate the pupil, and so can the LEA, although only after consulting the governors. There are rights of appeal against these decisions. The governors also have to inform the LEA about pupils who do not attend regularly.

Funding Agency for Schools — ave atque vale

The Funding Agency for Schools came — and then went! The Conservative Government's Education Act 1993 established a new *Funding Agency for Schools* in England, and a similar body for Wales, which took over some of the responsibilities of the DfE and some from LEAs. The Agency was a quango and had between 10 and 15 members appointed by the Secretary of State. Initially, the role of the Agency was to distribute grant to grant-maintained (GM) schools, but then gradually extended its role to take over responsibility for the rationalisation of places in GM schools and for securing sufficient school places over the whole of the State sector. When developed on these lines, the Agency was intended to be rather like an LEA with enhanced powers, but fully controlled by the Government.

The plan was that where more than 10% of primary or secondary pupils in an LEA area were at GM schools, then the LEA and the Agency would have had shared responsibility for securing sufficient places. This could, if past experience of shared functions was anything to go by, have been a source of considerable friction. When 75% of those pupils were at GM schools, then the Funding Agency would have taken over full responsibility and the LEA would have lost its role in the organisation of schools in its area. There were similar provisions for special schools that opted out, with the Agency and the LEA sharing responsibility for special educational provision or, if the 75% point was reached, the LEA losing its responsibility altogether.

These provisions represented a considerable diminution in the powers of an LEA — but the danger never materialised because with the abolition of GM schools (see later), the Funding Agency for Schools also disappeared, before it could make any inroads into the LEA area of responsibility.

Training and Enterprise Councils — QUANGOS.

The Training and Enterprise Councils (TECs) are quangos responsible for providing training schemes to meet local needs; for encouraging schools to bridge the gap between the world of school and the world of work; and for helping new businesses. They influence schools and further education institutions. The TECs usually have 15 members, of which 13 are prominent businessmen, and the remainder include a leading trade unionist, a chief executive and a chief education officer.

Teachers

The initial training of teachers is undertaken in a variety of higher education institutions, on courses funded by an executive agency of the DfEE, the *Teacher Training Agency*. Apart from funding higher education institutions, the Teacher Training Agency provides information and advice aimed at promoting teaching as a career.

Teachers' salaries are fixed at national level by the government but they are employed by LEAs/governors of voluntary aided schools. The School Teachers' Pay and Conditions Act 1991 established new national negotiating machinery after a long period of disputes and settlements imposed by the government. There is a review body, appointed by the Prime Minister, that reports to the Secretary of State who may give it directions to which it must have regard, including financial considerations, and the date by which it must report. A teacher's contract of employment cannot include any terms other than those specified in an order of the Secretary of State.

New Labour, as part of its effort to improve standards in schools, also made new arrangements for improving the quality of the teaching force. The Teaching and Higher Education Act 1998 created a new General Teaching Council (GTC) for England (with a parallel body for Wales), a quango appointed by the Secretary of State. The remit of the GTC included: standards of teaching and teacher conduct; the role of the teaching profession; the training, recruitment, career development and performance management of teachers; and medical fitness to teach. The 1998 Act also brought those institutions involved in teacher training into a new inspection regime.

One of the more significant features of the 1998 Act was to formalise and transfer some aspects of teacher competence and discipline from the local employment context (LEA and school governors) to a new national context under the GTC. The GTC deals with cases of unacceptable professional conduct, serious professional incompetence or conviction of a relevant criminal offence. The process involves the use of a variety of orders — conditional registration, suspension and prohibition — with appeals to the High Court. The context for the GTC was not only teacher competence but also child protection. For many years the DfEE had maintained a non-statutory list of people regarded as unsuitable for teaching — the so-called 'List 99' — to which LEAs and governors could refer before making an appointment (if they remembered to do so).

The arrangements under the Child Protection Act 1999 (see the Chapter on *Personal Social Services*) for a statutory national list also extended to prospective teachers.

Types of schools — pre School Standards and Framework Act 1998

For a full appreciation of the system of school classification introduced by the SSFA 1998, it is useful to understand the categorisation system in operation prior to the Act, especially since the old titles will probably still be referred to for some time. At times, the names used to describe schools and colleges can be confusing, but the picture can make sense, if the issue is approached systematically, by considering the different types of educational institution and, then, how they are organised.

In overall terms, schools can be in the private sector or State sector. Schools in the private sector are usually called 'independent' or even 'public', charge tuition fees and are usually selective. They had no connection with LEAs and that is still the case after SSFA 1998.

The schools in the State sector (not private or independent schools) were usually referred to as 'maintained' — either maintained by the LEA or grant-maintained directly by central government. LEA maintained schools could be 'county' schools, or 'voluntary' schools, or 'special' schools.

County schools were those established by the LEA itself, by initially providing and retaining the ownership of the school site and buildings. The word 'county' more often than not appeared in the school's name, especially if it was a primary school. However, it should be appreciated that 'county' was a term of art and 'county' schools occurred throughout England and Wales, not just in the shire counties.

There were three types of *voluntary school*: 'controlled', 'aided', or 'special agreement'. The essential feature of the voluntary school part of the LEA-maintained sector was that although the LEA now met the running costs of the voluntary schools in its area, it had not provided the original land or buildings, the ownership of which remained vested in the school's trustees, who were separate from the school governing body.

Voluntary schools were usually established in the way described earlier in the historical commentary section, but have since been absorbed into the State sector. The school trustees still retained the ownership of the immediate school site and buildings, although the LEA might later have provided playing fields for the school and, in that case, may have retained ownership of those playing fields. The essential difference between controlled and aided voluntary schools was the degree of responsibility and influence which the LEA had over the school — the LEA had more influence over a controlled school than an aided one.

Voluntary Controlled schools were usually connected with the Church of England or the Free Churches — although sometimes a local landowner or charitable body would have established the school, as explained earlier. In most cases, there would also have been close links with the relevant church with, for example, church representatives on the governing body, and the relevant local minister or vicar maintaining a working association with the school. The school might also have had historic connections such as celebrating the original founders, or receiving income from a trust. The word 'controlled' usually appeared in the names of such schools. The LEA met all of the school's running costs, employed the teachers, paid for the internal and external repairs and, consequently, had slightly greater representation on the governing body than on an aided school. Religious education was usually according to the *Agreed Syllabus* (which applied in county schools) or the school's trust deed, if there was one.

In the case of *Voluntary Aided* schools, as their name implied, the influence which the LEA exerted in their running was rather less than their voluntary controlled counterparts. The word 'aided' also usually appeared in the name, and although there were many Church of England aided schools, the majority were Roman Catholic, since that church made separate arrangements when its voluntary schools were absorbed into the State sector. The LEA paid the teachers' salaries, although the teachers were technically employed by the school governing body; the LEA paid for the internal repairs, while the school governors met the cost of external and major repairs and improvements which were partly financed by grants from the DfEE, with the governors (in reality the relevant church authorities) paying 15% of the cost. The LEA paid all the other running costs. The composition of the governing bodies reflected the increased involvement of the church and there was more emphasis on religious education for the pupils in accordance with the tenets of the relevant church, rather than according to the Agreed Syllabus.

Voluntary Special Agreement schools were fairly rare. They were only established where a particular set of circumstances made the usual controlled or aided type of voluntary school inappropriate — special agreement schools were established as a joint Church of England/Free Churches project. The Special Agreement establishing the school defined the relative responsibilities of the LEA for meeting the school's running costs.

Special schools were schools provided specifically to meet the needs of children with mental and/or physical disabilities, or some form of learning disability. In recent years, much had been done to integrate such youngsters, so far as is possible, into their local neighbourhood school. With children who were very ill or frail, the special educational provision which they needed might be more appropriately provided at home or in hospital.

Grant maintained (GM) *schools* were an addition to the types of schools and resulted from the Conservative Government Education Reform Act 1988, which provided the opportunity for the governors and parents of an LEA school to apply to the Secretary of State for permission to 'opt out' of the control of their LEA. The importance of such a move was the impact which it would have on other schools in the areas — would a GM school attract their best pupils, for example? GM schools continued to offer free education but were funded directly from central government. The stated intention of the Conservative Government was to widen the choice for parents within the state system and, by introducing an element of competition to attract pupils, to improve standards. Any state school with at least 300 pupils could apply to 'opt out' and become a GM school. Special schools which had delegated management, under the Education Act 1993 (see later), could ballot for GM status.

The number of GM schools fell well short of the Conservative Government's original target. Some applications for GM status were made by schools seeking to avoid the consequences of closure or amalgamation proposals made by the LEA to remove surplus school places, as required by the Secretary of State. Some of the early decisions of the Secretary of State in approving GM status betrayed a greater interest in increasing the number of GM schools, than in removing surplus places — viewed as ironic by the LEA involved. Other schools saw that GM schools enjoyed relatively generous (and unfair) capital allocations from the government — much more generous than the government allocated for LEA maintained schools. Even the inducement of generous capital allocations did not increase the number of new applications for GM status, so the Conservative Government introduced a new requirement upon governing bodies to discuss, each year, holding a parental ballot about opting out. Even that did not increase the rate of GM applications to any significant extent.

The formal application to the Secretary of State for GM status needed the support of a majority of parents eligible to vote in a secret ballot. The Secretary of State then had to decide if the school had a secure future and that the governors and the head and the staff were competent to run it. Skegness Grammar was among the first to be granted permission to opt out. If opting out was approved, then ownership of the school transferred from the LEA to the school governors. In the case of the voluntary schools, however, the churches or trusts involved retained site ownership, but like the other GM schools, it was the governing body, working closely with the head teacher, which actually managed the school, receiving direct from the Secretary of State a grant equivalent to the amount which the LEA would have spent on its running costs.

All local parents were able to apply for a place at a GM school, and each school decided how it allocated places if it was over-subscribed. Parents retained a right, as with LEA schools, of appeal to an independent committee against a refusal of admission. The governors had to account to the Secretary of State and to parents for their management of the school, and the ultimate sanction was the Secretary of State withdrawing the grant. If ever such cases occurred, pupils at the school would once again become the responsibility of the LEA.

The arrival of the New Labour Government marked the end of any new GM schools, with their status being altered by the SSFA 1998, as explained in the next section.

Types of schools — after the School Standards and Framework Act 1998

The SSFA 1998 was a major piece of legislation (145 sections and 32 schedules) and had several purposes, arising out of the White Paper, *Excellence in Schools,* which preceded it. This section is about the consequences of the SSFA 1998 for the way in which schools are categorised. The other aspects of SSFA 1998 are dealt with elsewhere in this Chapter.

The SSFA 1998 required schools to be re-categorised as 'community', 'foundation', 'voluntary aided', 'voluntary controlled', 'community special' or 'foundation special', following the following principles:

old	new
County	Community
Controlled	Voluntary Controlled
Aided	Voluntary Aided
Special Agreement	Voluntary Aided
Maintained Special	Community Special
GM (previously county/controlled)	Foundation
GM (established by Funding Agency)	Foundation
GM (previously aided/special agreement)	Voluntary Aided
GM (established by promoters)	Voluntary Aided
GM Special	Foundation Special

The governing body of a GM school could accept the SSFA 1998 allocation or could opt, after balloting the parents, to apply to the Secretary of State for a different category.

The relative responsibilities of the LEA and the governors, as described in the previous section, remained unchanged by the SSFA 1998 — with the exception of foundation schools, which were a new category. The allocation of responsibilities between the LEA and the governors of a foundation school is similar to that for community and voluntary controlled schools — reference to the table above demonstrates that this merely reflects the position before the school concerned obtained GM status.

City Technology Colleges

Again, with a belief that standards of education would improve with wider choice, the Conservative Government introduced in October 1986 an experiment with a new kind of secondary school called a *city technology college* (CTC). Kingshurst, Birmingham was first, followed by one in Nottingham. Conceived specifically for urban areas, the CTCs are open to all pupils, and have an emphasis on technology, science and mathematics. Computer technology figures prominently and courses are designed to fit youngsters with the skills that industry requires. The controlling bodies define their own admission policies and select those pupils likely to take full advantage of science and technology.

That is why they are run by bodies closely linked to industry and commerce. Like GM schools used to be, they are independent of the LEAs and receive their running costs directly from central government, capital costs being shared between government and private sponsors (eg. Dixons CTC in Bradford). This initiative also turned out below the government's expectations — commerce and industry were less willing to put up the money than the government had hoped — with the result that most of the CTCs were financed largely by the government. At the end of March 2000 there were 15 CTCs.

Sixth Form Colleges and FE Colleges

Both sixth form colleges and further education colleges used to be maintained by LEAs. Sixth form colleges are schools providing secondary education for pupils in the 16 to 19 age range. FE colleges are establishments providing further education for students over the age of 19. FE colleges also provide a range of 'leisure occupation' courses adults. Due to changes brought about by the Conservative Government, all sixth form colleges and FE colleges were removed from LEAs, to become self-governing corporations.

Selection, Grammar Schools, Specialist Schools and Academies

The SSFA 1998 made provision for increasing the selection of pupils — rather odd, one might think, for a Labour government to do, given the antipathy of previous Labour governments to the issue and their enthusiasm for complete coverage of comprehensive education. Post-16 selection (for admission to the sixth-form) has never been an issue, since education after that age is voluntary.

The 166 maintained secondary schools still operating some form of selection (by ability or aptitude) at the beginning of the 1997/1998 school year could continue to do so and were designated as 'grammar schools'. New Labour decided that any decision to make a change in the character of the admission arrangements those grammar schools should be put in the hands of the **relevant** parents, rather than the Secretary of State, following a ballot.

At the beginning of 2000, grammar schools existed in Ripon, the London Boroughs of Barnet and Sutton, Birmingham, Trafford and Kent. Two types of ballot are involved, an 'area ballot' (involving all parents resident in a predefined area) or a 'feeder school ballot' (involving parents of children in those schools (State or private) which have transferred at least five pupils to the grammar school over the previous three years). The type of ballot depends upon the extent to which the grammar school(s) impact on the local education system: area ballots would be appropriate in Trafford, Kent and Sutton, where the impact is total; feeder school ballots would be appropriate in Ripon, Barnet and Birmingham, where the impact is partial. A ballot can be petitioned by at least 20% of the relevant parents. The Secretary of State has designated that ballots will be administered by Electoral Reform (Ballot Services) Ltd (the commercial arm of the Electoral Reform Society) and interested parties are expected to comply with the Ballot Information Code (on pain of the ballot being declared void if non-compliant actions have affected the result). A ballot cannot be re-run for at least five years.

The first ballot under the SSFA 1998 took place in Ripon — a feeder school ballot in respect of the future of one grammar school, Ripon Grammar School, said to have been founded in 1555. Ripon was apparently chosen by CASE (Campaign for State Education) as a starting point because the number of petition signatures for a feeder school ballot there was quite modest (587) — an area ballot in Kent, covering the whole county, would need 45,959 signatures. In the event, when the result of the ballot was declared on 10 March 2000, the relevant parents who voted in the ballot decided by a two-thirds majority that the Ripon Grammar school should remain unchanged. CASE complained about the feeder school ballot system but it is unlikely that the Government would be willing to change it. It remains to be seen whether the Ripon experience causes CASE to reconsider its next target, which is apparently Barnet where 7,209 signatures are needed for a feeder school ballot there.

The 1998 Act introduced the concept of 'permitted selection' which could be used by schools other than grammar schools — such schools would be called 'specialist schools' (not to be confused with special schools for pupils with special educational needs). The 1998 Act drew a distinction between 'selection by ability' and 'selection by aptitude'. Where a school is regarded as having a specialism for a specific subject, up to 10% of that school's pupil intake can be selected by their aptitude for that particular subject.

In case the distinction between the two forms of selection is too subtle to be immediately obvious, the then Minister for School Standards, Mr Byers, explained it all to the Commons Standing Committee examining the SSFA 1998 when it was still a Bill: *"Ability is what a child has already achieved. Aptitude is natural talent and interest that a child has in a specific subject: in other words, the potential to develop a skill or talent. That is the distinction in the Bill. I am pleased to put that on record. With ability, we are talking of where a child is already. With aptitude, we are talking of a child's scope for development in the future — an innate talent in a particular area"*. At the end of March 2000 there were reported to be 480 specialist schools.

The grammar and specialist schools will now be joined by 'academies', announced by David Blunkett in mid-March 2000. The new 'academies' would be established in partnership with private business, the churches and charities — not unlike the CTCs to which New Labour objected when in Opposition; indeed, New Labour will use the Conservatives' CTC legislation to set up the academies. Their announcement was seen by some commentators as an admission of the failure of the 'Fresh Start' initiative — three 'Superheads' had resigned in the two weeks before the announcement. The academies would be similar to the US Charter Schools and would be expected to develop their own approaches to governance, management, teaching and the curriculum, specialising in at least one curriculum area. The Government envisages that the new academies will appear in the larger cities; less than ten initially but more, if the demand is there.

The organisation of the education system

The organisation of the education system varies from area to area, but the phases are broadly: primary; secondary; further/tertiary; and higher. Although the LEA no longer has responsibility for further/tertiary and higher education, it still retains responsibility for deciding how primary and secondary education is to be delivered in its area — usually this aspect is referred to as school 'organisation'.

Primary phase

The primary phase is delivered through primary schools (five to 11 year olds); or infant schools (five to seven) followed by junior schools (seven to 11). In some areas, there are 'first' schools (five to eight or nine) and 'middle' schools (eight or nine to 12 or 13). Middle schools can be classified as primary or secondary schools. There is no selection in the primary phase.

The SSFA 1998 enabled the Secretary of State to limit infant classes on a national basis to 30 or less. Each LEA was required to produce plans of how it proposed to reduce infant classes of the schools it maintained to bring them within the new limit. The additional cost of reducing class sizes (employing more staff and possibly more accommodation) would be met through a specific grant for that purpose.

Also, in some areas, there may be nursery **schools** (or, alternatively, nursery **classes** in primary or infant schools) for children under five. The 1944 Act expected there to be an expansion of nursery education, but did not make it compulsory, and therefore its provision is spread unevenly. Some local education authorities expanded their provision by adding nursery classes to existing primary or infant schools.

The New Labour Government announced its planned extension of nursery education so that it would be available for all, including a voucher system. Although this was laudable, it threatened to have unintended consequences, with the complete collapse of the childminding sector, as parents sought to move their children to free nursery education, instead. The government was obliged to announce the injection of £1m into the sector to keep pre-schools and playgroups going until the Working Families Tax Credit (see *Essential Central Government*) came into effect in October 1999. In the event, the voucher system was never introduced and instead the SSFA 1998 made provision for the general expansion of 'early years provision' — nursery education and childcare places, achieved through partnerships between LEAs and the private and voluntary sectors. The government was able to announce that, by January 1999, 98% of four year olds were in early years provision, with the planned expansion in the number of three year olds in such provision to 66%, by 2002. The *Early Years Development and Childcare Partnerships* which gave registered providers access to Nursery Education Grants, were initiated through the *Early Years Development and Childcare Plan* prepared by each LEA for approval by the Secretary of State.

Secondary phase

The secondary phase runs from 11 or 13 to 16 or 19. In some areas, selection may still remain for admission to the secondary phase: grammar schools for those who pass a selection test, or secondary modern/technical schools for the remainder. In the absence of selection, the secondary phase involves comprehensive schools to which the pupils transfer at 11 or 13. All secondary schools, selective or comprehensive, can cater for pupils through to 16 or 19, or they can end at 16.

Some secondary schools will offer some form of 'community education' provision (basic further and leisure occupation education) for their surrounding adult population in the evenings (but sometimes during the day as well). To confuse matters, such schools will usually call themselves 'community college' or 'college'. In spite of their modified title, they are still, in essence, secondary schools.

In some areas, post-16 studies for secondary pupils are provided by sixth form colleges, or by tertiary colleges, which have come about through a merging of local comprehensive sixth forms and part or whole of a college of further education. Such colleges are no longer maintained by LEAs.

Further education

LEAs used to be responsible for a variety of further education colleges leading to recognised vocational or professional examinations and leisure interests. Their powers were severely curtailed by the Further and Higher Education Act 1992 which removed further education and sixth form colleges out of LEA control to new Funding Councils, directly funded by central government. LEAs retain their responsibilities for certain kinds of **non-advanced** further education by funding courses in FE Colleges, adult centres and schools.

Higher education

Colleges or polytechnics offering degree courses have not been run by LEAs since 1987 and, as a result of the Further and Higher Education Act 1992, the funding distinction between universities, polytechnics and colleges was abolished and all of these institutions are funded by the Higher Education Funding Council.

Institutions other than the then existing universities were allowed to include the word 'university' in their title, subject to Privy Council approval, and the Secretary of State could extend to such institutions the right to award their own degrees — many of the larger polytechnics followed this course of action.

National Curriculum

The National Curriculum was another important requirement in the Education Reform Act 1988, causing a great deal of controversy — especially with the extension of the concept of school performance league tables.

The move to a national curriculum was based upon a belief that British pupils were under-achieving; that teachers' expectations of their pupils were too low; and that the curriculum was too narrow. Statistics were produced to show that pupils and their parents, when faced with choices, gave up important subjects like modern languages and, particularly in the case of girls, the physical sciences.

The introduction of a national curriculum was intended to guarantee that a broad and balanced education was provided everywhere, and by setting standards to be reached and monitoring progress, to raise the standard of education. The curriculum comprises three 'core' subjects (English, mathematics and science) and seven 'foundation' subjects (history, geography, technology, a modern foreign language (in secondary schools), art, music and physical education).

For these subjects, the government issued programmes of study and attainment targets. Pupils are tested in the core subjects and some of the foundation subjects at the ages of 7, 11, 14 and 16. Results of these tests are published. The government had to simplify both the national curriculum and the tests, because they were too burdensome. For primary school pupils there is now a baseline assessment scheme. The national curriculum is overseen by the *Qualifications and Curriculum Authority* which superseded the School Curriculum and Assessment Authority and the National Council for Vocational Qualifications.

Religious education is to be provided for all pupils in State schools, with daily collective worship for all pupils — though parents can opt to withdraw their children from this.

Each LEA has to publish a policy statement on the curriculum being followed in its schools, which the governors may adopt or modify. However, the headteacher will have to ensure that the pupils' curriculum is in line with the LEA's general policy —

which in many areas will be the national curriculum in a largely unaltered form, with some additional subjects. The non-biological aspect of sex education, however, is a matter for the governors alone, and they have to publish a statement on this.

The Secretary of State can waive or modify the national curriculum in relation to a particular school, to permit experiments or development work. A headteacher is allowed to suspend the requirements of the national curriculum to help a particular pupil with learning difficulties. In such cases, the parents, the LEA and the governors must be informed. Parents have a right to appeal against this to the governors and if still dissatisfied, the LEA.

School Organisation

The government and the Audit Commission will, from time to time, suggest that the LEA remove surplus places in the local primary/secondary system. This reduction can be achieved in a number of ways which might involve the complete closure or amalgamation of schools. To achieve any change along these lines, the LEA has to follow a formal statutory process and publish its proposals and undertake a wide public consultation exercise. Prior to the SSFA 1998, if there are any objections to the LEA proposals, the proposals were referred to the Secretary of State for final decision.

The Secretary of State no longer takes the final decision in disputes over school reorganisations. Instead, the SSFA 1998 provided a new process. The LEA is now under a duty to prepare a School Organisation Plan (this should not be confused with the Education Development Plan) which has to be endorsed by a local School Organisation Committee and an Adjudicator appointed by the Secretary of State. The School Organisation Committee is a local quango consisting of representatives of the LEA, the Church of England and the Roman Catholic Church (reflecting the interests of their voluntary schools). The Committee not only approves the Plan but also determines any reorganisation proposals to which objections have been made. The voting system in the Committee is odd — block and unanimous votes — and the Adjudicator is the person who cuts the Gordian Knot. When the SSFA 1998 was still a Bill, Frances Rafferty outlined these proposals in an article in the *TES* for 27 February 1998, under the headline *"Four-tier 'monster' fear"*.

Parental choice and school admissions

'Parental choice' was one of the flagship education reforms introduced by the Conservative Government. The pity was that 'parental choice' was not really that at all. In its propaganda at the time, the government implied that parents had the right to send their child to whatever school they chose — 'parental choice'. In fact, parental rights were limited to the right to express a **preference** for a place at the school of their choice and then a right of appeal if their expressed preference was denied. Many parents were understandably somewhat disillusioned when they discovered the true position. The whole admission process is now to be conducted in compliance with a national Code of Practice issued by the Secretary of State under the SSFA 1998 (the first version came into force in July 1999).

The LEA decides, according to national guidelines, the number of the pupils to be admitted to the community and voluntary controlled schools which it maintains; the governing body of each foundation or voluntary aided school does the same for its own school. In this context, the LEA or governing body (as the case may be) is known as 'the admission authority' in respect of the school involved.

Each year, the admission authority must publish its admission arrangements. These admission arrangements explain to parents how to go about expressing a preference for a place at the school of their choice; how any applications for oversubscribed schools will be prioritised (usually called 'admission criteria'); and how parents can appeal to an independent appeal panel, if their application is unsuccessful. The admission arrangements have to be drawn up in consultation with other interested parties (LEA and governors), with any objections or failure to agree being determined by an Adjudicator appointed by the Secretary of State.

The admission authority must comply with the parental preference unless refusal can be justified on certain grounds: admission would prejudice the provision of efficient education or the efficient use of resources; admission would reduce the religious character of a foundation or voluntary aided school; the school is permitted to operate a selection process; or the school is reducing its infant classes to meet the national limit. In addition, the SSFA 1998 introduced an additional reason for refusal — that, during the previous two years, the child had been permanently excluded from two or more schools. Arguments about the efficient use of resources derive from the fact that schools cannot be expanded or contracted instantly and teachers cannot be moved around from school to school at little or no notice, just to meet parental demand for places from one year to the next.

Ofsted and quality

The inspection of schools has always been important and, until 1992 was carried out by inspectors employed in Her Majesty's Inspectorate and by the local inspection and advisory staff of the LEA. That system was changed by the Education (Schools) Act 1992 (now the School Inspections Act 1996), which established a new *Her Majesty's Chief Inspector of Schools for England* (HMCIS) (and a similar appointment for Wales linked to the Welsh equivalent to Ofsted, *Estyn*) as head of a new statutory *Office for Standards in Education* (Ofsted). Inspections are now carried by Ofsted through its staff (still probably referred to as HM Inspectors of Schools) or by contracting with teams of suitable people registered by the Chief Inspector. LEAs can continue to inspect their schools, but many find it difficult to do so out of the retained part of the LMS budget not delegated to schools.

Ofsted was required to complete the first round of inspections within four years, with subsequent inspections every six years, except for schools where the inspection raised concerns. Inspectors follow a standard *Framework for Inspection* and the detailed guidance in Ofsted's *Handbooks of Inspection*. The summary reports produced by the inspection team have to be considered by the governing body, which has to produce an *Action Plan* within 40 working days — in effect the school's response to the inspection report. The summary report and the action plan are open to public inspection. Sometimes, the LEA may also be required to produce its own Action Plan addressing any issues over which it has control.

Where an Ofsted inspection report determines that the school is *'failing to give its pupils an acceptable standard of education'* (usually referred to as a 'failing' school) the school concerned can be deemed to be *'in need of Special Measures'*. In such a case, the school's Action Plan has to be submitted to the Secretary of State and its performance is then closely monitored by Ofsted. If the school shows no improvement to an acceptable standard within two years, it will, in all probability, be dealt with under the *Fresh Start* initiative described in the earlier section on the Secretary of State. Ofsted inspections can now report 'serious weaknesses', even though the general standard of education provided by the school is otherwise thought to be acceptable.

The Education Act 1997 extended the concept of inspections so that LEAs, as well as schools, could be inspected by Ofsted. The subject of the inspection is the performance of the LEA in discharging its responsibilities for the education of pupils of compulsory school age in its maintained schools. Inspections can also be carried out by Ofsted in collaboration with the Audit Commission. The report of the inspection is published and the LEA has to produce a report for the Secretary of State on any action it proposes to take to meet any criticisms in the report.

Ofsted's sphere of influence is set to expand. The Care Standards Bill (see the Chapter on *Social Services* for a description of the remainder of the Bill) proposes to transfer the existing responsibilities of local authorities for the regulation of childminding and day care provision. In England, those responsibilities will be transferred to HMCIS under a new arm of Ofsted, covering childcare and early years education. In Wales, these responsibilities will be transferred to a new regulatory body established as part of the National Assembly for Wales, although Estyn will continue to inspect early years education.

The kinds of action which can be taken to raise standards in schools was extended by SSFA 1998, implementing a number of ideas in the 1997 White Paper *'Excellence in Schools'* The SSFA 1998 included limits on the maximum size of infant classes in maintained schools. The Act also introduced the concept of *Education Action Zones* (EAZ), which are partnerships between clusters of schools (up to 20, but not necessarily all of the schools in an area), businesses, parents and LEAs aimed at improving education standards in specific problem areas. A local *Education Action Forum* would provide the impetus for the partnership.

The Secretary of State approves the EAZ bids, some of which have been very imaginative. The incentive for schools to participate in this initiative is the fact that EAZ status brings with it the promise of an extra £500,000 to £750,000 a year for the next three years — with a possible extension of a further two years. Nobody is sure what is going to happen when the extra money stops. However, participation by business was not as great as the New Labour Government hoped (rather like the Conservative Government's previous experience with CTCs) and of the 41 EAZs announced in November 1999, only two were business-led; of the remainder, 19 were led by schools, 15 by LEAs and five by partnerships.

Religious education and the daily act of collective worship

In most areas, county and voluntary controlled schools will follow the *Agreed Syllabus* of religious education drawn up by the local *Standing Advisory Committee on Religious Education* (SACRE). The Agreed Syllabus must, by law, be non-denominational. In voluntary aided schools, religious education will be given in accordance with the tenets of the church or the school's trust deed. There may be some minor differences in some church schools to meet parents' wishes, or, for example, to meet the provisions of a trust deed or other historical covenants when a church school was originally founded.

Arrangements have to be made for pupils to be excused from the particular form of religious education offered in the school, if their parents so request — the only school subject from which pupils have the right, in effect, to opt out.

The SACRE is a local quango, consisting of groups of representatives of the LEA, school governors, teachers and appropriate religious bodies — each group having a single block vote. Apart from drawing up the Agreed Syllabus for religious education, the SACRE also deals with applications from schools to be excused from holding the daily *Act of Collective Worship*, which the Education Reform Act 1988 required to be predominantly Christian in its character. Such applications are made by schools with a majority of children of non-Christian faiths and for whom a predominantly Christian act of collective worship would not be particularly useful.

There has, recently, been a degree of controversy over the Christian churches' significant involvement in the state education system. The reasons for this significance are given in the historical commentary section at the beginning of this Chapter. The Agreed Syllabus, apart from being non-denominational will now, given the multi-ethnic nature of most parts of the country, include material aimed at improving awareness of other religions.

However, even allowing for that, the issue of state funding for non-Christian schools is, understandably, an important issue within ethnic minority communities. Those communities have sought, from time to time, to obtain from the government voluntary aided status for private schools which they have established themselves and which offer the type of education which they prefer. There were particular issues about the breadth of the curriculum offered within those schools and all previous applications were unsuccessful — until recently. The New Labour Secretary of State has now approved the granting of voluntary aided status to a muslim school and it is to be expected that more will follow, now that the principle has been conceded.

Special educational needs

Many pupils are identified as having a 'learning difficulty' and, therefore, special educational needs (SEN). The majority of such pupils are (as recommended by the Warnock report in 1978) educated within the primary/secondary mainstream school system alongside pupils without such needs, although they may need some additional tuition or ancillary support at the school to meet their particular needs.

Some children will require the protection of a *Statement of Special Educational Needs,* which defines the learning difficulty, the special educational provision needed to meet that difficulty and the place where the LEA proposes that provision should be made, at its expense. The Statementing process can take some time, since it involves a multidisciplinary assessment of the child involving education and health professionals. Parents are consulted at various stages of the process and have the right of appeal to the independent Special Educational Needs Tribunal if they do not accept the final Statement. Even if a child has a Statement, he or she may still be educated in a mainstream school but with the additional support and tuition mentioned in the Statement.

Some problems can arise with Statements which often receive fairly high profile publicity. The parents may believe that their child has a learning difficulty which the LEA or health professionals are not prepared to recognise as such at all — an example of this was dyslexia, a condition which many medical professionals did not accept existed, until fairly recently. Also, some parents may believe that the only way to meet their child's needs is for the child to be sent abroad for some unusual educational treatment — and they then expect the LEA to pay the costs involved; for its part, the LEA sees no need to pay for this treatment if suitable facilities exist in the UK, which can be funded from within its capped revenue budget.

Locally Managed Schools

Local Management of Schools (LMS), is a phrase which figures largely in school communities in the State sector. LMS was a move which followed the belief that decisions on running schools were best made by governors, headteachers and their staff, and by parents. From September 1987, LEAs were required to give delegated powers to governors, under a scheme made by the LEA but approved by the Secretary of State. All secondary and primary schools with more than 200 pupils took responsibility for their own revenue budgets. The Secretary of State had the power to extend the arrangements to smaller and special schools.

There will be variations from area to area, but broadly, the governors take responsibility for the appointment and dismissal of staff, staff salaries, books and equipment, heat and light, furniture, Rates, and so on. New buildings, maintaining the fabric of the building, and home-to-school transport remain with the LEA, and the LEA has the discretion to retain responsibility for services like school inspection, welfare and psychology services — which are probably run more cost effectively on an area, rather than school, basis.

The LEA determines the size of the Aggregate Schools Budget (ASB) and then delegates a proportion (at least 85%) to each school, as its 'School's Budget Share'. The remaining, undelegated, part of the ASB is used to fund activities such as the school psychological service and advisory services. Attempts were made to increase the school's budget share to 90%, but this proved to be very difficult to operate, because the LEA retained share was not adequate to fund retained LEA activities.

Student awards and loans

Grants to students are also administered by LEAs. Anyone taking a first degree or similar course at a university or other institution of higher education is normally entitled to a *mandatory award*. Student and parental income are taken into account in assessing the amount of grant, and the authority receives 90% reimbursement from central government.

LEAs also have the power to make *discretionary awards* to students following courses which do not carry mandatory awards. The courses which are supported by discretionary awards vary from LEA to LEA, as does the value of the award, since the LEA has to meet 100% of the cost of discretionary awards granted.

The Education (Student Loans) Act 1990 provided for, as from 1990, a gradual replacement of mandatory grants by loans which the student has to repay after the end of the course. Loans are not managed by local government, but by the Student Loans Company. Grants were not increased for 1990-91, or in subsequent years, but loans will be. No real interest will be payable on the loans but as their value is increased annually by the rate of inflation, this means that effectively the student pays an interest rate equivalent to inflation. The normal repayment period is five years but this may be extended for courses where the student borrows for more than four years or in cases of hardship. The Education (Student Loans) Act 1998 provided for the transfer of public sector student loans to the private sector.

Independent schools

Independent schools are outside the State education system and receive no grant from public funds, but they all have to be registered with the DfEE. In addition to this they can, if they choose, be inspected and be 'recognised as efficient' by the DfEE.

LEAs can, although not many do these days, arrange with particular independent schools for a number of places to be allocated to pupils whose fees are paid, in whole or in part, by the LEA.

The Conservative Government's Education Act 1980 introduced the *Assisted Places Scheme*. Independent schools applied to the DfEE to enter the scheme. If they were approved, pupils who passed the entrance examination, and whose parents' income was below a certain level, had their fees (but not boarding fees) reduced on a set scale. The DfEE reimbursed the schools for any money lost to them through reduced fees. The Assisted Places Scheme was extended to independent primary schools by the Conservative Government through the Education Act 1997, but this did not last for long, because the Assisted Places Scheme as a whole was ended by the New Labour Government enacting the Education (Schools) Act 1997 when it came into office.

10 Town and Country Planning

The relevant bodies — the Secretaries of State — local planning authorities — development plans — development control and enforcement — planning gain — building regulations — listed buildings — conservation areas — CPOs — blight — inquiries — consultation

The relevant bodies

In the field of land use planning, the relevant bodies in England are:

- Central government departments: (for planning) the Department of the Environment, Transport and the Regions (DETR) and its Secretary of State; and (for listed buildings) the Department for Culture, Media and Sport and its Secretary of State.
- Quangos at national level: (for listed buildings) English Heritage.
- Local planning authorities: all local authorities.

The Scottish Executive, the Welsh Assembly; and the Northern Ireland Secretary/Executive carry out similar functions.

Introduction

The regulation and control of land development, as a local government function, is a product of the 20th century, having a relatively recent origin, compared with functions such as public health or housing. Although there was a Planning Act in 1909, which was extended by subsequent Acts, the first comprehensive piece of town and country planning legislation was the Town and Country Planning Act 1947. The law on town and country planning was consolidated by four Acts passed in 1990 and further adjusted by the Planning and Compensation Act 1991. These Acts, together with the regulations and orders made under them constitute the Town and Country Planning Code, under which all development in England and Wales is controlled.

The purpose of town and country planning is not confined to preserving the appearance and amenity of the environment. Control is exercised to ensure that development is: correctly placed in terms of the infrastructure needed to support it; sustainable in terms of its impact on the environment; and correctly located on suitable land unlikely to be affected by such factors as flooding.

Planning consists of two components:

- *forward planning,* which entails local authorities describing, in the form of various *Development Plans* (structure, local and unitary plans), the future development of their area over the plan period; and
- *development control,* where local authorities respond to individual *planning applications* for consent to make a material change in the use of existing land or buildings or to carry out physical development such as the construction, adaptation or demolition of buildings. Most development control decisions are informed by the relevant Development Plans.

In areas which do not have a two-tier system of local government, the local authority is responsible for all aspects of the planning process. Where there is a two-tier system, the position is rather less clear-cut.

Secretary of State

The Secretary of State oversees the land use planning process in overall terms. The DETR lays down guidance on how local planning authorities are to carry out their responsibilities and will act as arbiter in the case of certain disputes between the individual and the local planning authority about planning issues. The Secretary of State can also 'call in' planning applications for determination at DETR level.

The views of central government on the issue of land use planning tend to swing from time to time — especially on issues such as development in the Green Belt, the location of new shopping facilities (existing town centre or out of town), and the location of new housing to meet future housing needs (both distribution across the nation and the use of new green field sites or the redevelopment of land previously used for that or another purpose — brown field sites). For example, the attitude of the last Conservative Government seemed to be in favour of granting planning consent rather than refusing it. New Labour appears to be more interested in preserving existing town centres and the countryside — and yet, occasional decisions or policy statements by the Secretary of State will seem to be at odds with the government's stated approach.

The government sets out its view of the principles to be followed by local planning authorities, in a series of *Planning Policy Guidance Notes* (PPGs). Although PPGs are only guidance, they are, nevertheless, widely followed by local planning authorities, if only to improve their chances of winning a planning appeal to the Secretary of State against their refusal of planning consent or to avoid an objection to their development plans. The development plan process is also informed by Regional Planning Guidance (RPG) produced by the relevant Government Office for the Regions in collaboration with the strategic planning authorities in the region.

The Secretary of State also makes regulations (statutory instruments or delegated or subordinate legislation) which provide the detailed legal provisions to cover various aspects of the planning process. Two examples of this are described in the section on development control.

Under the Local Government, Planning and Land Act 1980, local authorities have to keep registers of land which is not used or is insufficiently used. The Secretary of State can direct the local authorities to dispose of any such land at market value.

The Secretary of State (for Culture, Media and Sport, in this case) maintains the list of buildings of historical or architectural interest.

Development Plans

There are three types of Development Plan:

- *Structure Plans*, which are the responsibility of county councils (or joint strategic planning authorities) in two-tier areas;
- *Unitary Plans*, which cover the areas of metropolitan boroughs and London boroughs — and will gradually appear in unitary authority areas, certainly in Wales and probably elsewhere; and
- *Local Plans*, which are usually prepared by shire borough/district councils in two-tier areas, except for Minerals and Waste Local Plans which are prepared by strategic planning authorities.

It is possible to produce joint Structure or Unitary Plans covering the area of more than one strategic planning authority. In this context, 'strategic planning authority' means a planning authority other than a shire borough/district council.

Development Plans — who does what

In London borough council, the City of London and metropolitan borough council areas, a Unitary Development Plan combines the features of Structure and Local Plans in a single document. In the new unitary authority areas, there is likely to be an existing Structure Plan which may continue for several years until it is replaced by a new Unitary Plan. However, in those counties where there is a mix of the new unitary and the two-tier system, county-wide development planning will in most cases be dealt with on a joint basis between the strategic planning authorities. The abolition of the metropolitan county councils meant that the metropolitan borough councils became responsible for all planning functions in their area. In London, the position was slightly different when the GLC was abolished; the Joint Planning Committee for London was established, principally with a consultative role. The new Greater London Authority will have London-wide strategic planning responsibilities.

In two-tier areas, the rôles are shared. The main responsibility of county councils is to draw up a County Structure Plan and two special types of Local Plan — for minerals extraction and for waste management. Shire borough/district councils have responsibility for producing a Local Plan for their area. County councils also tend to take the lead in countryside facilities and economic development within the county.

Development control — who does what

In London borough council, the City of London, metropolitan borough and unitary council areas, the local authority takes the development control decisions.

The 1974 reorganisation introduced a system which involved a measure of overlap and duplication, especially in the field of development control, which was the subject of later criticism. In two-tier areas, shire borough/district councils are the development control authorities to whom applications for planning consent are made. The shire borough/district council has to pass on to the county council only those applications which relate to 'County Matters' or on which the shire borough/district council is obliged to consult the county council. Consultations between authorities is consistent with a Code of Practice drawn up by the Secretary of State.

Planning applications which are 'County Matters' are still decided by the county council but the definition of a 'County Matter' was made much narrower by the Local Government, Planning and Land Act 1980 Act — mineral working, waste disposal, development by the county council itself and development which straddles a National Park boundary. Shire borough/district councils are only obliged to consult the county council on proposed development which adversely affects: the Structure Plan; land affected by mineral extraction; or land which is to be used for waste disposal. However, the county council can no longer direct the shire borough/district council how to determine a planning application on which it has been consulted. For all other applications, the shire borough/district council will not consult the county council and will determine the application itself with no input from the county council.

Functions shared by county councils and shire borough/district councils include: the acquisition of land, either voluntarily or by compulsory purchase, for development or redevelopment; land disposal; caravan sites; conservation areas; historic building control; tree preservation; registration of local land charges; and schemes to reclaim derelict land.

Structure Plans

Structure Plans are forward-looking (15 year) documents which show how the county council (in collaboration with any other strategic planning authority within the county) thinks the whole of its area should develop over the plan period. Housing allocations are particularly contentious, with developers (usually backed by the National Housebuilders Federation) wanting more generous allocations of green-field sites which are easier and cheaper for them to develop and with the county council (usually backed by the local residents' pressure groups) wanting to encourage the redevelopment of brown-field sites and reduce the amount and impact of new development on open land.

In addition to housing allocations, Structure Plans will include proposals for employment initiatives and for developing communications and transport. The plans will also include policies for the conservation of the natural beauty and amenity of land, the preservation of the physical environment, and for traffic management; and will identify particular areas where these policies are to be applied. When preparing, or altering the Structure Plan, regard must be had to national policies, regional guidelines and the resources likely to be available to implement the plan's proposals.

Consultation is an important part of the exercise of preparing, or amending, Structure Plans. There is informal consultation with the public and with the shire borough/district councils when work starts (sometimes called the 'Consultation Draft stage') and then full consultation when the draft proposals are published and put on deposit for public inspection (sometimes called the 'Deposit Draft stage') as part of the formal statutory process for Structure Plan preparation. Apart from being on deposit for public inspection at council offices and public libraries, copies of the draft plan will be available for sale. The formal stages of the process will inevitably produce public objection, support or comment on the plan's draft proposals and the county council will then appoint an independent inspector (nominated by the Secretary of State from the Planning Inspectorate) to hold an *Examination in Public* (EIP).

The EIP is a special kind of reasonably informal local inquiry at which the Inspector leads a series of discussions on the plan's draft proposals, with the objectors and supporters being able to supplement their written comments by making an oral contribution to the discussion, if they wish. The Inspector then submits a formal report to the county council, suggesting any modifications to the original draft plan. The county council then decides whether or not to accept the Inspector's findings; has to publish its conclusions; and may have to commission a further EIP, if it does not follow the Inspector's suggestions and there is significant public opposition about this. The Structure Plan preparation process is completed when the county council formally adopts the final (if necessary, modified) Structure Plan.

The Secretary of State has power to 'call in' all, or part, of a Structure Plan while it is being prepared and either approve, modify or reject those parts of the plan called in.

When finally approved, the Structure Plan in its final form must be published, with copies available for inspection and sale. A challenge to the approved Structure Plan can be made to the High Court, but only on a point of law.

Local Plans

Local Plans are the means by which flesh is put on the Structure Plan skeleton. For many years, the coverage of Local Plans was very patchy, with some authorities having no Local Plan at all, until the 1991 Act required authorities to produce a single authority-wide Local Plan. Even now (April 2000), there is still no nation-wide coverage of Local Plans and Unitary Development Plans and, according to a ministerial policy statement 'Modernising Planning' in January 1998, complete coverage will not be reached for some years. The latest DETR survey (December 1999) showed that there was still a fifth of councils with no adopted Local Plan. In May 1998, the DETR published a consultation document aimed at speeding up the Local Plan process; whether its suggestions tackle the root causes of delay and achieve that result remains to be seen — revised regulations were published in January 2000. The Local Plan/Unitary Development Plan process is complex and time-consuming, to comply with DETR PPG12 and the statutory regulations.

The number of staff allocated to forward planning within a capped budget is relatively small when compared with the more immediate development control applications, which have to be dealt with within two months and which count towards performance indicators. When the draft Local Plan is put on deposit, some authorities are swamped by literally thousands of objections and this delays the inquiry process, while they try to sort them out and attempt to resolve as many of the objections as possible through negotiation. Even then, there can still be a problem — as explained in the public inquiries section later, the Bradford Unitary Development Plan inquiry had to have five inspectors to deal with the objections in anything like a reasonable time. In some cases, the Local Plan preparation process is so prescriptive and time-consuming that the Local Plan, when it is finally adopted, can be in need of almost immediate review.

Local Plans are a guide to how the shire borough/district council wants its area to develop in a way which is in general conformity with the Structure Plan. The Local Plan shows where development or redevelopment is intended, any other major works proposed, and how the whole environment is to be managed and improved. For example, the Structure Plan may provide for a particular shire borough/district council area to provide an additional number of housing units to meet the projected demand for additional housing for the whole county over the Structure Plan period; the Local Plan will indicate where, within the shire borough/district, that additional demand is to be met, including the phased release of land to meet the target.

Local Plans were originally envisaged as supplementing Structure Plans at local level and, therefore, being prepared after the Structure Plan had been approved. However, it is now possible for Local Plans to be prepared in advance of the adoption of the relevant Structure Plan, because the Structure Plan process itself can take a long time to complete and Local Plans (even if they have yet to achieve final adoption) are important documents for the purposes of development control. Local Plans have to pay regard to the Structure Plan, but the approval of the county council (or the Secretary of State) is not needed for their adoption.

The county council (in collaboration with any other strategic planning authority in the county) also prepares special kinds of Local Plans itself, for minerals and waste, covering the whole county.

The process of preparing an area-wide Local Plan is similar to that for a Structure Plan, although there are a few differences. The shire borough/district council must also consult the county council and other interested bodies. The county council has to say whether or not the draft Local Plan is in general conformity with the Structure Plan — if there is a dispute, this is first dealt with by the Inspector at the Local Plan Inquiry. If the dispute continues after the inquiry, the county council can invite the Secretary of State to act as referee. If there is a conflict between the Structure Plan and the adopted Local Plan, the Local Plan prevails, provided that it post-dates the Structure Plan.

Public consultation and participation also have a very important part to play in the Local Plan preparation process and the consultation process is more detailed, because the Local Plan proposals (especially those for new housing or industry) can have a more direct effect on individual residents. Even before the formal stages of the process, there will usually be informal consultation with local societies and groups and with local residents through the local media or through a specially produced newsletter. Once the formal stages have been reached, local authorities have to advertise details of what the draft Local Plan contains and will usually produce a special leaflet delivered to every household in the area, explaining what the draft plan contains and where the deposited draft plan can be inspected. There may also be a series of local meetings and exhibitions at which presentations are made by officers and councillors on the draft plan.

The formal stages of the Local Plan process are broadly similar to those described earlier for a Structure Plan — a period for objection/support/comment; a Local Plan Inquiry (rather than an EIP); consideration of the Inspector's findings; publication of any proposed modifications to the original draft; another local inquiry, if necessary, to consider objections to the proposed modifications; and adoption of the final version of the Local Plan. When the Local Plan is adopted, it is printed and published and objectors, other local planning authorities and the Secretary of State are informed and copies of the Local Plan are put on sale. As in the case of Structure Plans, the plan can be challenged, on a point of law only, in the High Court.

The new regulations published in January 2000, mentioned earlier, now provide for a two-stage formal deposit process, aimed at speeding up the remainder of the Local Plan process. Objections must be made to the original deposit and the council will seek to negotiate on those objections and will produce a revised version as a second deposit draft. At this stage, only objections to the revisions (not the original version) can be made. The Inspector considers the objections to the revisions and can only consider the original objections where the council has not dealt at all with the issues raised by those objections.

Unitary Development Plans

Unitary Development Plans have replaced the Structure Plan system in London and the metropolitan county areas and will ultimately do so in the new Welsh unitary authority areas and possibly in other unitary authorities. These are, in effect, Structure and Local Plans rolled into one, in what are, virtually, all-purpose authorities. Their preparation follows the Local Plan process.

In London, the Joint Planning Committee for London exists to advise the London borough councils on matters of common interest and to inform the Secretary of State of borough views on planning matters. The new Greater London Authority will have London-wide strategic planning responsibilities.

Development control

In principle, any material change in the use of land or any development which changes the physical appearance of land or buildings will require planning consent. However, regulations made by the Secretary of State can, in effect, grant deemed planning consent for specified changes of use or specified physical development, but only if that the change of use or development is within the limits specified by the regulations. However, these *permitted development rights* are only granted if the conditions in the regulations are satisfied. The two main regulations/orders involved are the Town and Country Planning (Use Classes) Order 1987 (modified in 1995) and the Town and Country Planning Act (General Permitted Development) Order 1995, which are closely linked and complex.

A very simplified explanation of the rather complex Use Classes Order is that various kinds of land or property are categorised into classes; a material change of use from one use to another use within the same class will not require planning consent; a change in use from one class to another class will usually require planning consent, but not always — there are exceptions. For example, Class A covers uses to be found in a shopping area. Class A1 contains a series of definitions of most, but not all, shops. Class A2 covers premises offering financial and professional services to visiting members of the public (banks and estate agents). Class A3 covers pubs and hot food outlets such as restaurants and take-aways. A change of use within each subclass (A1, A2 and A3) does **not** require planning consent. A change from A1 to A2 or A3 **does** require planning consent. This enables the local planning authority to consider whether the appearance and viability of shopping area would be adversely affected by the proposed change to class A2 or A3 use. A change of use in the opposite direction, from A2 to A1, say, does **not** require planning consent, because the presumption is that a change in that direction is unlikely to be damaging. Other kinds of office, which are not routinely visited by the public, fall within class B1, emphasising that this kind of use can have an even greater effect on a shopping area than a class A2 use.

The General Permitted Development Order describes the kinds of development (including material changes of use under the Use Classes Order) which can be carried out without planning consent. For example, the extension of a dwelling house can constitute permitted development provided that it complies with the conditions in the 1995 Order: in the case of a terraced house, say, the extension must not exceed 50 cubic metres or 10% of the original, whichever is the lower; the height of the roof-line of the dwelling must not be increased; and the extension must not be nearer to the highway than the original building or within 20 metres of the highway, whichever is the nearer. There can be limited exceptions for porches. Another example of permitted development relates to gates, fences or walls: it is not necessary to obtain planning consent to erect them provided their height does not exceed 1 metre next to a highway, or two metres elsewhere.

It is possible, in certain circumstances, for the local planning authority to make a special kind of order (called an 'Article 4 Direction'), removing some of these permitted development rights, but the landowner may be able to claim compensation from the local planning authority if a planning application is then refused. For example, garden sheds are usually covered by permitted development rights, but these rights might be removed by an Article 4 Direction if the circumstances justify it — say, to prevent an explosive accumulation of methane gas leaching out of an adjoining landfill site.

Development control can also be tighter in relation to a listed building or in a Conservation Area (see the later sections for what these involve). For example, provided that a building is not listed, planning consent is not needed to alter its interior, although building regulation approval may still be needed to ensure the stability and safety of the building. If the building is listed, then listed building consent will be needed before any part of it can be altered.

Planning consent is not usually required to lop or cut down a tree — but it may be needed if the tree is the subject of a tree preservation order or the property is in a Conservation Area.

Planning consent

Applications for planning consent must be made on forms obtainable from the local planning authority responsible for development control — unitary authority, London borough council, metropolitan borough council, or shire borough/district council in a two-tier area — and must be accompanied by a plan. A fee is payable. The application will appear in the register of applicants and immediate neighbours will be notified. For certain kinds of development, it must be advertised in local newspapers that the application is being made, to enable people who would be affected by it to make representations to the local planning authority.

The Secretary of State has the right to 'call in' any planning application for decision. This right is exercised, for example, when an application raises issues of national or regional importance; arouses more than local opposition; where it might be unreasonable to ask the local planning authority to adjudicate (for example an application for development by a foreign government); or where the proposed development raises unusual issues.

Planning authorities must deal with planning applications within two months, unless an extension of time is agreed with the applicant. Once the two month period (or any agreed extension) has expired, the applicant can appeal to the Secretary of State on the grounds of non-determination, and the appeal will be treated as if the application had been refused. However, most applicants will be prepared to give the local planning authority a reasonable time to reach a decision. Some of the more complex applications (for an out-of-town shopping centre, say) could never be decided in two months anyway, if proper consultations are to be undertaken and appropriate technical evidence commissioned and obtained.

Most planning authorities will have a system of delegation in order to meet the two month deadline, with uncontentious applications being determined by officers. More controversial and complex developments will be dealt with by the planning committee and really major applications will be determined by the full council. Parish/community councils are also routinely consulted on applications in their area. Officers play a key role in advising councillors of technical matters and will usually present the case at any subsequent planning appeal. Officers can sometimes be in a difficult position in giving technical evidence at a planning appeal inquiry, if they had recommended the approval of an application which the councillors decided to refuse, giving rise to the appeal.

A local planning authority has three options when considering planning applications: to give unconditional consent, to give conditional consent, or to refuse consent. In coming to its decision, the local authority will take into account such matters as: the structure and local plans; the appearance of the proposed development; representations received from the public; and the effect on public safety.

A local planning authority may also grant *outline* planning consent (consent in principle), reserving until later its approval (*detailed* planning consent for *reserved matters*) of any matters not particularised in the outline planning application. This two-stage approach is often used by developers to test the water with the local planning authority, to establish whether planning consent would be forthcoming, and avoiding abortive work on producing detailed proposals for the development itself.

Apart from any other conditions which it might contain, every planning consent is granted on the condition that the development is started within five years (or such other time as the local planning authority may direct), otherwise the consent lapses. Planning consents which have lapsed can be renewed, but a fresh application (and fee) is necessary and circumstances may have changed over the intervening period to such an extent that refusal would then be justified.

If planning consent is refused, or if only conditional consent is granted, the applicant has six months to lodge an appeal, free of charge, against the refusal or the conditions, with the Secretary of State. The appeal will be dealt with by an Inspector appointed by the Secretary of State from the Planning Inspectorate. The appeal will either be determined on the basis of the written material or the appellant may opt for an informal oral hearing or a formal public local inquiry. The Inspector can decide certain kinds of appeal or it may be necessary for him to produce a report for consideration by the Secretary of State, who can decide whether or not to accept the Inspector's recommendation. The decision of the Secretary of State can be challenged in the High Court through judicial review and the Secretary of State's decision not to follow the Inspector's recommendation can sometimes be an important part of the challenge. The right to challenge the Secretary of State's decision in the High Court is sufficient to ensure that the planning appeal process satisfies the requirements of the Human Rights Act.

The appellant or the local planning authority can apply for the other side to pay its costs in making or responding to the appeal. If the Inspector believes that the circumstances justify it (the appeal or the local planning authority's decision was without merit) then costs will be awarded.

To reduce the number of repetitive planning applications sometimes made for the same piece of land, local planning authorities have power to decline to consider an application on the grounds that the Secretary of State has refused a similar one, on appeal, within the two preceding years.

Planning gain

'Planning gain' is a vague term. In the 1960s, the approach to development was that developers would be expected to provide the infrastructure within their site and the relevant local authorities would provide the infrastructure off-site. However, constraints on public expenditure meant that many local authorities could not afford to provide the infrastructure and therefore consent had to be refused for the development. With the later inflation in house prices, developers became increasingly prepared to contribute towards the cost of off-site infrastructure as a means of tipping the balance in favour of planning consent. At the time, many professionals were concerned that this was tantamount to buying planning consent, which had to be unlawful. This view would be (and still is) entirely justified if the offered 'gains' had no real connection with the proposed development.

However, planning gain is now an established feature, with developers regarding it as normal practice to contribute to off-site infrastructure costs, including schools and community centres, where appropriate. The use of this practice has now been extended, with Government approval, so that developers of large housing estates are usually asked to provide some low-cost housing within the development, as well as the other planning gain items.

The Planning and Compensation Act 1991 gave a **unilateral** right to developers to volunteer to enter into *planning obligations* (usually called a 'section 106 agreement') to carry out works or contribute to the infrastructure, if their development went ahead. This process usually happens if there is likely to be a planning appeal. This is an alternative to the normal process of a *planning agreement,* freely negotiated between the developer and the local planning authority. The intention of this alternative is that the content of the planning obligation, which is binding on the developer, will be particularly useful in enabling the developer to clarify his, her or its intentions at any appeal against refusal or non-determination by a recalcitrant local planning authority.

Enforcement of development control

A person who wishes to find out whether the existing use of land, or the way in which it is proposed to be developed, is lawful, can apply to the local planning authority for a *Certificate of Lawfulness of existing Use or Development* (CLEUD) or a *Certificate of Lawfulness of Proposed Use or Development* (CLOPUD). The local planning authority can either grant the certificate or refuse the application. Appeals against failure to determine the application within the two month time limit or a refusal are dealt with in the same way as other planning appeals. The content of the certificate will determine whether planning consent is needed to continue the present or proposed use of the land — effectively giving assurance that an enforcement notice is not on its way.

Changing the use of land to a material extent or carrying out works of development without planning consent (where such consent is required) can result in some adverse consequences for the person or body involved in the change or development. In the case of contravention of a tree preservation order, prosecution of the individual for a criminal offence is an option immediately open to the local planning authority.

Occasionally, where there is some doubt about the use or development of the land, the local planning authority may suggest that the necessary planning application is made and, if planning consent is granted, the position can be regularised in this way.

However, where no planning application has been made or an application has been refused or granted subject to conditions which have been breached, then the local planning authority has to decide what to do about the contravening development. Where the contravention already exists, the usual course of action is to serve an *Enforcement Notice* on the individual, which will describe the nature of the contravention and explain the steps to be taken within a specified period, to remedy the breach of planning control. If the contravention is in the process of being committed and the local planning authority has served an enforcement notice which has not yet expired, the local planning authority can go further and serve a *Stop Notice* on the individual, before the enforcement notice expires. Contravention of a stop notice constitutes a criminal offence. The local planning authority may be liable to compensate the individual for any loss if the enforcement notice upon which the stop notice depends is quashed, varied or withdrawn.

The individual concerned has a right of appeal to the Secretary of State against an enforcement or stop notice and a local inquiry is usually held to determine the appeal. Occasionally, the issue of an enforcement/stop notice can prompt the individual to make a belated planning application which, in all probability, will be refused. To avoid a series of appeals about the same issue, an appeal against an enforcement/stop notice will be combined with any appeal against the refusal of planning consent.

If the appeal to the Secretary of State succeeds, then planning consent is granted and the change of use or development no longer contravenes the planning law. If the appeal is dismissed, the local planning authority will then take further enforcement action, if the individual fails to remedy the situation. That further action can be prosecution for a criminal offence. On conviction at a Crown Court, the fine is unlimited and at a magistrates court the maximum fine is £20,000. In either case, in fixing the fine, the court can have regard to any financial benefit accruing to the individual. Alternatively, or in addition, the local planning authority can enter the land itself and remove the contravening development, at the expense of the individual. Obstruction of the local planning authority at this stage constitutes a criminal offence. This is the background to the occasional stories of new houses built in the countryside without planning consent being demolished against the owner's wishes.

Building Regulations

Building Regulation approval is almost always needed for new building works or adaptations to existing buildings — even where planning consent is not required. Building Regulation approval is granted by those local planning authorities which are responsible for development control.

The reason for building control is to ensure that a building is structurally sound. In this sense, building control has a longer history, in local government terms, than town and country planning, since it has its origins in public health. A charge is made for the service, and building control officers inspect a building while it is being put up, to ensure it complies with the Building regulations. It is now possible to opt for private inspection — by the NHBC.

The standards for control of buildings are national, applied throughout the country — except in inner London which has its own mode of control — and are contained in Building Regulations made by the Secretary of State under the Public Health Act 1961 and the Health and Safety at Work Act 1974. Before the 1961 Act, public health authorities made their own building by-laws. It was felt that this system was too haphazard, so it is now subject to ministerial control. Building Regulations govern the specifications of new buildings — and alterations and additions to old ones — from the standpoint of safety, health and design. They cover, amongst other things, materials, method of construction, sanitation and fire precautions.

Plans for new building work must be submitted for approval. If the plans comply with the Building Regulations, and are not defective for any other significant reason, they must be approved. Equally, if they do not conform to the Regulations in any way, they must be rejected. There will usually be a process of discussion and negotiation between the applicant and the Building Inspector to iron out any difficulties. Councillors never consider Building Regulation applications which are rightly regarded as highly technical.

It is an offence to build in contravention of the Building Regulations. Local authorities can order buildings built without Building Regulation consent to be demolished, or for remedial work to be done. Local authorities, alternatively, may do the work themselves at the owner's cost.

Buildings of architectural or historic interest

Buildings of architectural or historical interest can be destroyed or neglected to such an extent that the only sensible course of action is demolition. However, there is a process by which such buildings can be given a degree of protection, although even this process can sometimes fail to achieve the desired objective, if the owner is sufficiently determined.

The process involves having the building *Listed* by the Secretary of State (for Culture, Media and Sport) under the Listed Buildings Act 1990. A building does not have to be very old to be listed — there are, for example, some early designs of BT telephone boxes which have been given listed building status because of their contribution to a particular street scene; and some 1920s /1930s factories have been listed as important examples of the industrial architectural style in vogue at that time. Originally, the Secretary of State was reluctant to list buildings constructed after the Second World War unless there were exceptional circumstances. That changed in 1988, when a rolling 30 year rule was introduced and there have been competitions since that date to identify buildings for listing.

Buildings are listed because of: their architectural interest; their historical interest; their close historical association with nationally important people or events; or their group value as an architectural or historical unity or a fine example of planning (such as squares, terraces or model villages). The lists are published and notified to local planning authorities and owners and occupiers of the buildings concerned.

The relative importance of the building will determine which of the two grades is applied to it. The most significant is Grade I ('exceptional' — only 2% are Grade I). Grade II is allocated to buildings which are of 'special interest', with Grade II* being given to buildings which are 'particularly important'. Once a building is listed, the owner must obtain *Listed Building Consent* from the local planning authority to alter or extend the building in any way; negotiations with English Heritage may also be involved. The degree of control over what the local planning authority is prepared to permit and the materials which can be used, will depend upon the building's listing grade — the lower the grade, the more latitude which may be allowed. If the local planning authority refuses the listed building consent, the applicant can appeal to the Secretary of State and any appeal can include a claim that the building does not justify listing.

If a local planning authority wants to protect a non-listed building of architectural or historic interest from threatened demolition or alteration, it can put a *Building Preservation Notice* on it. This is sometimes referred to as *Spot Listing*. This notice lasts for six months and has the same practical and legal effect as listing by the Secretary of State. During the six month period, the Secretary of State has to decide whether the building should be listed. If the Secretary of State does not approve the listing, then the owner may be able to claim compensation if they have suffered loss as a result of the notice.

If unauthorised work is carried out on a listed building, the local planning authority can serve an *Listed Building Enforcement Notice* requiring the building to be returned to its former condition. The local planning authority can acquire the building by CPO, if it has the necessary resources. The authority may find itself in the position of having to acquire it anyway, if the owner of a listed building serves a purchase notice on the local planning authority, requiring it to acquire the building on the grounds that it is incapable of reasonably beneficial use in its present state.

Maintaining a listed building can be an expensive business, and so grants may be paid by central and local government to help with repairs and maintenance — although the price for this may be a measure of limited public access to the building.

Conservation Areas

The concept of Conservation Areas was introduced by the Civic Amenities Act 1967, which recognised that broader forms of protection were needed for buildings which were important but which did not justify listing. Conservation Areas are designated by local planning authorities as areas of special architectural or historic interest, where the character or appearance of the area and the buildings within it should be preserved or enhanced.

Once a designation has been made, special attention is paid when the local planning authority carries out its development control functions. Some permitted development rights under the General Permitted Development Order do not apply in Conservation Areas and the local planning authority can make an Article 4 Direction to increase the degree of control which it can exercise over the external appearance of buildings, in such matters as replacement windows. In addition, the demolition of certain buildings requires the approval of the local planning authority (a *Conservation Area Consent*) and it is a criminal offence to cut down, lop or wilfully damage any tree in the Conservation Area.

Authorities have to advertise, in a local paper, notice of any planning application in a Conservation Area which they feel would affect the character or appearance of the area. The public have 21 days from the date of advertisement to make representations about such applications. Local planning authorities must take any representations into account when making a decision.

Compulsory purchase

Compulsory purchase is one of the most emotive aspects of local government. Any public authority — local authority or government department — is entitled to issue a *Compulsory Purchase Order* (CPO) on any land or buildings which it wishes to acquire for its statutory purposes. The CPO requires the confirmation of the Secretary of State and the local authority which made the CPO may be called upon to justify it and, if it fails to do so, the CPO will not be confirmed.

Any proposed CPO must be advertised in two successive issues of local papers. A copy of the order must be sent to every owner and tenant affected. The CPO and a map must be deposited with the local authority for public inspection. Anyone affected by the CPO has the right to object to the confirming government department — the objection must be sent within 21 days of the notice first being advertised.

If formal objections are received, the relevant Secretary of State will appoint an Inspector to hold a public local inquiry. This inquiry must be advertised and be open to anyone affected by the CPO, who must be given a chance to explain their opposition. The Inspector will make a report to the Secretary of State, who then decides whether or not to confirm the CPO. If the CPO is confirmed, then there may be grounds to refer the matter to the High Court, on judicial review.

Compensation is available to owners affected by a confirmed CPO. The amount of the compensation payable will be the full market value of the property (determined by the Inland Revenue Valuation Agency), disregarding any adverse effect on the value of the property caused by the existence of the CPO or the proposals which gave rise to it. In addition, owners are entitled to reimbursement of expenses for such items as fees for professional legal and valuation advice and removal costs.

Additional compensation may be payable where land which has been compulsorily acquired within the past 10 years, increases in value as a result of a later planning decision.

Planning blight

When the value of property suffers as a result of a planning decision by a public authority, it can be regarded as having been 'blighted', because it may be more difficult (or even impossible) to sell. Owners of property suffering from planning blight can, under certain conditions, force the relevant local authority to acquire the property (a CPO in reverse). The conditions which must be satisfied are related to the nature of the property, the nature of the owner's legal interest and the length of the owner's occupation.

Cases can include:

- property threatened by CPO for public schemes such as road building; the local authority which made the CPO can be forced to buy the property, earlier than it might otherwise have done, at the full market price, unaffected by the scheme which gave rise to the CPO;
- land where planning consent has been refused and consequently is incapable of reasonably beneficial use; the local planning authority can be forced to buy the property.

Although not strictly planning blight, compensation can be claimed by people owning property whose value has been reduced by a minimum threshold amount due to noise or fumes from new public works which began after 1971; in these cases, only compensation can be awarded..

Owners seeking to force the relevant local authority to acquire their property, have to serve a *Blight Notice* on the local authority, giving details of their claim. If the claim is contested by the local authority, it serves a counter-notice objecting to the blight notice and disclaiming its intention to acquire the property. The owner then has two months in which to refer the case to the Lands Tribunal for adjudication; if the owner fails to do this, the original blight notice is void.

Public local inquiries

Public local inquiries have already been mentioned in relation to applications for planning consent and objections to CPOs and structure and local plans. In addition, they are common with proposals for new roads. Such inquiries will also take place if, as mentioned earlier, the Secretary of State 'calls in' a major planning application, as with the Sizewell Inquiry, which concerned a nuclear power station.

Most public local inquiries are primarily of local interest, concerned with appeals against the refusal of planning consent in individual cases. Occasionally, they are of national interest, for example the location of a third London airport. They may last for months and cost millions of pounds.

The procedure is the same for all types of inquiry. The inquiry must be publicised — in addition to the applicant and the local planning authority, those entitled to attend and be heard include formal objectors to the proposed development, anyone who has a legal interest in the site and the parish/community council concerned. Very occasionally, groups of objectors try to disrupt proceedings — the most noteworthy cases of this have been over new road proposals. Objectors and applicants may be represented by barristers and call expert witnesses but are not entitled to legal aid. They may cross examine anyone giving evidence.

Inquiries are conducted by independent Inspectors appointed by the Secretary of State. They may allow people other than those with a right to be heard to give evidence; they listen to the evidence both for and against and will make a site visit. In the more complex inquiries involving technical issues, the Inspector may be assisted by one or more technical Assessors. If the inquiry is likely to be a long one, it can be shortened by appointing more than one Inspector — for example, the Bradford Unitary Development Inquiry had five inspectors assigned to it.

In many minor cases, the nature of the issue means that the Inspector conducting the inquiry is allowed to make the decision on it. In all other cases, the Inspector will report with recommendations to the Secretary of State, who will make the decision. This happens in significant matters of national importance; for example, the application by the British Airports Authority to develop Stansted, or the National Coal Board's desire to mine in the Vale of Belvoir. The Secretary of State is usually guided by the Inspector's report, but is not bound by it and may overturn the Inspector's recommendations.

Public participation and consultation

Public participation was urged upon local authorities by the Skeffington Report in 1969. Local planning authorities may have to consult with the public — indeed, most of them welcome the chance to do so — but they cannot, and will not, involve members of the public in policy decisions. That is what councillors are elected to do.

Local planning authorities, as mentioned earlier in this Chapter, are under a duty to consult with the public and keep them informed at all stages of the preparation of both Local and Structure Plans. Members of the public may also object to the Secretary of State and give evidence at a public inquiry should it be decided to hold one.

With planning applications, people affected by the proposed development may make representations, which the local planning authority must consider before a decision is made. The individuals concerned may also give evidence at a public inquiry, should one be held.

In the final analysis, however, it is the planning authority, or the Secretary of State (or the Inspector) who decides — not the public.

11 Personal Social Services

The relevant bodies — child protection — fostering — adoption — wardship — community care — elderly, disabled and mentally ill people — the private sector

The relevant bodies

In the field of personal social services, the relevant bodies are:

- Central government departments: the Department of Health (DoH) and its Secretary of State; the Scottish Executive; the Welsh Assembly; and the Northern Ireland Secretary/Executive.
- Local social services authorities: unitary authorities, London borough councils, metropolitan borough councils, county councils in two-tier areas, and the Corporation of the City of London.
- Local housing authorities have a contribution to make in terms of providing sheltered housing and providing improvement grants for home adaptations.
- Quangos at local level: NHS authorities and trusts collaborate with local social services authorities and local housing authorities through Joint Consultative Committees (JCCs) in jointly planning for and providing a range of community-based services, which are a very important contribution to personal social services at local level.
- Quango at national level: (proposed by the Care Standards Bill) Ofsted for the regulation of childminders and day care for children).
- Voluntary organisations at national and local level: very many, connected with specific client groups, such as NSPCC, Age Concern, MENCAP and Home Start; the contribution of voluntary organisations to personal social services should not be underestimated.

The background

The long tradition of local authority social welfare was dramatically updated following the report of the Inter-Departmental Committee on Local Authority and Allied Personal Social Services. The report, named the *Seebohm Report*, after the chairman of the committee, was published in 1968. It led to the Local Authorities Social Services Act 1970, which created new generic social services departments out of the traditional separate health and welfare and children's departments. The former Medical Officer of Health and the Children's Officer were replaced by a new chief officer, the Director of Social Services.

Social services departments are now responsible for a wide range of personal social services for families, children, people with physical and mental disabilities, elderly people, and people who are mentally ill. They can only provide these services effectively by working in close collaboration with the local housing authority (in all but the county council, another department of the same local authority) and with the NHS, through joint planning and joint funding arrangements.

Social services authorities are required to appoint a director of social services and to establish a social services committee and department to provide and administer the services.

The National Health Service and Community Care Act 1990 introduced a new system of community care and placed major new responsibilities on local social services authorities. It aimed to develop, using private sector facilities wherever possible, new extensive care and support services to allow people to continue to live in the community in their own homes, rather than in institutions, mostly NHS hospitals. Because of the significant costs involved in developing community-based services to replace the hospital provision, and the need to shift substantial resources from the NHS to local government, the introduction of the 1990 Act's provisions was delayed until 1993.

Although the various social services are managed under a single generic social services department, this account of the way the services have developed will be continued in the sections which follow, dealing with the various client groups.

Children

Social services authorities work in concert with the police, the NSPCC and a range of other agencies, including NHS trusts and local education authorities to protect and help children. The various agencies come together in the *Area Review Committee* (ARC) which establishes the child protection procedures which all the agencies should follow and carries out reviews of cases where the procedures appear to have failed to prevent *non-accidental injury*, to see if any lessons can be learned. On a day-to-day basis, information is collated and shared between the various agencies through the *Child Protection Register* maintained by the ARC.

The Children Act 1989 made the most far-reaching and comprehensive reform of the law relating to children within living memory, bringing together the public and private law on the care, protection and upbringing of children and the provision of services for them and their families. The 1989 Act stated that, when matters come to court, the *paramount* consideration is the child's welfare, and that courts should only make orders if doing so would be better for the child than making no order at all. The Act covers cases such as divorce and whether to place a child under the supervision or care of a local authority. Parental responsibility is redefined in a modern manner, so that unmarried fathers can acquire equal parental responsibilities as mothers.

Courts can make four types of orders:

- *Residence* — settling with whom the child should live.
- *Contact* — allowing the child to have visits or contact with a named person.
- *Specific Issue* — determining a specific question concerning the care of the child — for example, attending a specific school.
- *Prohibited Steps* — forbidding specified actions by the parent in relation to the child.

Social services authorities have a duty to promote the upbringing, where possible, of children by their families, as well as the general duty of promoting the welfare of children in their area, who are in need. Regard must be had to the wishes and feelings of the child and of anybody with parental responsibilities for the child. The idea is that there should be a partnership between the parents and the social services authority where this is possible. Assistance can be given either by cash or in kind; and day care may be provided for children under five who are not at school and care and supervision for those at school who need it.

Local social services authorities must provide accommodation for any child who needs it, if there is nobody with parental responsibility; or the child is lost or abandoned; or because the person who is responsible is unable to provide the care. Where parents make voluntary arrangements with a social services authority to care for a child, then they can withdraw the child from the arrangements without giving notice. When the social services authority has been looking after a child, its responsibilities do not end when the child leaves its care. The social services authority then has a further duty of advising, assisting and befriending, including giving financial assistance for accommodation, for example.

Care and supervision of children

Before a court can make a care or supervision order, it must be satisfied that the prescribed grounds exist. These grounds include that a child is likely to suffer significant harm from receiving care of a standard below that which would be given by a reasonable parent, or that the child is beyond parental control. Care or supervision orders cannot be made for anybody aged 17 or over.

Under a *Care Order*, the social services authority assumes parental responsibility for the child, but it must allow parents reasonable access to the child, unless there is an emergency or a court denies access. A *Supervision Order* puts a child under the supervision of the social services authority, which then has a duty to advise, assist and befriend the child. The actual day-to-day supervisor will be a social worker or, under certain circumstances, a probation officer. An order directing with whom the child should live, may be attached to a Supervision Order.

Emergency protection of children

The 1989 Act provided major reforms in the rules governing *Emergency Protection*, aimed at striking a balance between the need to protect children from harm in emergencies, and allowing aggrieved parents to challenge any action.

If the court is convinced that there is reasonable cause to believe that the child is likely to suffer significant harm, then it may make an *Emergency Protection Order*, giving the parent's responsibilities to another person, usually the social services authority. However, the emphasis is always on the need to return children to their parents as soon as continued removal proves unnecessary. Emergency protection orders are limited to eight days but can be extended for a further seven days, but only if the court is satisfied that the likelihood of significant harm still exists.

The Family Law Act 1996 extended the range of powers available in connection with an emergency protection order. Instead of removing the child from the home and source of danger, the source of danger itself is removed, thus obviating the need for the child to be removed from home. This is achieved by the court making a non-molestation order or attaching an exclusion requirement to an emergency protection order. The person suspected of causing the threat is excluded from the home and from the surrounding area.

Providing accommodation for children

Social services authorities have a duty to provide, themselves, *Community Homes* for children looked after by them. They are also responsible for the registration of residential children's homes provided by other persons for profit. Social services authority, voluntary, and certain other kinds of public sector children's accommodation (such as hospitals) are exempt from registration. Anybody who is prohibited from fostering a child privately cannot be involved with the management or finances of a registered children's home, without the consent of the social services authority.

Children in the care of a social services authority can be accommodated in a community home (which may also have education facilities on the premises (CHE)) or with foster parents.

In very special circumstances and only with the specific approval of the court through a *Secure Accommodation Order*, a social services authority can restrict the liberty of a child in their care by placing them in secure accommodation. The availability of the specially-provided secure accommodation is limited (although the DoH is increasing it) and it is often the case that a place can only be found at short notice in a secure unit some distance away. The secure accommodation orders have a limited life (initially not more than three months) and have to be renewed (for up to six months at a time) by the court if the child is to remain in secure accommodation. In addition, in between court appearances, the continued need to keep the child in secure accommodation is reviewed by the social services authority at frequent intervals (after the first month and every three months thereafter) by a special 'review panel' of 'suitable persons', which includes an independent member.

Fostering children

Fostering children can be arranged by a social service authority, a voluntary agency or privately. Social services authorities use fostering for children in their care, as an alternative to residential care in a community home. Official foster parents must be approved by the social services authority and the approval process involves investigations into the prospective foster parents' family life — prospective foster parents are visited in their homes by social workers. References are needed and prospective foster parents must agree to inquiries being made about them with the doctor and the police.

There are severe restrictions on who may become foster parents. Among those prohibited from fostering children are people who have been convicted of causing or permitting bodily harm to a child. If there is someone else living in the same house who has been convicted of such an offence, then that also is enough to prohibit a fostering arrangement there. The prohibition also operates in respect of anyone who has had an order, to remove a child from their control, made against them.

Social services authorities approve a range of people as foster parents: married couples, single or widowed women, and sometimes men. Social workers have the right to see foster children on request at regular intervals. They can remove a child from foster parents at any time, if they believe it to be in the child's interests. However, this course of action may prompt the foster parents to apply to court for a residence order.

Social services authorities use foster parents on both a short-term and a long-term basis. Allowances are paid to foster parents for feeding and clothing the children. Most councils also make extra payments to cover birthdays, holidays and Christmas. For children with special needs, enhanced payments are made.

Private fostering arrangements are not unlawful, but where fostering is arranged privately, the social services authority must be informed when a child has been looked after for more than 27 days by someone not related to it. Failure to notify the social services authority is a criminal offence. Once notification has been given, the child comes under the supervision of social workers.

Adoption of children

Children can, by law, only be adopted through an *Adoption Agency*. An adoption agency is any social services authority and any voluntary adoption society approved by the Secretary of State. Not all adoption agencies arrange adoption **placements**, although they will carry out assessments. For example, the British Agencies for Adoption and Fostering is an adoption agency, but it makes no placements itself. Adoption agencies will usually establish an adoption panel to reach conclusions on specific issues: whether adoption is in the particular child's interests; and whether particular prospective adopters are suitable to be adoptive parents either generally or for a specific child.

The formal adoption process can be carried out in one or two stages. The single stage process involves the placement being made with the full co-operation of the natural parent(s) and resulting in an *Adoption Order* made by the court. However, sometimes the parent wishes the process to be completed as quickly as possible or cannot accept that adoption is in the child's best interests — in such cases, a two stage approach is used. Firstly, the adoption agency applies to the court for a *Freeing Order,* freeing the child for adoption. If the court grants such an order, when the time comes to make the adoption order itself, the natural parent plays no part in the proceedings. At the time that the freeing order is made, the prospective adoptive parents may not have been identified. The freeing order puts the child in a sort of legal limbo and this is causing increasing concern to the courts, who much prefer to know the identity of the prospective adoptive parents when being asked to make a freeing order. The Adoption Bill which was lost due the 1997 General Election was intended to address this issue.

Anyone over 21 is legally entitled to adopt a child, but, in practice, adoption is usually confined to married couples, where the wife is under 35 and the husband is under 40, although much will depend upon the age of the child. Babies in good health are easy to place for adoption, since most prospective adopters prefer to adopt that kind of child. Older children and those with medical problems or displaying challenging behaviour are more difficult to place. The adoption of children by two partners in a single-sex relationship raises considerable difficulties.

Before a couple who wish to adopt a child are approved, they will have several meetings, both together and separately, with a social worker who will investigate their backgrounds and their reasons for wanting to adopt. Once they have been approved, the child is put into their provisional care. If this is done through an approved adoption society, the social services department, or its own adoption panel, must be notified. The child then becomes protected: it is visited regularly by social workers to make sure that the relationship between the prospective parents and the child remains good and that the material conditions at the home are suitable. An adoption order, made by a family proceedings court sitting in private (the press are not allowed to be present), cannot be made until at least three months after notification to the social services authority.

Wardship of children

This normally occurs in parental disputes over the future upbringing of a child; for example, a child is made a Ward of Court to prevent a parent taking it out of the country. These days, social services authorities are rarely involved in Wardship proceedings, since the law now requires social services authority involvement in the future of the child to be achieved through the procedures under the Children Acts. A social services authority's participation in Wardship proceedings is limited to those circumstances where the desired objective is impossible to achieve under the Children Acts.

Wardship proceedings are normally held in private, but the judge may, if the applicant wishes, permit the press to be present so that maximum publicity is given.

Registration of childminders

Social services authorities must keep a register of all people who receive payment for looking after children under the age of five. When an application to be registered is made, a social worker will inspect the applicant's home. Registration may be granted subject to conditions about the facilities to be provided, the number and qualifications of staff, and the maximum number of children who can be minded. Registration may be refused if the home, or the applicant, is not considered to be suitable.

Inspection can take place at any time and if the registration conditions are breached, then registration can be revoked or modified to reduce the maximum number of children who can be minded. Carrying on as an unregistered childminder is a criminal offence.

The Care Standards Bill proposes to establish a new independent regulatory body for social care and private and voluntary healthcare services in England, the National Care Standards Commission. In Wales, an arm of the National Assembly will undertake a similar role. In the case of childminding and day care provision, the Bill proposes to transfer the existing responsibilities of local authorities. In England, those responsibilities will be transferred to HMCIS under a new arm of Ofsted, covering childcare and early years education. In Wales, these responsibilities will be transferred to a new regulatory body established as part of the National Assembly for Wales, although Estyn (the welsh equivalent of Ofsted) will continue to inspect early years education. National standards will be applied and there will be a right of appeal to a Tribunal established under the Protection of Children Act 1999.

Community Care for elderly and disabled people — a joint approach

The National Health Service and Community Care Act 1990 placed major responsibilities on local social services authorities in respect of community care aimed at:

- the promotion of domiciliary, day and respite services to allow people to live in their own homes;
- ensuring that those who provide services make practical support a high priority;
- a proper assessment of a person's needs and then good case management;
- the development of a flourishing independent sector alongside good public services;
- a clarification of responsibilities, better value for money and a new funding structure.

Social services authorities, as well as NHS authorities, are under a duty to prepare plans for their community care arrangements and are positively encouraged to undertake the plan preparation as a joint exercise. Plans must be published and kept under review and, in their preparation, the social services authority must consult widely with a whole range of bodies including the voluntary sector.

In suggesting the Community Care approach and the production of joint plans, the 1990 Act was building upon a foundation which had been there for some time — from about 1974. In the mid 1970s, the DHSS (as it then was) decided to promote joint working between the NHS and aspects local government (social services, housing, education and transport) to improve non-hospital based services for the benefit of the clients. The mechanism which was chosen to deliver this new way of working was the Joint Consultative Committee (JCC) and the additional money made available to health authorities could only be spent on JCC recommendation. Initially, JCCs were informal bodies operating under a DHSS circular, but later they were given statutory recognition.

The JCCs consist of representatives of all the relevant statutory agencies in the NHS and local government, supplemented by representatives elected by voluntary sector organisations and, latterly, the private sector. The JCCs meet in public and follow much the same procedural framework as a local authority committee. The JCCs are not just talking shops — apart from approving the joint plans, they approve the expenditure of significant sums of NHS money on jointly-financed projects to give the plans substance.

Community Care in action — services for elderly and disabled people

There is a duty on social services authorities to assess the needs of a person requiring care, by reason of their age, infirmity, disability or other circumstances and to make arrangements to provide suitable services to meet those needs within the limit of the resources available.

If the assessment shows that the person is disabled, then the social services authority must determine the services required under the Disabled Persons (Services, Consultation and Representation) Act 1986 and inform the disabled person of what they are doing and the rights of appeal. The social services authority is under a duty to provide the services which it has determined are required under the 1986 Act and so arguments can arise if it is suspected that the social services authority has been economical with its assessment, in order to save money. However, the courts have now decided that the resources available to the social services can be taken into account when assessing need.

Services cover a wide range of activities including home helps, hot meals, telephone, cheap travel, parking, holidays and home modifications and aids to daily living. Employment can be provided for disabled people in sheltered workshops, and day nurseries and day centres can be provided for children and people who are disabled.

In recent years, measures have been taken to move people with a mental disability out of long-stay hospitals into small group homes to enable them to live together in ordinary family-sized homes, with a substantial degree of independence. Where services need to be provided by the social services authority or the local housing authority, then they must be notified and invited to take part in the assessment and decisions. Where there is a need for temporary care, this can be provided without waiting for an assessment.

Many carers of elderly or disabled people are relatives who undertake that responsibility voluntarily, without regard to the effect on their own lives. The strain on the carer can be enormous. The Carers (Recognition and Services) Act 1996 was introduced to provide additional support for carers in their own right. Anyone who is providing, or intends to provide, a substantial amount of regular unpaid care to a person who is being assessed for community care, can request an assessment of their own needs and ability to provide that care. The carer's assessment may lead to additional help (such as respite care, to enable the carer to have some time to themselves) which recognises the carer's needs as much as the needs of the person being cared for.

Social services authorities were given additional flexibility by the Community Care (Direct Payments) Act 1996. This Act effectively puts the client in the driving seat, by enabling the social services authority to pay cash to the client, rather than provide services. The client can then use the cash to make their own arrangements for their care in the way, and at the time, that suits them best.

Private sector residential care

While social services authorities can (and do) provide residential care homes themselves and meet the full costs of maintaining them, it was the intention of the last Conservative Government to increase substantially the use made of private sector facilities. Social services authorities already possessed the power to make arrangements with private suppliers and voluntary organisations and pay the charges involved, but the main emphasis was on direct provision.

As a result of the 1990 Act, when an elderly person reaches the point of requiring residential accommodation, they are assessed by a social worker and placed in a residential care home that best suits their needs — local authority or private. Where a social services authority enters into an agreement with a private sector operator to provide residential accommodation, it must assess the ability of the person accommodated to pay towards the cost of the care which they receive. This will be the full economic cost, unless the resident cannot afford to pay it. Residents in private homes may claim a social security residential care allowance and will have to pay the amounts over to the homeowner, less a personal allowance, which they can keep for themselves. Residents in local authority homes cannot claim the residential care allowance. The implications of that are explained below.

The government, consistent with its view of the 'enabling authority', pursued the concept of a 'mixed economy of care', in so arranging matters that the public sector provision declined and the private sector provision increased.

The government achieved its objectives by various means. The different treatment of residents in private and local authority homes in relation to the social security residential care allowance meant that charges for people in local authority homes were inevitably higher and were then presented by the government as being excessive when compared with the private sector.

Social services authorities received a *Special Transitional Grant* (STG) from the government for the expansion of community care and they claimed at the time that the extra money allowed by the government for this purpose fell short of the extra costs that they were having to incur. Partly, this was due to people living longer and to underestimates of the numbers for which local authorities would be responsible. It was a source of friction with NHS trusts which, for their own financial reasons, wanted to move as many elderly people as possible out of hospital. In addition, when the STG was first introduced, it was paid by the government subject to the condition that 85% of it had to be spent in arranging private sector residential placements.

At the same time, social services authorities were made responsible for registering private care homes, applying standards which did not, as a matter of law, apply to the social service authority's own homes. Perhaps if the same standards had applied to social services authority homes, the government might have felt obliged to make available the capital allocations necessary for upgrading the social services authority homes. Private sector care homes were physically more attractive, being new, built to modern standards, while social services authority care homes were in need of modernisation to meet modern registration standards.

It is against that background that many social services authorities saw the number of residents in their care homes dwindle, making them even more expensive to run. In the end, some social services authorities looked at the possibility of transferring their care homes to a third party, in the hope that any new residents in them would then have access to the residential care allowance and the new owners might be able to raise the finance needed to upgrade them. Some have done so.

Mentally ill people

Local social services authorities have very limited powers in relation to people who are thought to be in need of treatment for mental disorders.

Specially trained *Approved Social Workers* have the right to apply to a hospital for a person to be admitted for up to 28 days for **compulsory observation**. The application must be supported by two doctors, but in an emergency, where it would be unsafe to wait for two doctors, the approved social worker, with the support of one doctor, can apply for emergency admission. This only lasts for 72 hours, but after examination by the hospital psychiatrist, it can be replaced by a 28 day observation order or long-term treatment. Compulsory observation orders, unless replaced by admission for long-term treatment, lapse at the end of 28 days when the patient must be discharged.

If an approved social worker believes that a mentally disordered person is being ill-treated or neglected on private property, then an application can be made to a magistrate for a warrant allowing a policeman to enter the premises.

An approved social worker may make an application for a mentally ill person to be admitted to hospital for **treatment**. This must be with the consent of the nearest relative, but if the social worker believes that this consent is being withheld unreasonably, the social worker may apply to the courts for an order appointing someone else to have the rights of nearest relative. Where children in care suffer mental disorders, the social services authority may exercise the rights of nearest relative.

A social services authority can be appointed guardian to a mentally disordered person who is not likely to respond to hospital treatment, but who is in need of protection. Where a private person is appointed as guardian, this must be with the consent of the social services authority.

Social services authorities have a duty to provide for the care and after-care of mentally disordered people. Some run their own residential hostels; others take up places in hostels controlled by voluntary organisations. Social services authorities also run adult fostering or supervised lodging schemes under which ex-patients are boarded privately. Day care centres are provided or sponsored by social services authorities. These can provide sheltered employment for people with untreatable disorders.

Protection of Children Act 1999

A series of notorious cases involving the systematic abuse of children by staff in children's residential care homes led the Secretary of State to consider the introduction of a statutory list of people considered to be unsuitable to work with children. Such a list, called the *Consultancy Service Index,* had been maintained by the Secretary of State on a non-statutory basis since 1993 and the legality of the Index was confirmed by the Court of Appeal in a judgment issued on 1 March 2000 when it dismissed a judicial review challenge mounted by an unqualified social worker who objected to the inclusion of his name on the Index — R v Secretary of State for Health, *ex parte C.*

However, the issue was put beyond doubt by the Protection of Children Act 1999. The 1999 Act gave statutory authority to the Secretary of State to maintain a list of people who are considered to be unsuitable to work with children. The names of people on the Consultancy Service Index were automatically transferred to the list maintained under the 1999 Act. A child care organisation is under a duty to inform the Secretary of State where it has transferred or dismissed someone guilty of misconduct which has harmed a child or put a child at risk. The duty also applies where the individual has evaded formal disciplinary action by resignation or retirement. A person whose name is added to the list (or whose name the Secretary of State refuses to remove from the list) has a right of appeal to an independent Tribunal. There is a cross reference to a similar list kept by the DfEE in respect of teachers and to criminal conviction searches authorised under the Police Act 1997. Employment for work with children must be refused for any person whose name appears on either of the lists.

Care Standards Bill

This Bill has already been mentioned in relation to Ofsted in the section dealing with childminding. However, the Bill has much wider implications which affect most aspects of local authority social services and some aspects of the NHS. The Bill derived from a series of White Papers, the most important of which were *Modernising Social Services* (November 1998) and *Building for the Future* (March 1999) — with similar documents for Wales.

The main purpose of the Bill is to reform the regulatory system for care services in England and Wales — covering residential care homes, nursing homes, children's homes, domiciliary care agencies, fostering agencies, voluntary adoption agencies, private and voluntary healthcare services (including hospitals, clinics and primary care premises (including, for example, dental practices where general anæsthesia is used)).

In its focus on premises and services, the Bill proposes:

- the creation of a new independent quango regulatory body, the *National Care Standards Commission* (in Wales, an new arm or executive agency of the National Assembly), registering and applying new national standards to the care services mentioned in the previous paragraph;
- local authority community homes will now be regulated;
- local authority adoption and fostering services will now be subject to inspection;
- welfare arrangements in boarding schools and FE colleges accommodating children will be subject to inspection.

In relation to social workers and other working with vulnerable groups, the Bill proposes:

- the creation of a new *General Social Care Council* (GSCC) in England and a *Care Council for Wales* (CCW), in place of the Central Council for Education and Training in Social Work (CCETSW), which is abolished;
- the new Councils will regulate the training and standards of social workers;
- each new Council will maintain a completely new national register for social work staff;
- the Secretary of State will maintain a joint England and Wales list of people considered to be unsuitable for working with vulnerable adults (similar to the list maintained under the Protection of Children Act 1999 in relation to workers with children);
- specified care providers (registered with National Care Standards Commission/National Assembly) and employment agencies providing people to work in care positions will be under a duty to refer dubious people to the Secretary of State for possible inclusion in the list;
- care providers will be under a duty to check potential recruits against the list and to refuse employment to anyone on the list.

Appropriate rights of appeal against decisions under the Bill's regulatory regime will lie to the Tribunal established under the Protection of Children Act 1999.

12 Emergency Services

Police — Fire and Rescue — Ambulance — Emergency Planning

Relevant bodies

In the field of the police service, the relevant bodies are:

- Central government departments: the Home Office and its Secretary of State, the Home Secretary (England and Wales); the Scottish Executive and the Scottish Minister for Justice.
- Quangos at national level: the Police Complaints Authority.
- London, excluding the City of London: the Metropolitan Police Service, under the command of the Commissioner (equivalent to the Chief Constable elsewhere) and under the supervision of the Metropolitan Police Authority under the Greater London Authority (GLA), formerly the Home Secretary (equivalent to the Police Authority elsewhere).
- The City of London: the City of London Police, under the command of the Commissioner of Police for the City of London and under the supervision of the Corporation for the City of London.
- Outside London: the Chief Constable, under the supervision of the Police Authority, either county-based or combined to cover more than one county.
- In Scotland, the Chief Constables and Combined Police Authorities, under the supervision of the Scottish Executive and the Minister for Justice.
- In Northern Ireland, the Chief Constable of the Royal Ulster Constabulary (RUC), under the supervision of the Northern Ireland Secretary/Executive (if it exists).

In the field of the fire and rescue service, the relevant bodies are:

- Central government departments: the Home Office and its Secretary of State, the Home Secretary; the Scottish Executive.
- London: the London Fire and Emergency Planning Authority (formerly the London Fire and Civil Defence Authority) under the Greater London Authority.

- Outside London: in the metropolitan counties: Fire and Civil Defence Authorities; elsewhere: either the county council or a Combined Fire Authority covering more than one county or an area containing one or more unitary authorities.

In the field of the ambulance service, the relevant bodies are:

- Central government departments: the Department of Health (DoH) and its Secretary of State Scottish Executive; Welsh Assembly.
- London: the London Ambulance Service.
- Outside London: an NHS Trust.

N.B. The ambulance service has not, since 1974, been part of local government.

In the field of emergency planning, the relevant bodies are:

- Central government departments: the Home Office and its Secretary of State, the Home Secretary (England and Wales); Scottish Executive.
- London: the London Fire and Emergency Planning Authority (formerly the London Fire and Civil Defence Authority) under the Greater London Authority.
- Outside London: in the six metropolitan counties: Fire and Civil Defence Authorities; elsewhere: all local authorities, usually co-ordinated by the Chief Executive of the county council and acting in collaboration with the police, fire and ambulance services.

Police historical background

The present distinctive arrangements for police reflect the origins of the service. Prior to 1830, the maintenance of civil order had rested in the hands of the local magistrates and parish watchmen and constables; the usual response to crime was to increase the number of offences carrying the death penalty and the only way to deal with civil disturbance was to call out the militia.

In London, the position was even worse and *ad hoc* arrangements like the Bow Street Runners set up by the Fielding Brothers and the Thames Police failed to address the problem. When Robert Peel became Prime Minister in 1829, he set up the Metropolitan Police Office at Scotland Yard, the first effective UK police force, under the charge of the Home Office — it was paid for by a new 'police rate' levied on all people within the Metropolitan area who paid the poor rate. Although the force was initially greeted with derision, its effectiveness in reducing crime and maintaining the security of the ordinary citizen of London became self-evident.

Over the next 30 years, the example of London was followed first by the borough councils (as criminals moved out of London) and then by the county magistrates (as criminals moved out of the boroughs). Crime was thus controlled by certainty of detection, rather than severity of punishment.

The modern police

The police service still has strong links with local government, except in the Metropolitan Police area, which is larger than that of the former GLC, but excludes the City of London (which has its own police force). Previously the Home Secretary was the 'police authority' for the Metropolitan Police; the Home Secretary has now handed over responsibility for the Metropolitan Police to the new London Police Authority, working under the auspices of the Greater London Authority (GLA). The remainder of this section deals with the position outside London.

Local police forces are subject to great control by the Home Office (or the Scottish Executive). In addition, Chief Constables have freedom of action in 'operational matters', independently of their police authority. In that respect, they are completely different from local authority chief officers.

Until 1995, the framework of the police system was set out in the Police Act 1964, which had swept away the previous system of county and borough forces and watch committees, replacing it by forces based predominantly on counties. The Chief Constable reported to the Police Committee of the county council. Although the Police Committee was constitutionally part of the county council and received its budget from the county council like any other committee, it was a special committee with its own arrangements and Standing Orders and had a composition fixed by the 1964 Act: two-thirds county councillors, one-third magistrates.

There were, however, some combined forces like Devon and Cornwall Police and Thames Valley Police, with their own Combined Police Authority, which settled its own budget and levied a precept on the collection authorities. The Combined Police Authorities had a composition similar to police committees: two-thirds of the membership consisted of councillors from the area concerned, the remaining third being magistrates.

The system was modified by the Local Government Act 1985, because five of the abolished metropolitan counties — Greater Manchester, Merseyside, South Yorkshire, West Midlands and West Yorkshire — had their own police forces, while the sixth — Tyne and Wear — was already part of the Northumbria Police, with Northumberland County Council. New police authorities were set up in the five metropolitan county areas. They had the same composition as existing county and combined forces.

The Police and Magistrates' Courts Act 1994 (now consolidated into the Police Act 1996) introduced changes to the police authority system, aimed at reducing the local authority elected member involvement in police authorities. The previous two-thirds councillor to one-third magistrates composition of police authorities was replaced on 1 April 1995 by a new independent Police Authority arrangement, usually involving nine councillors, three magistrates and five independent co-opted members.

The councillor members are appointed from the 'relevant authorities' in the police area covered by the new Police Authority. The relevant authorities are: any county council, metropolitan borough council or unitary authority. Where there is only one relevant authority, that authority makes its own appointments. Where there is more than one such authority, the appointments are made by a special joint selection committee on which each authority is represented. The political balance of the councillors on the Police Authority has to reflect the overall political balance of the relevant authorities, so far as practical.

The magistrate members of the Police Authority are appointed by a selection committee of the local Magistrates Courts Committee. The independent members are co-opted by the councillor/magistrate members following a complex selection procedure — which includes the Home Secretary approving the short-list from which the final selection is made. In some parts of the country, the decisions of the then Home Secretary on the initial appointments attracted some criticism. The chairman of the Police Authority is appointed by the members of the Police Authority.

The previous requirement that there should be a public inquiry before police areas could be amalgamated has now been removed, making it easier for the Home Secretary to amalgamate police forces if he so wishes.

Role of Police Authority

The Police Authority is a body corporate in its own right and raises its revenue by fixing and levying a *precept* on the collection authorities, which then include the Police Authority precept in the Council Tax bills which they issue.

The statutory obligation of the Police Authority is to maintain an efficient and effective police force for its police area. There are substantial powers vested in the Home Secretary and the Home Office Inspectorate to act in default, where the Police Authority is considered to have failed to carry out this obligation.

The Police Authority has to publish an annual *Policing Plan*, after consulting the Chief Constable. It also has to publish its local *Policing Objectives* which have to be consistent with *National Objectives* laid down by the Home Secretary. The Police Authority is responsible for monitoring both the implementation of the Policing Plan and the attainment of the local Policing Objectives — and has to publish an Annual Report.

Each Police Authority has a duty to appoint a Chief Constable, subject to the approval of the Home Secretary. The Police Authority also appoints the Assistant Chief Constables, one of whom is then designated by the Chief Constable to act as his or her deputy. The Police Authority has to appoint, for itself, a Clerk, a Treasurer and a Monitoring Officer.

The meetings of the Police Authority are open to the public in the same way as local authority meetings. A member of the Police Authority is nominated to attend meetings of the 'relevant authorities', to answer questions on Police Authority activities asked by councillors at the meeting.

The land and buildings used for police force purposes are owned by the Police Authority, but are managed by the Chief Constable.

Role of the Chief Constable

It is important to understand that the Chief Constable has always had his or her own statutory responsibilities in relation to police operational matters — separate from the Police Authority. The Chief Constable has to have regard to the policing plan approved by the Police Authority, but otherwise has very wide powers as an individual. When police officers misbehave, it is the Chief Constable who is sued, not the Police Authority.

The Chief Constable appoints all officers below the rank of Assistant Chief Constable and exercises considerable control over staff numbers and grades — both uniformed and civilian staff.

The Chief Constable has to produce an annual report. This usually includes crime and vehicle accident statistics, comments on growing problems such as violence and drink driving; how the force is deployed; and details of any major incidents. In addition, the Police Authority may ask the Chief Constable for a special report on any policing matter. The Chief Constable can refuse to provide this (but needs the Home Secretary's approval before doing so), if the Chief Constable considers that it is not in the public interest to disclose the material concerned.

Role of Home Secretary in relation to Police

Mention has already been made of Home Office control. The Home Secretary is responsible for the overall supervision of all police forces in England and Wales — in Scotland, the Minister for Justice undertakes this role. This includes procedures for promotion and discipline, demanding reports from Chief Constables and ordering inquiries. The Home Secretary may also require a Police Authority to call for a Chief Constable's retirement (subject to proper inquiry).

The new police authorities are now statutory authorities in their own right, each with its own Standard Spending Assessment (SSA) limiting the amount which it can spend. However, they differ from local authorities in that a large proportion of their budget is funded by a specific, rather than a general, government grant. The Home Secretary determines both the SSA and the amount of specific grant.

The Home Secretary has a general duty to exercise powers in the way best calculated to improve efficiency. HM Inspectors of Constabulary are appointed to report to the Home Secretary on the efficiency of individual police forces.

Police Complaints

The 1996 Act sets out the procedure for investigating complaints against police officers. The Act effectively restates parts of the Police and Criminal Evidence Act 1984, which established the Police Complaints Authority (PCA).

A complaint first goes to the Chief Constable whose first task is to obtain and preserve all the evidence relating to the conduct complained of. The Chief Constable then has to decide whether the complaint is one which he or she can have investigated or dealt with or whether it should be referred either to the Police Authority or to the PCA. If the complaint relates to a 'senior officer', an officer above the rank of Superintendent, then the complaint is referred to the Police Authority. If the complaint alleges conduct causing death or serious injury (or is of a kind specified by the Home Secretary), then, regardless of the rank of the officer, it is referred to the PCA.

If the complaint is one which the Chief Constable can deal with, and it cannot be resolved informally with the agreement of the complainant, then the Chief Constable appoints an officer of that force or another force to investigate the complaint and produce a report for the Chief Constable. However, at any time, the Chief Constable or the PCA can decide that the complaint should be referred to the PCA.

If the complaint is one which the Police Authority can deal with, then the Police Authority will appoint an officer of that force or an officer of another force (not lower than the rank of the officer complained of) to investigate the complaint and produce a report. Again, at any time, the Police Authority or the PCA can decide that the complaint should be referred to the PCA.

If the complaint is referred to the PCA, then the PCA is in a position to object to the appointment of any officer already appointed to investigate the complaint and require the appointment of someone else. Where no officer has yet been appointed, the PCA approves the appointment when it is made. The PCA can impose conditions on the way the investigation is to be handled. When the investigating officer produces a report, the PCA adds its own 'appropriate statement', which confirms its satisfaction about the conduct of the investigation and comments upon any criminal or disciplinary aspects of the case. The PCA paperwork is sent to the Chief Constable or Police Authority as appropriate.

At the conclusion of an investigation, either under the auspices of the Chief Constable, the Police Authority or the PCA, the Crown Prosecution Service (CPS) may become involved if the investigation has produced evidence of alleged criminal activity on the part of the officer being investigated.

The taking of disciplinary action is a matter for the Police Authority in relation to senior officers or the Chief Constable in relation to all other officers. The Police Authority must follow a formal disciplinary procedure and can impose disciplinary sanctions on the senior officer (including the Chief Constable). If the Chief Constable is unwilling to take disciplinary action in a case where the PCA has been involved, then the PCA, if it wishes, can direct the Chief Constable to take disciplinary action. Police officers may still face disciplinary charges even if criminal charges are not brought, or, if found not guilty when they have been. Disciplinary charges are heard by the Chief Constable and punishment can include a caution, reduction in rank or dismissal. There is a right of appeal from the Chief Constable's decision to a police disciplinary appeals tribunal.

One issue which is coming to the fore is the standard of proof required before any disciplinary charges can be found proven and disciplinary sanctions applied by the Chief Constable to the police officers concerned. Even some Chief Constables have commented on this, frustrated at what they see as an obstacle which prevents them from rooting out unsatisfactory or even corrupt police officers from their police force. In all internal employment-related disciplinary processes which cover the remainder of the population, apart from police officers, the standard of proof is the civil standard: *"is it more likely than not, on the balance of probabilities, that the police officer committed the disciplinary offence?"*. In the case of police officers, the standard of proof is the much stricter criminal one: *"Did the police officer commit the disciplinary offence, beyond all reasonable doubt?"*. There are moves being made to change this, but it will require legislation and any such change is likely to be heavily resisted by the Police Federation.

The only course of action open to a member of the public who is not satisfied with the way a complaint has been dealt with is to apply for a private summons to prosecute the police officers involved in the events complained about, alleging the commission of a criminal offence. The criminal courts then adjudicate on the facts of the matter — but, of course, applying the criminal standard of proof.

Fire and Rescue

It was not until 1938 that local authorities outside London were compelled to provide a fire brigade — the Fire Brigades Act 1938 made it a compulsory duty for county borough councils, non-county borough councils and urban district councils. Before that, fighting fires was a haphazard affair — the local parish or town might have a volunteer fire brigade, or a fire insurance company might run its own brigade. The insurance company brigades would, however, only fight fires in houses belonging to their policy holders — usually indicated by a fire mark plaque fixed to the outside of the house.

During the Second World War, all fire brigades were combined as part of the National Fire Service, but they went back to local authority control in 1947. The difference then was the Fire Services Act made county councils the Fire Authorities. This Act was updated by the London Government Act 1963, (which created the GLC), by the Local

Government Act 1972, (which made metropolitan county councils the Fire Authorities) and by the Local Government Act 1985 (which abolished the GLC and the metropolitan counties). As a consequence, seven new Fire and Civil Defence Authorities were established.

In the six metropolitan counties, the Fire and Civil Defence Authorities are made up of councillors nominated by each metropolitan borough council involved. Numbers are based on the size of each authority and are required to reflect the political balance of the councils as far as is practical. In Greater London, the London Fire and Civil Defence Authority consisted of one councillor nominated by each of the 32 London boroughs, plus one from the City of London — this changed when the Greater London Authority arrived.

The introduction of new unitary authorities, as a consequence of the 1992 rolling programme of local government review, has resulted in the creation of new combined fire authorities to preserve the existing county-wide fire services in those counties where the two-tier status quo has not been maintained.

Combined fire authorities can cover two or more counties — this is done either by agreement or by direction of the Home Secretary. A fire brigade which is the responsibility of a county council in a completely two-tier county, will be supervised by a committee of the county council and have its budget managed by the county council, like any other service which the county council provides. Fire and civil defence authorities and combined fire authorities determine their own budget in the same way as police authorities and issue precepts to the collection authorities. Fire authorities bear the cost of local fire services but receive an Exchequer contribution within the RSG. There is no specific grant similar to that given for the police service.

Role of the Home Secretary and Fire Authorities

Each Fire Authority has to notify the Home Secretary each year of its brigade establishment scheme; the Home Secretary decides whether the provision is adequate and efficient. The Home Secretary may make such a scheme for any brigade, if necessary, and any brigade intending to reduce its services must obtain the consent of the Home Secretary before it can do so. In addition, the Home Secretary maintains a system of fire brigade inspectors, similar to those for the police service. The Home Secretary also has a general power to make detailed regulations on the running of fire brigades, particularly with regard to staffing.

Each of the Fire Authorities in England and Wales must:

- equip and train a fire fighting force;
- make arrangements for dealing with calls for assistance;
- gather information about 'risk' buildings in the area;

- give advice on fire protection; and
- make sure that the local water company maintains an adequate supply of water at a pressure suitable for fire fighting.

Each Fire Authority must also draw up reinforcement schemes with neighbouring fire services to deal with big fires. Similar arrangements operate in Scotland.

In addition to their main function of fire fighting and fire prevention, fire brigades may be called on to deal with other emergencies. Special services are divided into two categories — humanitarian and non-humanitarian (not urgent). An example of the former is a serious road accident in which people are trapped. A non-humanitarian incident could involve pumping out a flooded basement.

The Fire Precautions Act 1971 laid down that various kinds of premises, for example, offices, sports grounds, hotels and theatres, could not be used without a Fire Certificate. Certificates are issued by Fire Authorities after an inspection, to see if there are adequate fire precautions and fire escapes. This provision runs parallel to two others: the requirement for adequate fire precautions in new buildings under the Fire Regulations; and the requirement under the Public Health Act 1936 that fire escapes must be provided in buildings like theatres and hotels.

The disaster at Bradford City Football Club in 1985 helped concentrate minds on the provisions of the 1971 Act, implementation of which had been very slow. An immediate result was that many football grounds were forced to reduce attendance limits until further safety precautions were taken.

Ambulance Service

Prior to the 1974 reorganisation, local authorities had responsibility for the ambulance service, along with other public health responsibilities under the direction of the local authority's Medical Officer of Health. Those responsibilities transferred to District Health Authorities in 1974 and became part of the National Health Service. Many ambulance services are now managed by NHS trusts as explained in *Essential Central Government*.

Although the ambulance service is not strictly part of local government any more, nonetheless the long tradition of close co-operation between the three emergency services — police, fire and ambulance — continues. The ambulance service plays a full part not only in everyday incidents but also in the exercises undertaken as part of the emergency planning activities of what used to be called Civil Defence.

Emergency Planning and Civil Defence

Civil defence, like the other emergency services, is a local authority function which the Home Secretary closely controls. But for this, there would be no civil defence provision in some authorities.

The Civil Defence Act 1948 empowered the Home Secretary to take the necessary measures to implement an effective means of civil defence. It also empowered the Home Secretary to direct local authorities to take appropriate measures.

Local authority powers were extended by the Civil Defence (Planning) Regulations 1974, which imposed on county councils — in the metropolitan areas the Fire and Civil Defence Authorities — the duty to make plans to deal with hostile attacks, so as to preserve essential services and look after the victims. The county council has to consult the shire borough/district councils about its emergency plans, and the plans cannot be implemented without authorisation by the Home Secretary.

Recently, the Home Office has made a major policy change and now seeks to integrate peace time disaster and war planning, the emphasis on the latter having declined as part of the 'peace dividend' resulting from political changes in Eastern Europe. The Home Office is also seeking to encourage emergency planning to become an integral part of local authority work, instead of 'semi-detached', as in the past. This change may make it more acceptable to those local authorities who have had political objections to the old civil defence concept.

All county councils in England and Wales have an *emergency planning officer* who is responsible for co-ordinating the emergency services, in accordance with the various civil disaster plans.

The Home Secretary has some discretion in reimbursement of local authority costs; in some cases they get all the money back, but in others only 75%. These arrangements are likely to be reviewed by the Home Office. In view of the policy change, the future of the present specific grant must be in doubt.

13 Environmental Health and Consumer Protection

Relevant bodies — environmental health — waste collection and disposal — pollution control — contaminated land — statutory nuisances — clean air — food hygiene — trading standards — food and drugs — slaughterhouses — animal health — shops — weights and measures — trade descriptions — fair trading — consumer credit

The relevant bodies

In the field of environmental health, the relevant bodies are:

- Central government department: the Department of the Environment, Transport and the Regions (DETR) and its Secretary of State; the Scottish Executive and the Welsh Assembly.
- Quangos at national level: the Environment Agency (EA) and the Scottish Environmental Protection Agency (SEPA).
- Local authorities:
  - — *(waste collection, pollution control, statutory nuisances, contaminated land and clean air)* unitary authorities, London borough councils, metropolitan borough councils, shire borough/district councils in two-tier areas, and the Corporation of the City of London;
  - — *(waste disposal)* unitary authorities, joint boards in London and metropolitan county areas, and county councils in two-tier areas.

In the field of food and animal health, the relevant bodies are:

- Central government department: the Ministry of Agriculture, Fisheries and Food (MAFF) and its Secretary of State; the Scottish Executive and the Welsh Assembly.
- Local authorities:
  - — *(food safety)* unitary authorities, London borough councils, metropolitan borough councils, shire borough/district councils in two-tier areas, and the Corporation of the City of London;

— *(food in consumer protection and animal health)* unitary authorities, London borough councils, metropolitan borough councils, county councils in two-tier areas, and the Corporation of the City of London *(in animal health, plus importation of animals within former GLC area).*

In the field of consumer protection, the relevant bodies are:

- Central government department: the Department of Trade and Industry (DTI) and its Secretary of State, the President of the Board of Trade; the Scottish Executive and the Welsh Assembly.
- Local authorities:
  — *(trading standards, weights and measures, consumer credit)* unitary authorities, London borough councils, metropolitan borough councils, county councils in two-tier areas, and the Corporation of the City of London;
  — *(shops)* unitary authorities, London borough councils, metropolitan borough councils, shire borough/district councils in two-tier areas, and the Corporation of the City of London.

Environmental health — background

The modern system of shire borough/district councils grew out of the local boards of health and other sanitary authorities set up under the Public Health Acts 1872 and 1875. Local government lost most of its health functions in 1948 and 1974 with the establishment and reorganisation of the NHS, leaving it only with a responsibility for environmental health. The principal statute under which local authorities worked then was the Public Health Act 1936, but the main statutory provisions are now to be found in the Environmental Protection Act (EPA) 1990. Environmental services overlap many other duties of local authorities, particularly trading standards and housing. Many all-purpose authorities will have departments of environmental services, which cover environmental health and all aspects of trading standards and consumer protection. Others, including some shire borough/district councils, have combined environmental health and housing departments.

Waste collection

The environmental health services which are most familiar to the general public are those for street cleaning and the collection and disposal of domestic and trade refuse.

The collection authorities arrange for the collection of household waste in their area and can arrange for the collection of commercial or industrial waste, if asked to do so. The collection of household waste is covered by the Council Tax; the collection of commercial or industrial waste is subject to a charge. The waste collection authorities also arrange for the emptying of privies and cesspools.

Once collected, the waste has to be delivered to places designated by the waste disposal authority. However, most collection authorities now operate some sort of recycling scheme, diverting recyclable waste from the waste delivered to the waste disposal authority.

Waste disposal

As already explained, special arrangements exist in London and the metropolitan county areas. In the remainder of England and Wales, the EPA 1990 required waste disposal authorities to form arm's-length *Local Authority Waste Disposal Companies* (LAWDCs) and then transfer most of their operational activities to the LAWDC. Waste disposal authorities were obliged to carry out their functions through *Waste Disposal Contractors* — either their LAWDC or, if they preferred, entirely through private sector contractors. The process adopted was a form of CCT.

Waste disposal authorities are responsible for the disposal of waste collected by the collection authorities; for providing waste transfer sites and sites where householders can take their waste; and for recycling waste or selling it for scrap. The waste disposal contractors, if they operate waste disposal sites, have to obtain a *Waste Management Licence* from the *Waste Regulation Authority*. In managing the waste within their control, waste management contractors have to comply with the *Duty of Care Code of Practice*, issued by the Secretary of State.

Waste regulation

The waste regulation authority (EA or SEPA) regulates the management of *controlled waste* (household, commercial or industrial waste) by issuing *Waste Management Licences* — either a site licence or a mobile plant licence. Licences can be refused or granted subject to conditions. Arrangements for enforcement are similar to those for other forms of pollution control under the EPA 1990 (see later).

Pollution control

Interest in the environment has increased significantly in recent years and the EPA 1990 consolidated earlier legislation, aiming to produce an integrated, centrally operated, pollution control policy and air pollution control by local authorities. Much of the EPA 1990 was shaped by the obligations of the UK government to translate EU legislation and Directions into UK domestic law. This EU approach resulted in the Act containing the formula *"best available techniques not entailing excessive cost"* (BATNEEC) in place of the previous requirement to use *'best practical means'*.

The regulatory regime is similar to the town and country planning system and relates both to processes and to the release of substances into the environment, whether to land, air or water. However, processes are divided into two lists: list A contains those processes which are subject to central enforcement through the EA/SEPA (oil refineries, steel works and large chemical plants); list B contains those processes which are subject to local authority enforcement — mostly small power plants, glass works and municipal and hospital incinerators. Even in relation to list B processes, the Secretary of State specifies the standards, objectives and requirements to be applied by local authority inspectors and can direct local authorities how to discharge their responsibilities in specific cases. The BATNEEC approach means that enforcing authorities have to keep up to date on developments in pollution abatement technology and in techniques in relevant processes.

No process can be carried on without an authorisation issued by the relevant enforcing authority. Applications can be granted subject to conditions or refused, with appeals to the Secretary of State by dissatisfied applicants. The enforcing authority can withdraw the authorisation at any time.

If the enforcing authority believes that an operator is in breach of the authorisation, it can serve an *Enforcement Notice*, specifying the nature of the breach, the steps to be taken to put matters right and the time within which those steps are to be taken. Even where the process is being carried out satisfactorily, there may be external factors which the enforcing authority believes create an imminent risk of serious pollution to the environment and, in that event, the authority must serve a *Prohibition Notice*, effectively withdrawing the authorisation while the prohibition notice subsists. There are rights of appeal to the Secretary of State against these notices.

Failure to obtain an authorisation or to comply with an enforcement or prohibition notice constitutes a criminal offence, with a maximum fine of £2,000 in the magistrates court or an unlimited fine and/or imprisonment for up to two years in the crown court.

Contaminated land

The EPA 1990 required relevant local authorities to inspect their area to identify and register any contaminated land. If the contamination problems were thought to be particularly serious, then the local authority could designate the site as a 'special site'. In both cases, the EA/SEPA had to be notified. The enforcing authority for 'special sites' is the EA/SEPA; for others, the local authority. The enforcing authority is obliged to serve a *Remediation Notice* on the appropriate person, specifying the required remedial action and the time in which that action has to be taken. The provisions for appeal and enforcement are similar to other EPA provisions.

Statutory nuisances

These have already been referred to in the Chapter on *Housing*. The EPA 1990 enables relevant local authorities to deal with statutory nuisances such as the following which are prejudicial to health or a nuisance: premises; smoke, fumes or gas emitted from premises; dust, steam smell or effluvia; accumulations of rubbish; animals; and noise from premises or from a vehicle, machinery or equipment in the street. In relation to noise, the powers extend to seizing the equipment creating the noise.

Enforcement is through an *Abatement Notice*, served on the person responsible for the nuisance, specifying the nature of the nuisance, the steps to be taken to stop it and the time within which those steps are to be taken. Appeals against such notices are to the magistrates court. Unusually, any person who is aggrieved by a statutory nuisance can lay a complaint before the magistrates court direct.

The powers of the relevant local authority were taken one step further by the Noise Act 1996 which enables control over noise emitted from dwellings at night. An officer of the local authority investigates complaints and, if the measured noise level exceeds the statutory limits, immediately serves a *Warning Notice* on the person responsible for the offending noise. Failure to comply with the notice constitutes a criminal offence. After a warning notice, the local authority's officers' powers include right of entry without warrant to seize the offending equipment, and obstruction of the officer also constitutes a criminal offence.

Clean air

The Clean Air Act 1993 updated provisions which originally appeared in the Clean Air Act 1956, to eliminate the winter smogs which were a common occurrence before the 1956 Act was passed. The relevant local authority enforces the provisions of the Act — prohibiting the emission of 'dark smoke' from chimneys; limiting the emission of smoke, grit, dust and fumes from chimneys; regulating the height of chimneys; declaring *Smoke Control Areas* in which the emission of smoke is prohibited; and monitoring the exhaust emissions from vehicles in accordance with regulations laid down by the Secretary of State.

The Environment Act 1995 gave responsibilities to relevant local authorities to review present and likely future air quality in their area. Where air quality is not meeting prescribed standards or objectives, the local authority can designate an *Air Quality Management Area,* for which they then produce an *Air Quality Action Plan,* setting out measures to be taken to improve air quality.

Food safety

Food safety functions are, in two-tier areas, the responsibility of shire borough/district councils. The functions are related to the observance of proper hygiene in selling food for human consumption, and any other activities related to this — importing, preparing, transporting, storing, packing, wrapping, displaying, serving and delivering food.

The principal Act is the Food Safety Act 1990, although the detail is found in the regulations made under the Act, which now reflect EU requirements. The 1990 Act creates criminal offences connected with the safety of food: rendering food injurious to health; and selling food which does not comply with food safety requirements.

The local food safety authority enforces the requirements of the Act, usually through its environmental health inspectors. The inspectors can: inspect and seize suspect food; issue *Improvement Notices* to proprietors of food businesses; and issue *Emergency Prohibition Notices*, closing down a food business where there is a risk to health. In taking action, especially in relation to communicable disease, there will usually be close co-operation with the public health parts of the NHS. Additional enforcement obligations can arise at short notice — the recent ban on the sale of beef on the bone in shops and restaurants, in the wake of the BSE scare, was an example.

Food safety authorities are also responsible for functions relating to slaughterhouses, principally their licensing in accordance with EU regulations and to inspect the quality of the meat produced by the slaughterhouse. Food safety authorities have the power to provide, themselves, public slaughterhouses, cold stores and refrigerators.

Animal health

The functions of the relevant local authority under the Animal Health Act 1981 cover live animals and are intended to prevent the spread of specified types of disease by movement or importation.

The local authority's inspectors enforce the provisions of the 1981 Act and the various regulations made under the Act relating to specific forms of animal disease. Where the landowner suspects an outbreak of specified disease, he or she must inform the police, the local authority and MAAF. There is close co-operation between the police, the local authority and the MAAF Veterinary Service. Once an outbreak has been confirmed, the movement of animals from the land is prohibited and the movement of animals within and beyond the local area is prohibited, except by licence granted by a local authority inspector.

The local authority inspector can enter premises to check for the existence of disease, verify that there have been no movement licence contraventions, and that any importation restrictions have been satisfied. Contraventions of animal health legislation constitute criminal offences and are regarded as being so serious that they can be prosecuted by the police as well as the local authority.

Shops

The previous responsibilities of local authorities in relation to shops under the Shops Act 1950 have been removed by the Deregulation and Contracting Out Act 1994. The government believed that the shop owners were better able to control for themselves opening hours, goods permitted for sale and employment practices. The one exception to this is Sunday trading.

Sunday trading used to be a mess, with law enforcement entirely dependent on the determination or otherwise of each responsible authority (all principal authorities except county councils). A few years ago the government tried to clear up the legislation, but lost its Bill, which would have abolished all restrictions on Sunday trading, at second reading. The topic came back on the agenda when some national companies appealed to the EU, claiming that its laws allowed them to open on a Sunday. In the event, it was decided that the UK laws did not offend EU legislation — so the problem was back with the UK government. This resulted in the Sunday Trading Act 1994 which allows 'large shops' to open on Sunday, but subject to conditions.

Litter

There are strict controls over the leaving of litter on land under the EPA 1990 which requires local authorities, statutory undertakers and other owners of public land to keep their land free of litter. *Litter Control Areas* may be designated by principal authorities other than county councils and then it becomes an offence for any person to throw down, drop or otherwise dispose of litter on land owned by a public body within the control area.

General health risks

There is a close working relationship between environmental health departments and the NHS — the Medical Officer of Health, who prior to 1974 was a local government employee, has resurfaced as Community Physician or Director of Public Health (or similar) in the NHS. If measures for preventing damage to public health fail, and a disease like smallpox, dysentery or typhoid breaks out, local authorities must notify the NHS and take immediate steps to prevent its spread.

Other environmental health activities

Other environmental services provided by local authorities include the provision of public lavatories, the maintenance of cemeteries and crematoria, and dealing with dangerous dogs, vermin and insect infestations.

Trading standards and consumer protection

Consumer protection is fairly recent responsibility of local government which grew out of the traditional services provided by weights and measures departments. Achieving accurate quantities was the aim of three Weights and Measures Acts, but in the latter half of the 1960s, Parliament started to look at other ways of helping consumers. Very quickly, trading standards departments were set up. They became concerned with the accurate description of goods, fair trading practices, credit and the safety of goods.

A number of authorities went further than required by law by setting up consumer advice departments. These have frequently worked in conjunction with Citizens Advice Bureaux and bodies like the Consumers Association.

Trading standards officers are employed by trading standards authorities. In two-tier areas, it is important not to confuse their work with that of environmental health officers who work for shire borough/district councils, rather than county councils. As far as food is concerned, composition and labelling under the food and drugs legislation is a consumer protection responsibility of the county council, while food hygiene is the concern of environmental health officers of the shire borough/district council.

Food in the context of consumer protection

This is not the same as food safety, although, rather confusingly, the main statutory provisions are found in the Food Safety Act 1990. In two-tier areas, the relevant authority is the county council, which appoints a public analyst who is also available to undertake scientific analysis services for shire borough/district councils, in connection with food safety as well.

The 1990 Act creates two main offences: selling food which is not of the nature or substance or quality demanded by the purchaser; and falsely describing or presenting food — usually through advertisement or labelling. Again, the detail is in the subordinate regulations made by the Secretary of State under the 1990 Act. Contraventions are criminal offences, usually enforced by trading standards officers.

Trading standards

Weights and measures functions of local authorities are principally defined by the Weights and Measures Acts of 1963 and 1979. Weights and measures authorities have to keep standard weights and measures (usually kept in a secure and temperature-controlled metrology laboratory) against which all those used in their areas can be checked. All authorities have to appoint a chief inspector of weights and measures and other inspectors, as required. All inspectors must possess qualification certificates from the DTI and enforce compliance with the standards in a personal capacity.

Use of unauthorised weights and measures is a criminal offence — all scales used to measure goods for sale must be verified against the standards kept by the local authority and stamped. Inspectors, armed with consent from magistrates, can demand entry to premises to check and test equipment. Sale of food or other goods by short weight is also a criminal offence and market stalls and shops are regularly checked. Retailers do have a defence of mistake, if they can show they took all due care. The weight and measures of manufactured goods are checked at the factory; the weights and measures of other goods, such as loose food, fuel and beer are checked at the point of sale.

Trade descriptions

Trading standards authorities have a duty to enforce the controls imposed by the Trade Descriptions (not Trades Description) Acts of 1968 and 1972. These provisions make it a criminal offence to apply a false trade description to the item being sold or to give a false indication of its price. The most usual false trade description cases involve over-optimistic holiday brochures, 'clocked' cars and counterfeit goods (which can be seized, confiscated and later destroyed or recycled). The Acts also lay down the conditions under which goods may be offered at a special 'sale' price.

Fair trading and consumer credit

Setting up the office of Director General of Fair Trading by the Fair Trading Act 1973, proved a big help to local authority trading standards officers. Particularly, they welcomed the Director General's power to ask anyone in the course of business acting in a way detrimental to the interests of consumers, to give an assurance as to future conduct. Where an assurance is not given, the Director General can take the 'offender' before the Restrictive Practices Court or county court, which can accept an assurance or, failing that, make an order. Local authority officers regard this as a valuable supplement to their work, particularly where persistent complaints could not previously be adequately dealt with by prosecution under the Trade Descriptions Act.

Local authorities also work closely with the Director General in implementing the provisions of the 1974 Consumer Credit Act, the 1976 Resale Prices Act, the 1978 Consumer Safety Act, and the 1979 Sale of Goods Act.

Civil claims, such as those under the Sale of Goods Act, have to be brought by individual consumers in the county courts. However, contraventions of the Trade Descriptions Acts and the Credit Acts are criminal offences. Prosecutions in matters of purely local interest are brought by trading standards officers, but in cases which raise questions of general policy or issues of a national character, the prosecution is brought by the Director General of Fair Trading.

14 Highways, Transportation and Leisure

Relevant bodies — highways — planning of highways — creation, diversion and closure — lighting — traffic management — public transport, buses and taxis — libraries — museums and art galleries — performing arts — recreation

The relevant bodies

In the field of highways and transportation, the relevant bodies are:

- Central government department: the Department of Environment, Transport and the Regions (DETR) and its Secretary of State; the Scottish Executive and the Welsh Assembly.
- Local highways authorities: unitary authorities, London borough councils, metropolitan borough councils, county councils in two-tier areas, and the Corporation of the City of London. In addition, shire borough/district councils will usually be agent authorities for highways in part or all of their area and will have their own powers in relation to off-street car parking; and parish/community councils have limited powers in relation to footpaths and off-street car parking.

In the field of recreation and leisure, the relevant bodies are:

- Central government department: the Department for Culture, Media and Sport and its Secretary of State; the Scottish Executive and the Welsh Assembly.
- Quangos at national level: such as the Sports Council.
- Local authorities: all local authorities, but depending on the aspect of recreation and leisure in two-tier areas: county councils tend to deal with country parks, while shire borough/district councils deal with swimming pools and leisure centres.

In the field of museums, art galleries and the performing arts, the relevant bodies are:

- Central government department: the Department for Culture, Media and Sport and its Secretary of State; the Scottish Executive and Welsh Assembly.
- Quangos at national and regional level: such as the Arts Council and the Regional Arts Boards.
- Local authorities: all local authorities.

In the field of libraries, the relevant bodies are:

- Central government department: the Department for Culture, Media and Sport and its Secretary of State; the Scottish Executive and Welsh Assembly.
- Local library authorities: unitary authorities, London borough councils, metropolitan borough councils, county councils in two-tier areas, and the Corporation of the City of London.

Historical context of highways

Highways have a very long history, starting with the long-distance routes used as long ago as the Iron Age, mostly along ridgeways, because the going was easier on the drier ground found there. Any other route tended to be purely local in character, serving the needs of the settlement, since travel beyond the confines of the settlement was rare.

The first attempt at improving the road system came with the arrival with the Romans — their roads were intended for military purposes, followed straight routes across the country and were so well constructed that they could be used in all weathers. The Dark Ages followed the departure of the Romans and their roads fell into disrepair. For hundreds of years, travel by road using wheeled vehicles was impossible during the winter months in those areas where the soil conditions were heavy. During the Middle Ages that did not matter because long-distance commerce did not exist to any great extent. As commerce grew from Tudor times onwards, road conditions became more important but were so bad that most goods were taken by sea, navigable river and, later, canal. At that time, parish councils were responsible for the upkeep of the main routes which passed through their area, but they saw little point in carrying out work which benefited people passing through from elsewhere — so the standard of work was poor, or the work was not done at all.

The solution to the problem was to use private enterprise — the eighteenth century version of PFI. Turnpike companies were granted Parliamentary powers to remake and maintain specific sections of road, in return for levying tolls on the users of the road. There were 2,000 Road Acts passed between 1700 and 1790 giving these powers and this approach, coupled with the road-making techniques pioneered by the engineer Macadam, laid the foundation for the long-distance road system which we see today.

When the new county councils came into existence in 1888, they assumed responsibility for roads in their area — followed by the various types of all-purpose authorities which came into existence later. The road system was seen as vital for national communications and commerce and, to avoid a repetition of the original problem of variable maintenance, the government retained control over those roads which were considered to be the most strategic — the trunk roads. More recently, the trunk road system was supplemented, again by the government, by the construction of 'special' roads similar to the European autobahns/autoroutes — the motorways. Even more recently, the strategic view of the UK road system now transcends national boundaries and is considered from the standpoint of EU road communication infrastructure.

Highways and highways authorities

The historical commentary explains why responsibility for roads is shared by all tiers of government, central as well as local. In local government terms, highways are discussed by every type of local authority. A committee concerned with highways is to be found in all principal local authorities, although this will change as a consequence of the adoption of one of the executive models under the Local Government Bill.

The term 'highway' means some kind of road, bridleway or footpath over which there exists a public right of way — a highway can be maintainable at public expense or privately maintainable. The various types of highway can be loosely divided into:

- motorways and trunk roads (M and A roads);
- primary roads (most A roads);
- secondary roads (B roads);
- unclassified roads in rural and urban areas;
- bridleways and footpaths;
- privately maintained roads and streets.

Highways authorities are responsible for the planning and construction of highways, maintaining and closing them, street lighting, traffic management, off-street and on-street parking and road safety. The highways authority for a particular type of road will depend upon what it is and where it is:

- *motorways and trunk roads:* the Secretary of State;
- *primary, secondary and unclassified roads:* unitary authorities, London borough councils, metropolitan borough councils, the Corporation of the City of London, and county councils in two-tier areas except where powers have been delegated to a shire borough/district council for part or all of their area;
- *bridleways and footpaths:* all local authorities;
- *private roads:* no local authority — the owners of property fronting the road are liable for its maintenance.

Motorways are 'Special Roads' under the highways legislation and are subject to their own procedures for maintenance and improvement. Trunk roads pre-date motorways and are the basic network of roads linking major centres of population, industrial areas and ports, and are designated as such by the Secretary of State. The Secretary of State is responsible for overall policy, planning, improving, maintaining, financing and controlling the trunk road and motorway programme, with decisions often being taken in the relevant regional office. Some of the responsibilities for motorways and trunk roads have been delegated to the *Highways Agency*, an executive agency which acts on behalf of the Secretary of State for maintenance and improvement. County councils used to maintain most motorways and trunk roads as agents of the Secretary of State, but now maintenance is contracted out by the Highways Agency to a variety of contractors; if county councils are still involved in this maintenance work, it is because they put in the cheapest quote. The role of the Highways Agency has now been redefined by the New Labour Government, as explained in a later section.

For primary, secondary and unclassified roads in London, the Secretary of State can designate certain roads to ensure a smooth flow of traffic: the London borough councils have to inform the Secretary of State of any proposals for these roads. For such roads in two-tier areas, agency arrangements can exist between the county council and a shire borough/district council. These agency agreements define the extent of delegation. Under the Local Government Act 1972, shire borough/district councils could claim agency powers over roads subject to a 30mph speed limit. Most county councils believed that this would produce an uneconomic result and so offered much broader agency arrangements (including traffic management) to those borough/district councils interested in undertaking highways functions.

Planning major highways

There are special procedures for informing and consulting people about major road projects. In the case of new roads, there is co-operation between government departments, local authorities and public bodies, with alternative routes being publicised.

A consultative document is issued, describing the various routes and giving information on cost, an environmental impact assessment (now important in the EU context) and other relevant factors. The statement is publicised and sent to all local authorities affected by the proposals. A public exhibition to present and to explain any alternative solutions is arranged. Opponents to the proposals submit their views to the Secretary of State. At the end of the consultation period, all the views expressed are examined. The decision on the route is published in a statement giving a summary of the public response and the DETR's reasons for its choice. After further detailed work, the chosen route is normally subject to draft orders, including any necessary CPOs.

If there are objections to the draft orders, a public inquiry is held. The inquiry is concerned with the route, design and need for the road. The Inspector hears the case for and against the road and reports to the Secretary of State. The final decision is taken by the Secretary of State — an administratively demanding and time-consuming process that can take a number of years. Once the orders have been made, in some cases the problems are just starting — determined resistance to the actual construction of environmentally sensitive and unwelcome road schemes is now a regular occurrence.

It is now generally considered that new roads tend to generate traffic, because the convenience of the new roads encourages more people to use cars. The need to do something about the ever-increasing volume of traffic has finally penetrated to highways engineers. The Traffic Reduction Act 1997 requires the design of new highways to take account of the need to reduce traffic, although there is no real indication of how this is to be achieved, given that the real answer lies in improving public transport. The fairly common provision of park-and-ride schemes and bus-only lanes has now been joined by more experimental traffic regulation orders, such as having '+2' lanes — giving priority to cars containing more than just their driver.

A New Deal for Transport

In July 1999, New Labour introduced a DETR White Paper — *A New Deal for Transport: Better for Everyone.* This White Paper set out to explain a major shift in government policy towards a more integrated approach to roads and transport, with the main aim of reversing the decline in the use of public transport. A new *Commission for Integrated Transport* would be created, to advise the government on the implementation of integrated transport policy, monitor developments across the transport, environment, health and other areas and to review progress towards government objectives.

The Highways Agency's role would change from being a road builder to being a road network operator, contributing towards sustainable development by maintaining, improving and operating the trunk road network in support of integrated transport and land use policies. The system of trunk roads was reviewed and about 60% would be retained as being the 'core' network of nationally important routes; the rest would be de-trunked and transferred to local highways authorities. Future trunk road planning would be co-ordinated with land-use planning through *Regional Planning Guidance* (RPG), which, in turn, would bring in all of the other aspects of integrated transport and work on a cross-boundary basis. The Highways Agency will also be expected to work more closely with rail operators to make interchanges easier, facilitating park-and-ride schemes and freight transfer facilities.

Local authorities would be required to formulate a five-year *Local Transport Plan,* to: co-ordinate and improve local transport; promote walking and cycling; promote green transport plans for journeys to work, school and elsewhere; and reduce social exclusion, especially in rural areas. Local Transport Plans could include such initiatives as: bus quality partnerships; freight quality partnerships; traffic management and calming; road user charging; and improving air quality.

Local authorities were asked to prepare, during 1999, non-statutory Local Transport Plans in the first instance (the new process required legislation to give it the necessary statutory authority) covering the period 2000 to 2005. The Local Transport Plans process will replace the existing *Transport Policies and Programmes* (TPP) system as a means of resource allocation by central government

Private streets

Some private streets are just that — the public has no right of way over it and this status is maintained by closing the street at regular intervals to avoid the creation of a public right of way by protracted unchallenged usage or 'prescription' — in addition, there may also be notices displayed, making it clear that just because the public is allowed to pass and re-pass over the street does not mean to imply that the street owners intend to 'dedicate' the street as a public highway.

However, there are some private streets which are public rights of way and the owners of property fronting a privately maintained street, which is, nevertheless a public highway, are liable for its maintenance. Such streets are fairly obvious because of the condition of their surface and sometimes the sign 'unadopted' appears under the street name. 'Unadopted' means that the local highways authority has not adopted responsibility for maintaining the street. Such streets can be adopted by the highways authority under the Private Street Works Acts, but only after the owners have paid for the street to be improved to adoption standard — a very expensive business where the cost is measured in hundreds (if not thousands) of pounds per running foot of frontage. The highways authority must go through a statutory procedure to carry out the works and, very occasionally, the frontagers can escape financial liability if they are able to prove that the street was an 'ancient highway' — that is, was in existence as a public right of way before the passing of the Highways Act 1835.

Creating, diverting and closing highways

Most newly-created highways are either the result of new road schemes or as a consequence of housing or other development. In the case of road schemes, the relevant highways authority will construct the new road to a suitable standard and then adopt it as a publicly maintainable highway. In the case of housing or other development, the developer will want to ensure that, when the development is finished, the local highways authority will assume responsibility for the estate roads. The developer, therefore, enters into a formal agreement with the local highways authority which requires the developer to construct the estate roads to adoption standard and then maintain them until they are formally adopted, repairing any faults during that period. Such an agreement will be backed by a bond issued by a bank or insurance company, so that if the developer goes bust or defaults, the roads will be finished and adopted without expense to the new householders.

In certain circumstances, highways (usually footpaths or bridleways) can be closed where they are no longer used or closed or diverted to enable development (for which planning consent has been given) to take place. Where a highway is being closed because it is no longer used, the highways authority has to apply to the magistrates court for an *Extinguishment Order* under the Highways Acts. Such applications are published and if there is a proven objection on the grounds that the highway is still in use, then the magistrates will not grant the order.

The other process for closing (or, more often, diverting) a highway is by obtaining a *Public Path Diversion Order* under the Town and Country Planning Acts, if necessary, following a local inquiry. This order is used to realign a footpath, so that it runs around the edge of the development site or follows the estate road pattern. Some closures or diversions can be temporary, while development takes place, with reinstatement along the original route being made after the development has been concluded — for example, for mineral extraction.

Developers need to very sure about establishing the existence of any rights of way across their site and obtaining any necessary diversion orders **before** they start work. This is fairly easy to do by inspecting the *Definitive Rights of Way Map* maintained by local highways authorities. When mistakes are made, it is often difficult (and sometimes impossible) to correct them afterwards and this occasionally leads to stories about the new householders having to let people walk through their gardens or, even, through their houses, along the line of the pre-existing footpath.

Street lighting

Highways authorities are responsible for street lighting, but shire borough/district councils (even where there are no agency arrangements) and parish/community councils may also be responsible for lighting footpaths and footways.

Traffic management, parking and road safety

Highway authorities are responsible for traffic management measures. These measures include one-way systems, traffic lights, pelican crossings, roundabouts, bus-only lanes, speed limits, weight restrictions limiting use by heavy vehicles, traffic calming measures and restrictions on waiting and unloading. Traffic regulation orders made by the highways authority, and following a statutory procedure, are used to put in place most traffic management measures. In special circumstances, such as introducing a 20 mph zone, a traffic regulation order may require the approval of the Secretary of State.

One of the most common form of traffic regulation order is that used to limit or prohibit on-street parking — such measures can include the use of meters or discs. In addition, highways authorities, shire borough/district councils and parish/community councils may provide off-street car parks.

Highway authorities have a duty to study the causes of road accidents and take measures to promote road safety and reduce accidents. Such measures may include giving practical training to road users, giving out information on road safety (especially in schools), and improving and repairing roads which are under their control.

Public transport and buses

Under the Local Government Act 1972, county councils and the then metropolitan county councils were made responsible for the co-ordination of transport, although their rôles were slightly different. The metropolitan counties provided bus services through passenger transport executives and sought to bring an integrated approach to local transport in their area. County councils "promoted the provision of a co-ordinated system of public transport" in their area, because many shire borough/district councils provided their own bus services.

The 45 district councils who had provided a municipal bus service before 1972 were allowed to carry on — at least for a time. Local authorities were able to subsidise bus services and in the metropolitan county areas, subsidies were often high and fares low. Those local authorities which were heavily subsidising bus fares out of the Rates claimed that this was part of their integrated transport policy (to encourage the use of public transport) but it brought them into direct conflict with both Labour and Conservative Governments. The rapid increase in the fare subsidy cost falling on local taxation distorted the authorities' revenue budgets.

With the abolition of the metropolitan county councils in 1986, responsibility for transport (buses, airports, and docks) in metropolitan areas was transferred to joint boards. In London, different arrangements were made, which are outlined later.

As part of their broader transportation responsibilities, county councils and joint boards can subsidise local transport services, mostly buses but, sometimes, rail services, to ensure a transportation system able to meet local needs.

The Transport Act 1985 brought about the major changes in approach in relation to buses. The Act was based on the principle that local bus services should be provided by the free market, with local authorities responsible not for planning a comprehensive network, but only for securing socially necessary services which the market would not provide. The aim was that the cost of the service to the user should first be reduced by competition, before any subsidy was considered.

In order to permit greater competition, bus services were deregulated in October 1986, thereby allowing any number of operators to run on a particular route. Anyone wishing to provide a bus service was merely required to obtain a Public Service Operators Licence from the Traffic Commissioners. This shows that the operator is competent to run a service. The Traffic Commissioners comprise a permanent chairman (appointed by the Secretary of State) and two commissioners selected from a panel nominated by county and district councils in the area. In addition, the route or routes which are to be run commercially have to be registered with the county council or joint board. With this new procedure it is not possible for existing operators to object and prevent a new operator providing a service. This accounts for the sometimes bewildering variety of buses which appear in such numbers that they clog up town centre streets and for which timetables appear illusory.

Many would now argue that the deregulation and privatisation of buses and trains has gone so far that producing an improved integrated public transport system will be very difficult. Until a good quality public transport system, performing consistently, is widely available, it must be open to doubt how the increase in traffic can be stemmed.

As a result of the registration of the routes, county councils and joint boards at least know which routes are not covered commercially, and can then decide which additional routes they wish to subsidise. These routes are put out to competitive tender to get the best value for money — in other words, an operator who will provide an acceptable service with the lowest subsidy. Once the routes have been registered, the operators have to give the county council or joint board notice of variations or cancellation of services. Action can be taken against operators who run an unreliable service including termination of the contract.

The former local authority bus services have had to be transferred from local authorities to separate companies under the Companies Acts, with their own directors, and they now have to compete with private operators in the market. Indeed, many former local authority bus companies have now been taken over by private sector companies.

Local authorities (usually district councils) may provide concessionary bus fare schemes for elderly or disabled people, provided all operators can participate. New Labour's White Paper, *A New Deal for Transport: Better for Everyone,* envisages the introduction of a new national minimum standard for concessionary fare schemes.

The position in London is different from the rest of the country. In 1985, responsibility for the buses and underground was removed from the GLC and given to *London Transport* (London Regional Transport Act 1984). London Transport was a quango with members appointed by and responsible to the Secretary of State. Like other public bus operators, London Transport was obliged to privatise its bus operations and now organises the bus routes using private companies under contract. Full deregulation, along the lines adopted outside London was proposed for the long-term by the last Conservative Government, but with the pendulum now swinging in favour of encouraging better integrated public transport, that was not pursued by the New Labour Government. Certain aspects of transport — concessionary fares, parking management, lorry ban and traffic control systems — across the whole of London were made the responsibility of a new *Transport Committee for London*, established in 1998 by the London borough councils to replace four existing bodies. Transport in London has now been reintegrated with the creation of *Transport for London* (Underground, buses, taxis, most main roads, and Docklands Light Railway) under the auspices of the new Greater London Authority

Principal local authorities and joint boards may also provide and run airports and docks. Sometimes, joint committees may be set up for this purpose. Examples of such provision include Luton, Manchester and Leeds/Bradford airports, and Portsmouth's ferry terminal. These have also had to be converted into companies, some in the public and others in the private sector.

Hackney carriages (taxis, which can ply for hire on the street) and private hire vehicles (which can only be booked by telephone and cannot be hailed on the street) are licensed outside London by unitary authorities, metropolitan borough councils, and shire borough/district councils, who also set the fare structure. Licences can be refused on grounds of suitability of the applicant (a police records check is always carried out) or suitability of the vehicle (some licensing authorities outside London are attempting, in the case of taxis, to require the use of London-style cabs, which are easier for disabled people to use). In London, taxis are licensed by the Commissioner of the Metropolitan Police, while the fare structure is determined by the Home Secretary — although this may change when the proposed Greater London Authority comes into existence.

Under the New Labour White Paper *A New Deal for Transport: Better for Everyone* mentioned in an earlier section of this Chapter, the use of all aspects of public transport (as opposed to the ever-increasing use of private vehicles) will be encouraged as part of an integrated and sustainable transport system.

Leisure — libraries

This is one of the main leisure provisions of local authorities. Local authorities were first empowered to provide public libraries — but not to buy books for them — by the Public Libraries Act 1850. It was not until the Public Libraries Act 1919 that local authorities were given the power to spend more than a rating limit of one penny in the pound on books. Today, there is no statutory limit, although the library service (and particularly the book fund) tends to attract less priority at a time of scarce resources.

Library authorities have a duty to provide a comprehensive and efficient library service, which can include the loan of records, tapes and videos in addition to books.

They have to make the service available to all who live or work in the area, or study full time there. Books must be issued free — fines can be imposed on overdue returns — but authorities can (and do) make a charge for the loan of records, tapes and videos. Authorities can use library premises for meetings, exhibitions or concerts.

The Department for Culture, Media and Sport has a duty to superintend and promote the improvement of the public library service. Library authorities must supply information required, and must make premises open to inspection.

Leisure — museums and art galleries

All local authorities are empowered to provide museums and art galleries. They may also contribute to expenses incurred in the provision of museums and art galleries by other authorities. Because the power is discretionary, the provision of museums and art galleries is not uniform and the private independent and university museums make a significant contribution to the local provision. Museum activities are co-ordinated through a series of Area Museum Councils which also provide a range of specialist help and advice to member museums — both local authority and independent.

Leisure — the performing arts

Further powers to local authorities to establish orchestras, concert halls and other places of entertainment, to maintain a band or orchestra, and to foster arts and crafts, were given by the Local Government Act 1972. This Act also gives local authorities wide powers to promote tourism in their areas, and to provide facilities for such events as conferences and fairs.

There was a great deal of concern that local authority support for the arts would suffer following the demise of the GLC and the metropolitan counties who had provided major financial support since 1974. Their role was transferred to London borough councils and metropolitan borough councils, backed up by some additional central funding and, in Liverpool, the establishment of a trustee body to oversee the Merseyside County Museum and the Walker Art Gallery. The fears over the abandonment of funding have not materialised, although the attitude of different successor authorities has varied. The arts are, as always, at risk in times of financial stringency, when other services, such as social services or education, are regarded as having higher priority.

Recreation

Under the Local Government (Miscellaneous Provisions) Act 1976, local authorities have a general power to provide such recreational facilities as they think fit, both within or outside their areas. They are also given specific powers to provide:

- sports centres;
- pitches for team games and athletic events, swimming pools, tennis courts, cycle tracks, golf courses, bowling greens, riding schools, camp sites and facilities for gliding;
- facilities for boating and water skiing;
- premises for athletic or recreational clubs;
- staff, including instructors.

All local authorities, including parish/community councils, can lease or buy land for public walks or pleasure grounds. Local authorities, except parish/community councils, may use CPO powers to acquire the necessary land. They may have transferred to them, for use as open spaces, disused burial grounds and open spaces held on trust.

Parts of public parks can be set aside for team games, and individual clubs can be permitted to have exclusive use of the facilities. Local authorities can equip and maintain pavilions and other buildings, provide apparatus (and make a charge for its use), provide boating lakes in parks, and provide caravan sites.

Leisure centres are now subject to CCT, with private companies being successful in a number of cases. This does not lessen the local authority's responsibility for setting standards in its specification and for monitoring that these are maintained. In some instances, where the private contractor was not performing satisfactorily, the local authority terminated the contract and resumed direct provision.

Appendix A

Principal Local Authorities in England

31 March 2000

Key to abbreviations:

(B)	*Shire district with borough status in a two-tier area*
(CC)	*County council in a two-tier area*
(D)	*Shire district in a two-tier area*
(UA)	*Unitary authority*

County areas now composed entirely of unitary authorities:

Berkshire	Bracknell Forest Borough; Newbury; Reading Borough; Slough; Windsor and Maidenhead Royal Borough; Wokingham.
Herefordshire	Herefordshire Council.
Isle of Wight	Isle of White Council.

Former county areas completely replaced by unitary authorities:

Avon	Bath and North East Somerset; Bristol City; North Somerset; South Gloucestershire.
Cleveland	Hartlepool; Middlesbrough; Redcar and Cleveland; Stockton-on-Tees.
Humberside	East Riding of Yorkshire; Kingston upon Hull City; North East Lincolnshire; North Lincolnshire.

County areas now containing one or more unitary authorities:

Bedfordshire	Bedfordshire (CC); Luton (UA).	Mid Bedfordshire (D); Bedford (B); South Bedfordshire (D).
Buckinghamshire	Buckinghamshire (CC); Milton Keynes (UA).	Aylesbury Vale (D); Chiltern (D); South Bucks (D); Wycombe (D).
Cambridgeshire	Cambridgeshire (CC); Peterborough City (UA).	Cambridge City (D); East Cambridgeshire (D); Fenland (D); Huntingdonshire (D); South Cambridgeshire (D).
Cheshire	Cheshire (CC); Halton Borough (UA); Warrington Borough (UA).	Chester City (D); Congleton (B); Crewe and Nantwich (B); Ellesmere Port and Neston (B); Macclesfield (B); Vale Royal (B).
Derbyshire	Derbyshire (CC); Derby City (UA).	Amber Valley (B); Bolsover (D); Chesterfield (B); Derbyshire Dales (D); Erewash (B); High Peak (B); North East Derbyshire (D); South East Derbyshire (D).
Devon	Devon (CC); Plymouth City (UA); Torbay Borough (UA).	East Devon (D); Exeter City (D); Mid Devon (D); North Devon (D); South Hams (D); Teignbridge (D); Torridge (D); West Devon (D).
Dorset	Dorset (CC); Bournemouth (UA); Poole (UA).	Christchurch (B); East Dorset (D); North Dorset (D); Purbeck (D); West Dorset (D); Weymouth and Portland (B).

Durham	Durham (CC); Darlington (UA).	Chester-le-Street (D); Derwentside (D); Durham City (D); Easington (D); Sedgefield (D); Teesdale (D); Wear Valley (D).
East Sussex	East Sussex (CC); Brighton and Hove (UA).	Eastbourne (B); Hastings (B); Lewes (D); Rother (D); Wealden (D).
Essex	Essex (CC); Southend-on-Sea Borough (UA); Thurrock Borough (UA).	Basildon (D); Braintree (D); Brentwood (B); Castle Point (D); Chelmsford (B); Colchester (B); Epping Forest (D); Harlow (D); Maldon (D); Rochford (D); Tendring (D); Uttlesford (D).
Hampshire	Hampshire (CC); Portsmouth City (UA); Southampton City (UA).	Basingstoke and Deane (B); East Hampshire (D); Eastleigh (B); Fareham (B); Gosport (B); Hart (D); Havant (B); New Forest (D); Rushmoor (D); Test Valley (B); Winchester City (D).
Kent	Kent (CC); Medway Towns (UA)	Ashford (B); Canterbury City (D); Dartford (B); Dover (D); Maidstone (B); Sevenoaks (D); Shepway (D); Swale (B); Thanet (D); Tonbridge and Malling (B); Tunbridge Wells (B).
Lancashire	Lancashire (CC); Blackburn with Darwen Borough (UA); Blackpool Borough (UA).	Burnley (B); Chorley (B); Fylde (B); Hyndburn (B); Lancaster City (D); Pendle (B); Preston (B); Ribble Valley (B); Rossendale (B); South Ribble (B); West Lancashire (D); Wyre (B).

Leicestershire	Leicestershire (CC); Leicester City (UA); Rutland (UA).	Blaby (D); Charnwood (B); Harborough (D); Hinckley and Bosworth (B); Melton (B); North West Leicestershire (D); Oadby and Wigston (B).
Nottinghamshire	Nottinghamshire (CC); Nottingham City (UA).	Ashfield (D); Bassetlaw (D); Broxtowe (B); Gedling (B); Mansfield (D); Newark and Sherwood (D); Rushcliffe (B).
North Yorkshire	North Yorkshire (CC); City of York (UA).	Craven (D); Hambleton (D); Harrogate (B); Richmondshire (D); Ryedale (D); Scarborough (B); Selby (D).
Shropshire	Shropshire (CC); Wrekin (UA).	Bridgnorth (D); North Shropshire (D); Oswestry (B); Shrewsbury and Atcham (B); South Shropshire (D).
Staffordshire	Staffordshire (CC); Stoke on Trent City (UA).	Cannock Chase (D); East Staffordshire (B); Lichfield (D); Newcastle-under-Lyme (B); South Staffordshire (D); Stafford (B); Staffordshire Moorlands (D); Tamworth (D).
Wiltshire	Wiltshire (CC); Swindon (UA).	Kennet (D); North Wiltshire (D); Salisbury (D); West Wiltshire (D).

County areas retaining a complete two-tier system:

Cornwall	Cornwall (CC); Caradon (D); Carrick (D); Kerrier (D); North Cornwall (D); Penwith (D); Restormel (B).
Cumbria	Cumbria (CC); Allerdale (D); Barrow-in-Furness (B); Carlisle City (D); Copeland (B); Eden (D); South Lakeland (D).
Gloucestershire	Gloucestershire (CC); Cheltenham (B); Cotswold (D); Forest of Dean (D); Gloucester City (D); Stroud (D); Tewkesbury (B).
Worcestershire	Worcestershire (CC); Bromsgrove (D); Malvern Hills (D); Redditch (D); Worcester City (D); Wychavon (D); Wyre Forest (D).
Hertfordshire	Hertfordshire (CC); Broxbourne (B); Dacorum (B); East Hertfordshire (D); Hertsmere (B); North Hertfordshire (D); St. Albans City (D); Stevenage (B); Three Rivers (D); Watford (B); Welwyn Hatfield (D).
Lincolnshire	Lincolnshire (CC); Boston (B); East Lindsey (D); Lincoln City (D); North Kesteven (D); South Holland (D); South Kesteven (D); West Lindsey (D).
Norfolk	Norfolk (CC); Breckland (D); Broadland (D); Great Yarmouth (B); King's Lynn and West Norfolk (B); North Norfolk (D); Norwich City (D); South Norfolk (D).
Northamptonshire	Northamptonshire (CC); Corby (B); Daventry (D); East Northamptonshire (D); Kettering (B); Northampton (B); South Northamptonshire (D); Wellingborough (B).
Northumberland	Northumberland (CC); Alnwick (D); Berwick-upon-Tweed (B); Blyth Valley (B); Castle Morpeth (B); Tynedale (D); Wansbeck (D).
Oxfordshire	Oxfordshire (CC); Cherwell (D); Oxford City (D); South Oxfordshire (D); Vale of White Horse (D); West Oxfordshire (D).
Somerset	Somerset (CC); Mendip (D); Sedgemoor (D); South Somerset (D); Taunton Deane (B); West Somerset (D).
Suffolk	Suffolk (CC); Babergh (D); Forest Heath (D); Ipswich (B); Mid Suffolk (D); St. Edmundsbury (B); Suffolk Coastal (D); Waveney (D).
Surrey	Surrey (CC); Elmbridge (B); Epsom and Ewell (B); Guildford (B); Mole Valley (D); Reigate and Banstead (B); Runnymede (B); Spelthorne (B); Surrey Heath (B); Tandridge (D); Waverley (B); Woking (B).

Warwickshire	Warwickshire (CC); North Warwickshire (B): Nuneaton and Bedworth (B); Rugby (B); Stratford-on-Avon (D); Warwick (D).
West Sussex	West Sussex (CC); Adur (D); Arun (D); Chichester (D); Crawley (B); Horsham (D); Mid Sussex (D); Worthing (B).

Greater London

Greater London Authority *(Mayor of London plus Greater London Assembly).*

London Borough Councils (except Corporation of London):

Barking and Dagenham; Barnet; Bexley; Brent; Bromley; Camden; Corporation of London; Croydon; Ealing; Enfield; Greenwich; Hackney; Hammersmith and Fulham; Haringey; Harrow; Havering; Hillingdon; Hounslow; Islington; Kensington and Chelsea Royal Borough; Kingston upon Thames Royal Borough; Lambeth; Lewisham; Merton; Newham; Redbridge; Richmond upon Thames; Southwark; Sutton;

Tower Hamlets; Waltham Forest; Wandsworth; Westminster City.

Former Metropolitan County areas (Metropolitan Borough Councils):

Greater Manchester	Bolton; Bury; Manchester City; Oldham; Rochdale; Salford City; Stockport; Tameside; Trafford; Wigan.
Merseyside	Knowsley; Liverpool City; St. Helens; Sefton; Wirral.
South Yorkshire	Barnsley; Doncaster; Rotherham; Sheffield City.
Tyne and Wear	Gateshead; Newcastle upon Tyne City; North Tyneside; South Tyneside; Sunderland
West Midlands	Birmingham City; Coventry City; Dudley; Sandwell; Solihull; Walsall; Wolverhampton.
West Yorkshire	Bradford City; Calderdale; Kirklees; Leeds City; Wakefield City.

Principal Local Authorities in Wales

31 March 2000

22 Welsh Unitary Councils:

Blaenau Gwent County Borough; Bridgend County Borough; Caerphilly County Borough; Cardiff County; Carmarthenshire County; Ceredigion County; Conwy County Borough; Denbighshire County; Flintshire County; Gwynedd; Isle of Anglesey County; Merthyr Tydfil County Borough; Monmouthshire County; Neath Port Talbot County Borough; Newport County Borough; Pembrokeshire County; Powys County; Rhondda Cynon Taff County Borough; City and County of Swansea; Torfaen County Borough; Vale of Glamorgan; Wrexham County Borough.

Principal Local Authorities in Scotland

31 March 2000

32 Scottish Unitary Councils:

Aberdeen City; Aberdeenshire; Angus; Argyll and Bute; Clackmannanshire; Dumfries and Galloway; Dundee City; East Ayrshire; East Dunbartonshire; East Lothian; East Renfrewshire; City of Edinburgh; Falkirk; Fife; City of Glasgow; Highland; Inverclyde; Midlothian; Moray; North Ayrshire; North Lanarkshire; Orkney; Perth and Kinross; Renfrewshire; Scottish Borders; Shetland; South Ayrshire; South Lanarkshire; Stirling; West Dunbartonshire, Western Isles; West Lothian.

Principal Local Authorities in Northern Ireland
31 March 2000

NB: The division of functions as between central government and local government is different in Northern Ireland (see Appendix B).

26 district councils:
Antrim; Ards; Armagh; Ballymena; Ballymoney; Banbridge; Belfast City; Carrickfergus; Casltereagh; Coleraine; Cookstown; Craigavon; Derry City; Down; Dungannon; Fermanagh; Larne; Limavady; Lisburn; Magherafelt; Moyle; Newry and Mourne; Newtonabbey; North Down; Omagh; Strabane.

Appendix B

Main Functions of Local Authorities in England, Scotland and Wales

Principal Local Authorities

**See the explanatory notes at the end of this appendix.*

Education *	Unitary authority London borough council Metropolitan borough council County council in two-tier area
Social Services	Unitary authority London borough council Metropolitan borough council County council in two-tier area
Housing	Unitary authority London borough council Metropolitan borough council Shire district/borough council in two-tier area
Highways and Transport	All authorities *
Planning	All authorities *
Environmental Services	All authorities *
Trading Standards *	Unitary authority London borough council Metropolitan borough council County council in two-tier area
Recreation and Arts	All authorities *
Libraries	Unitary authority London borough council Metropolitan borough council County council in two-tier area
Police	City of London Metropolitan Police Authority (Greater London Authority) Police Authority (outside London)

Fire and Rescue	London Fire and Emergency Planning Authority (Greater London Authority) Fire and Civil Defence Authority in metropolitan county areas County council, but only in complete two-tier county Combined Fire Authority (outside London, metropolitan counties and complete two-tier counties)
Emergency Planning	London Fire and Emergency Planning Authority (Greater London Authority) Fire and Civil Defence Authority in metropolitan county areas All authorities outside London
Allotments	Unitary authority London borough council Metropolitan borough council Shire district/borough council in two-tier area
Smallholdings	County council in two-tier area
Cemeteries and Crematoria	Unitary authority London borough council Metropolitan borough council Shire district/borough council in two-tier area
Registration of Births, Deaths and Marriages	Unitary authority London borough council Metropolitan borough council County council in two-tier area
Economic Development	All authorities
Electoral Registration	Unitary authority London borough council Metropolitan borough council Shire district/borough council in two-tier area
Council Tax collection	Unitary authority London borough council Metropolitan borough council Shire district/borough council in two-tier area
Superannuation	Joint arrangements in London and metropolitan county areas County Councils elsewhere

Explanatory Notes

Education

The functions likely to remain with the local education authority (LEA) have diminished over the last few years. Firstly, the general implementation of Local Management of Schools (LMS) gave individual schools control over their own budgets, including staff and building maintenance. Secondly, the ability of schools to opt-out completely from LEA control, by obtaining the Secretary of State's approval of Grant Maintained (GM) Status, meant that in some smaller authorities, the LEA had no responsibility for any of the schools in its area. GM schools have now been converted into foundation schools as a result of the School Standards and Framework Act 1998, so an LEA may have regained some of its lost responsibilities.

Highways and Transport

Highways includes the maintenance of roads, footpaths and bridleways, traffic management, off-street parking. Shire district/borough councils in a two-tier area can claim the statutory right of delegation from the county council to maintain unclassified roads in urban areas — this is usually supplemented by additional voluntary agency arrangements under which the shire district/borough council is given further highways agency responsibilities, to make the agency arrangement more sensible.

In completely two-tier areas, transport planning is usually the responsibility of the county council — including the payment of subsidies to transport providers to ensure the survival of some sort of co-ordinated public transport system. Where a county contains one or more unitary authorities, joint arrangements for this may exist.

In London, after 1948 and until 2000, public transport was run by London Regional Transport, a government appointed body. Certain aspects of transport — concessionary fares, parking management, lorry ban and traffic control systems — across the whole of London were the responsibility of a new *Transport Committee for London*, established in 1998 by the London borough councils to replace four existing bodies. The new Greater London Authority has responsibility for a new body, *Transport for London* (TfL) (covering the Underground, buses, taxis, most main roads, and Docklands Light Railway) from July 2000.

In each of the six metropolitan county areas, there is a passenger transport authority, to which the metropolitan borough councils appoint members.

Planning

Strategic Planning involves the production of Structure Plans, Local Plans or Unified Development Plans. The Structure Plan in a shire county area is the responsibility of the county Council, with the shire district/borough councils being responsible for producing a district/borough-wide Local Plan which conforms generally with the Structure Plan. Where a shire county has completely retained a two-tier system, that is still the case. Where any shire county now contains one or more unitary authorities, the Structure Plan process is likely to continue for the whole county, with the county council and unitary council(s) acting jointly. In metropolitan county areas, similar joint strategic planning arrangements, involving the metropolitan borough councils, are likely to exist.

In two-tier areas, the involvement of county councils in development control (the granting of planning permission) is very limited — to certain types of mineral extraction. Responsibility for providing gypsy sites is concurrent with both county and district/borough councils.

In London, development control is the responsibility of the London borough councils. The new Greater London Authority will have London-wide responsibilities for development plans.

Environmental Services

Those environmental services which include waste collection, building regulation, pollution control, food hygiene monitoring, control of diseases, monitoring of conditions in shops and offices and street cleansing. These functions are the responsibility of all authorities except county councils in two-tier areas.

Waste disposal (as opposed to collection) requires greater resources and is, therefore, usually the responsibility of a county council in a two-tier area and the responsibility of statutory or voluntary joint arrangements elsewhere. In London (except Bexley), there are four statutory waste disposal authorities and three voluntary joint bodies — under the supervision of the London Waste Regulation Authority. In the metropolitan county areas, there are voluntary joint arrangements in South Yorkshire, Tyne and Wear, West Midlands and West Yorkshire and statutory authorities in Greater Manchester (except Wigan) and Merseyside.

Trading Standards

In London and the metropolitan county areas, joint committees are likely to exist for the co-ordination of enforcement and the use of specialist facilities. In those areas where unitary authorities have been created, similar joint arrangements may also exist between the unitary authorities and any relevant county council.

Recreation and Arts

Recreation and Arts includes parks and open spaces, swimming pools, museums, encouraging tourism and supporting the arts. In two-tier areas, these functions are concurrent with both county and district/borough councils; in reality, the county council is more likely to provide country parks in rural areas, while the district/borough council is more likely to provide swimming pools and museums.

Functions of Parish/Community Councils

- provision of allotments. (They have a duty to provide allotment gardens if there is an unsatisfied demand);
- provision of public baths, wash houses and swimming pools;
- provision of cemeteries and crematoria;
- provision and maintenance of bus shelters;
- making by laws about parks and open spaces, cycle parks, baths and mortuaries;
- provision of public clocks;
- dealing with ponds and ditches;
- repair and maintenance of public footpaths, lighting of roads and public places; provision of litter bins; provision of parking places for bicycles and motor cycles; acquisition of rights of way, provision of roadside seats and shelters; provision of traffic signs and other notices;
- promotion of lotteries;
- provision of mortuaries and post-mortem rooms;
- provision of public conveniences;
- provision of village halls;
- acquisition of land for recreation grounds and open spaces, and the management and control of them; provision of gymnasiums, playing fields and sports centres; provision of boating pools;
- maintenance, repair and protection of war memorials.

In addition, the consent of parish councils is necessary for stopping or diverting a road.

Main Functions of Local Authorities in Northern Ireland

Local government in Northern Ireland was reorganised in 1973. Prior to that its structure and functions were broadly similar to that in England and Wales. The 1973 reorganisation resulted in the creation of 26 district councils and nine area boards.

The area boards owe their existence to the transfer of certain functions, in 1973, from local government to central government: four area boards look after health and personal social services and five area boards are responsible for education and libraries.

The remainder of what are regarded as a local government functions elsewhere in the UK are handled as follows:

- Planning, roads and water and sewerage services are the direct responsibility of the Northern Ireland Department of the Environment;
- Housing is the responsibility of the Northern Ireland Housing Executive;
- Fire is the responsibility of the Northern Ireland Fire Authority; and
- Urban arterial drainage is the responsibility of the Northern Ireland Ministry of Agriculture.

Index